Counterrevolution

COUNTERREVOLUTION

*The Crusade to Roll Back the Gains
of the Civil Rights Movement*

STEPHEN STEINBERG

STANFORD UNIVERSITY PRESS

Stanford, California

STANFORD UNIVERSITY PRESS
Stanford, California

© 2022 by Stephen Steinberg. All rights reserved.

Printed in the United States of America on acid-free, archival-quality paper
Library of Congress Control Number: 2021947843
ISBN: 9-781-5036-3002-4 (cloth)
ISBN: 9-781-5036-3003-1 (paper)

Cataloging in Publication Data available from the Library of Congress.

Cover design: David Drummond
Text design: Newgen North America
Typeset by Newgen North America in 10/15 Sabon LT

This book is dedicated to Derrick Bell
who neither surrendered to false optimism
nor allowed pessimism to diminish his struggle against white supremacy.

CONTENTS

ACKNOWLEDGMENTS

Writing a book may not take a village, but it does rely on friends, colleagues, and comrades who provide knowledge and indispensable feedback and criticism. It is also an occasion for remembering. Let me begin by paying homage to three professors who changed my life trajectory.

As a freshman at Brown University in 1958, I enrolled in an innovative course called The Identification and Criticism of Ideas, taught by Dennis Wrong. It was basically a great books seminar and we read Durkheim, Veblen, Freud, Fromm, Riesman, and other luminaries. In retrospect, Marx and Du Bois were absent from Dennis's pantheon, but then again, this was the regressive 1950s. Dennis's voice would resonate whenever ideas clashed around the table. This was my baptism in the contentious but liberating academic world.

In 1963 I came to know Bob Blauner, who was a new hire in the Sociology Department at UC, Berkeley. I attended his first class on racism, along with Gary Marx, an activist in CORE (Congress of Racial Equality), and David Wellman, a red-diaper baby from Detroit. The three of us absorbed Bob's penchant for challenging prevailing orthodoxies, and we witnessed the evolution of his tour de force, *Racial Oppression in America*.

As a graduate assistant at the Survey Research Center, I was delegated to work with Gertrude Jaeger Selznick on a national survey of anti-Semitism, sponsored by the Anti-Defamation League. Gertrude was trained in the philosophy of science and the logic of inquiry, which she applied to survey research. She was an intellectual to the core and was indefatigable when it came to unmasking obfuscation.

In 1971 I tore myself away from the seductions of California and morphed into a New Yorker, with the great opportunity of teaching at the City University of New York. I am indebted to Ben Ringer and Rolf Meyersohn for taking me under their wing and to Joe Bensman for his theoretical acumen and passion for "talking sociology." In 1978 I joined the Urban Studies Department at Queens College, a rare hub of interdisciplinarity. I am particularly indebted to two colleagues, both anthropologists: Jeff Maskovsky expanded my horizon with his mastery of poverty, grassroots activism, and political economy. Melissa Checker did the same with her critique of environmental gentrification and its consequences for racial and economic injustice. I could always rely on them for a dose of iconoclasm.

Much appreciation as well for Alyson Cole's friendship and intellectual scope and originality. Other colleagues in the Urban Studies Department shared decades of camaraderie: Sherry Baron, Dana-Ain Davis, Martin Eisenberg, Martin Hanlon, Tarry Hum, Madhulika Khandelwal, Len Rodberg, Alice Sardell, John Seley, and Alan Takeall.

In 1987 I was introduced to *New Politics*, a socialist journal founded and co-edited by Julius Jacobson and Phyllis Jacobson, two progeny of the nearly extinct Jewish blue-collar working class. Phyllis and Julie were fierce Trotskyists who rejected Stalin's authoritarianism and championed "socialism from below." For me personally, *New Politics* was a godsend—it bridged academic and political discourses and for over thirty years provided a venue for my research and writing. Julie and Phyllis were sources of inspiration and friendship, along with Herbert Hill who was the labor director of the NAACP and a frequent contributor to *New Politics*. Kudos as well to Barry Finger and Sam Farber for so many penetrating articles.

I met Derrick Bell at the Race Matters Conference at Princeton University in 1997. Derrick was teaching at NYU Law School. We frequently met for lunch, and conversation often drifted to the maddening contradictions of race in America. It is my honor to dedicate this book to his memory.

I came to know Charles W. Mills after reading *The Racial Contract*. I was bowled over by his ingenious concept of "an epistemology of ignorance." In my naivete, I was constantly puzzled that in matters of race, sociologists never got it quite right. Charles provided me with an epiphanic moment: that we are not *supposed* to get it right! How else can we explain sociology's proclivity for victim-blaming discourses?

Over the years I had extended dialogues with Adolph Reed, and though we sometimes sparred, I treasured his political acumen and trenchant prose.

It was my good fortune to meet Micaela di Leonardo, whose groundbreaking scholarship and vibrant prose merge into an eloquent amalgam. I cherish our long friendship.

For decades, Frances Fox Piven and I were colleagues at the CUNY Graduate Center. Knowing her has been an inspiration, and I have been shaped by her deep and indefatigable advance of progressive ideas and politics.

The academic enterprise is often solipsistic. However, students bring their diverse life experiences into our classes and in doing so inform or challenge our assumptions and point of view. I relish the memory of cohorts of students from the City College of New York, Queens College, and the CUNY Graduate Center. It is also a pleasure to acknowledge several graduate students who remain friends: Neil McLaughlin, Bruce Haines, Donal Malone, and Cody Melcher.

Two people generously read and commented on chapters of this book. Peter Taubman, a colleague and friend from Brooklyn College, provided thoughtful and candid criticism, in sharp detail and nuance. Heartfelt appreciation to Sharon Friedman, my partner in life, for her inimitable insight, close reading, and scrupulous editing. Perhaps a book takes a village after all, speaking of which, our children, Danny and Joanna, provided their ageing parents with perspective on the culture and politics of Generation Y. They shaped our values and sensibilities as much as the other way around.

Profound thanks to Kate Wahl, editor-in-chief of Stanford University Press, for her editorial wisdom, and Marcela Cristina Maxfield and Sunna Juhn for their indispensable support and keen judgment. Finally, words cannot convey my appreciation to Barbara Armentrout for her fastidious copyediting of the manuscript.

Counterrevolution

"RACE RELATIONS"
An Obfuscation

It was a stroke of genius really for white Americans to give Negro Americans the name of their problem, thereby focusing attention on symptoms (the Negro and the Negro community) instead of causes (the white man and the white community).

Lerone Bennett Jr., "The White Problem in America," 1966[1]

We use all manner of euphemisms and terms of art to keep from directly addressing the racial reality in America. This may be some holdover from a bygone time, but it is now time for it to come to an end.

Take for instance the term "race relations." Polling organizations like Gallup and the Pew Research Center often ask respondents how they feel about the state of race relations in the country.

I have never fully understood what this meant. It suggests a relationship that swings from harmony to disharmony. But that is not the way race is structured or animated in this country. From the beginning, the racial dynamics in America have been about power, equality and access, or the lack thereof. . . .

So what are the relations here? It is a linguistic sidestep that avoids the true issue: anti-Black and anti-other white supremacy.

Charles Blow, "Call a Thing a Thing," 2020[2]

In *The Feminine Mystique*, published in 1963, Betty Friedan came up with an ingenious formulation for the malaise that she observed among middle-class suburban housewives. She called it "the problem that has no name."[3] Except for a few articles by those rare women in American sociology—for example, Helen Hacker's 1951 article "Women as a Minority Group"—the wholesale subordination of women was not on the radar of the male professoriate.[4] *Sexism* had not yet entered the sociological lexicon.[5] The fact that women were consigned to uphold the patriarchal family and the suburban dream was beyond the sociological imagination. It was an unquestioned fact of life.

Thanks to Daniel Horowitz's assiduous biography—*Betty Friedan and the Making of The Feminine Mystique*—we now know that Friedan was no ordinary housewife who arrived at her epiphany through observation and introspection.[6] Indeed, she was a seasoned political activist who had been schooled in radical politics at Smith College in the 1940s, a period of heightened political awareness as the nation mobilized for war. Furthermore, Friedan worked as a labor journalist for two decades and was steeped in the feminist thought and politics of the 1950s. It is true that, by the 1960s, Friedan had morphed into a suburban housewife. However, she brought an ideological lens that allowed her to see what was opaque to most others.

As Horowitz documents, among the books in Friedan's library were Thorstein Veblen's iconoclastic *Theory of the Leisure Class* (1899) and Simone de Beauvoir's tour de force, *The Second Sex* (1963). In addition, she had a marked-up copy of Friedrich Engels's 1884 essay "The Origin of the Family, Private Property and the State" in a compendium of works by Engels and Marx; it included the following passage:

> We see already that the emancipation of women and their equality with men are impossible and must remain so as long as women are excluded from socially productive work and restricted to housework, which is private. The emancipation of women becomes possible only when women are enabled to take part in production on a large, social scale, and when domestic duties require their attention only to a minor degree.[7]

Alongside Engel's words "when women are enabled to take part," Friedan scrawled "along with men."[8] No ordinary housewife, she!

To be sure, Friedan grasped the malaise that she observed among suburban housewives, not to speak of her own discontents. But she also deployed her rhetorical skills as a journalist when she artfully wrote that this was a "problem that has no name."

Race in the United States presents quite another dilemma: a problem that had been *mis*diagnosed and *mis*labeled—a problem, one might say, with the *wrong* name: race relations. Let us examine the origins of this deceptively innocent designation. In their book *Racecraft*, Karen E. Fields and Barbara J. Fields unpack the hidden and perverse meanings embedded in *race relations*:

> Invented in the late-nineteenth-century heyday of the Jim Crow regime, the term "race relations" finessed the abrogation of democracy and the bloody vigilantism that enforced it.[9]

They continue:

> In a cognate maneuver, the formula "race relations" drew a sentimental curtain of Old South symbols across the New South's class relations and politics. While the curtain concealed the South's cheap labor, Black and white, it also muffled the noise of anti-democratic struggles to build white supremacy.[10]

This is the surreptitious racecraft that conceals oppression in a fog of theoretical abstraction.

How is it that we apply such benign language—"race relations"—to such a malignant problem? It is rather like diagnosing a melanoma as a skin rash and prescribing a topical salve. Indeed, putting the wrong name on a problem is worse than having no name at all. In the latter instance, one is at least open to filling the conceptual void. In the first instance, however, words lead us down a blind alley. They divert us from the facets of the problem that should command our attention, and as the analogy to melanoma suggests, they lead to remedies that are ineffectual or worse.

Sociology can hardly be accused of turning a blind eye to the problem of race. However, as Franklin Frazier pointed out in 1947, the first two treatises on sociology in America were pro-slavery tracts![11] Since then, sociology has produced a vast canon of learned scholarship on issues of race and racism. One might ask, with Kierkegaard, whether this is a case of seeing and still not seeing. What is the conceptual lens that the sociologist brings to the study of race? Does it illuminate or does it obscure? And is this obfuscation ideologically innocent, or does it provide perverse justification for the prevailing racial order, which is one of racial hierarchy and domination? And what are we to say of a scholarly field of inquiry whose very name, race relations, is an artful obfuscation?[12]

What terminology would more accurately capture the essence of race in America? The right name, I submit, is "racial oppression." This was the terminology used by Marxist writers in the 1930s, and it entered sociological parlance in the 1970s with the publication of Bob Blauner's *Racial Oppression in America*.[13]

Unlike *race relations*, *racial oppression* conveys a clear sense of the nature, magnitude, and sources of the problem. Whereas the race relations model assumes that racial prejudice arises out of a natural antipathy between groups on the basis of difference, *racial oppression* locates the source of the problem within societal structures that are racist. Whereas *race relations* elides the issue of power, reducing racism down to the level of attitudes, *racial oppression* makes clear from the outset that we are dealing with a system of domination, one that entails major political and economic institutions, including the state itself. Whereas *race relations* implies mutuality, *racial oppression* clearly distinguishes between the oppressor and the oppressed. Whereas *race relations* rivets attention on superficial aspects of the racial dyad, *racial oppression* explores the underlying factors that engender racial division and discord. Whereas the sociologist of race relations is reduced to the social equivalent of a marriage counselor, exploring ways to repair these fractured relationships, the sociologist of racial oppression is potentially an agent of social transformation.

The ultimate fallacy of the race relations model, as Thomas Pettigrew asserted in 1964, was that it placed more importance on reducing prejudice among whites than on improving conditions among Blacks.[14] Think about it: here was a praxis that ministered to the oppressor rather than the oppressed! In effect, Black aspirations for deliverance from poverty and racism were put on hold while whites underwent a therapeutic transformation. What clearer evidence that sociologists, against their intentions, have practiced a white social science?

More is involved here than a semantic quibble. I am taking issue not just with the term *race relations* but with the entire race relations paradigm. Other terms of discourse are equally problematic. In 1984 a psychologist at Brooklyn College, Barton Meyers, wrote an incisive paper entitled "Minority Group: An Ideological Formulation." He argued, much as I do here, that the term *minority group*, coined by Louis Wirth in 1945, presents "a distorted understanding of reality," whose effect is "to make obscure, especially to subordinate groups, the prevailing system of power and the intentions of the powerful."[15] Unfortunately, Meyers's proposal to expunge *minority group* from the sociological lexicon and to substitute *oppressed groups* has fallen on deaf ears. Is it that we hear, but still do not hear?

On close examination, even the terms *prejudice* and *discrimination* are ideologically laden. In the Marxist paradigm, prejudice and discrimination are mere epiphenomena of systems of racial domination. Oliver Cox stated the matter with his characteristic acumen: "Race prejudice, then, constitutes an attitudinal justification necessary for an easy exploitation of some race. To put it in still another way, race prejudice is the social-attitudinal concomitant of the racial-exploitative practice of a ruling class in a capitalistic society."[16] In contrast, the tendency in social science has been to reify prejudice, to treat it as a problem unto itself, and to pretend that racism could be ameliorated by disabusing whites of the distorted beliefs that they harbor about Blacks.[17]

This set of assumptions has given rise to a plethora of redundant studies conducted over six decades, which chart the prevalence and distribution of prejudiced beliefs. We measure—with meticulous care—but we measure the wrong things, or more precisely, we measure the ephemeras of racism. Or we measure the right things—glaring inequalities between Blacks and whites in wealth, status, and power—but we attribute them to the wrong causes: to deficits in human capital or to aberrant or dysfunctional cultures that are said to perpetuate poverty from one generation to the next.

Discrimination suffers from the same problem. Instead of focusing on the historical and structural processes that reproduce racial inequalities from one generation to the next, discrimination is reduced to the level of discrete acts by discrete individuals. However, far more is involved than individual acts of discrimination, even when they constitute larger aggregates. We are dealing here with the systematic exclusion of an entire people from whole industries and job sectors for all of American history. To depict this as "discrimination" is to trivialize it, to elide its institutional basis, and to obscure its sources and magnitude. It would be far more apropos to deploy the term *occupational apartheid*, which captures the systemic character of the problem and provides a logic for affirmative action—which is targeted not at atomized individuals but at social institutions such as corporations, unions, and universities.

As I argued in *Turning Back*, the racial crisis of the 1960s provided stark proof of the failure of the race relations paradigm to explain, much less do anything about, the forces that were tearing American society apart.[18] The result was a paradigm crisis, one that opened up the canon to radical and minority voices that had long been cast to the periphery. In *Racial Oppression in America*, Blauner explicitly rejected the race relations model and, picking up on the rhetoric and politics of Third World movements, he deployed the term *internal colonialism* to capture the encapsulation and plight of Blacks and other Third World groups in the United States.[19]

Another conceptual innovation had its origins in a book that was collaboration between a political activist and a political scientist. In *Black Power: The Politics of Liberation*, published in 1967, Kwame Ture and Charles Hamilton drew a distinction between "individual racism" and "institutional racism."[20] The latter, they held, did not depend on intentional acts of racial animus but was embedded in established and respected institutions of society. Here was a truly revelatory conception of racism, one that avoided the reductionist tendencies within sociology and treated racism as a *systemic* problem that required systemic change.[21]

Predictably, critics on the right railed against the whole idea of institutional racism. For example, in *The End of Racism*, Dinesh D'Souza dismissed institutionalized racism as "a nonsense phrase" and rebuked scholars "who have radicalized the definition of racism to locate it in the very structures of the American workplace."[22] To which his intellectual adversaries replied: "Damn right!"

Despite these theoretical advances, the insurgent sociology of the '60s never attained a fully developed alternative paradigm. Reflecting the racial backlash in the society at large, mainstream sociology reverted to the language and logic of "race relations," though often in new rhetorical dressing.

Like the Confederate flag, the race relations paradigm has endured the challenges of history. A study published in *Race and Society* examined the thirty-four course syllabi included in the 1997 edition of the American Sociological Association's publication on *Teaching Race and Ethnic Relations*. All but one course had prosaic titles such as Minority Groups, Minority Relations, Race and Minority Relations, Race and Ethnic Relations, and for a novel but equally obfuscating twist, Race and Ethnic Diversity. The exception was a course taught by Noel Cazenave entitled White Racism, which aroused fierce opposition when initially proposed at the University of Connecticut.[23]

One might argue that the Chicago sociologists who pioneered the study of race were "products of their times." No doubt this was the case, but it does not exonerate them from the judgment of history. The crucial question is why sociologists are still wedded to these same obfuscating categories seven decades later, as though the civil rights revolution never happened. Why is a course entitled White Racism seen as a provocation? Why has sociology failed to develop a discourse that illuminates, instead of obscures, the systemic character of racism?

To be sure, a number of sociologists have forged an alternative discourse centered on the concept of structural racism.[24] Its virtue and power is that it challenges the methodological reductionism that limits so much of sociological research on race.

Another major initiative with lasting impact came from Derrick Bell and his colleagues under the banner of critical race theory (CRT).[25] Centered among law professors, most of whom though not all were people of color, CRT generated an extensive body of theory and research on race and racism, particularly within the sphere of law, politics, and public policy. This movement lives on among legal scholars who have developed assiduous legal briefs arguing for reparations for past crimes whose tentacles extend to the present. Perhaps because of the balkanization that exists among academic disciplines, the struggles of the Black liberation movement were consigned to the cold storage of history until the recent upsurge of protest that has triggered "a national reckoning with race."

Thanks to affirmative action policies in higher education, there is a cadre of minority professors who appear, like spring flowers, at professional meetings, where they organize panels and practice their craft. With devotion and resolve, these dedicated scholars fulfill Edward Said's injunction to develop an antithetical discourse that represents the interests, experiences, and sensibilities of the subaltern.[26] Too often, however, like Du Bois, Cox, and scores of Black scholars, these truth tellers are left carping on the sidelines. It is fundamentally a question of intellectual hegemony: Which perspectives prevail? Which command resources? Which are central to intellectual discourse, both inside and outside the academy? And which are influential in the formation of public policy?

Nowhere was the hegemonic status of the race relations paradigm more evident than in the 1997 report issued by the advisory board for President Clinton's Initiative on Race. Here was a president who betrayed his antiracist claims and repealed welfare; removed billions of dollars of subsidies to poor minority families; affixed his signature to a crime bill that has increased the prison population to over two million people, two-thirds of them Black and Latinx; and promised to "mend, not end" affirmative action and yet presided over the quiet dismantling of affirmative action policy.

Instead of public policies to attack structural racism, Clinton provided us with the spectacle of a national conversation on race predicated on the assumption that dialogue "helps to dispel stereotypes" and is "a tool for finding common ground." However, "the problem isn't racial division or a need for healing," as Adolph Reed argued in his column in *The Progressive*. "It is racial inequality and injustice. And the remedy isn't an elaborately choreographed pageantry of essentializing yackety-yak about group experience, cultural difference, pain, and the inevitable platitudes about understanding. Rather, we need a clear commitment by the federal government to preserve, buttress, and extend civil rights and to use the office of the presidency to indicate that commitment forcefully and unambiguously."[27]

What can we hope from a presidential commission or the public at large if certified race experts still do not see that genuine race relations are unattainable—indeed, unfathomable—unless there is a basic parity of condition between the Black and white citizens of this nation?

Nor is "race relations" merely a relic of colonialism. In her 2015 study, *Managing Inequality*, Karen Miller brings to light the insidious ways in which politicians in cities with large Black concentrations don the mantle of racial liberalism in order to manipulate and manage "race relations" to the advantage of whites and the detriment of Blacks. Miller is a historian and her focus is on Detroit between the First and Second World Wars, which witnessed a massive influx of Southern Blacks seeking jobs in the burgeoning automobile industry. To quote Miller:

> Soon after the end of the Second World War, "race relations" became the language through which seemingly well-intentioned white liberals managed African American complaints about structural inequalities. State actors helped to produce and sustain racial inequality at the same time that they said they were producing institutions designed to improve race relations or even extend new resources to African Americans and other people of color in cities.[28]

According to Miller, liberal leaders created governmental and nongovernmental agencies that "ostensibly addressed racial inequality but were actually a cover for managing and containing Black protest and African American political participation."[29] Their thinly disguised purpose, like that of imperial powers of yore, was to "keep the natives happy." To preempt protest. And if or when it became necessary, to use their monopoly over the instruments of violence to stomp out any threat of revolt, however justified.

Miller points out that "liberals have historically claimed that part of their project is to remedy capitalism's most grotesque manifestations of inequality."[30] However, the Detroit Commission on Community Relations "remained small, underfunded, and less powerful than its mandates would require." Miller has this scathing assessment: "The agency was designed to quell racial conflicts with the aim of upholding the current urban order and saving the city from the negative economic and political consequences of discord. It was decidedly *not* an effort to reorganize municipal resources or power along more racially just lines."[31]

Worse than empty promises, these liberal institutions were guilty of "casting themselves as allied with 'the downtrodden' . . . but simultaneously working to sustain and extend deep inequalities."[32]

In the final analysis, *race relations* is a classic Orwellian example of the sinister use of a euphemism to serve as a smokescreen, in this case for camouflaging and perpetuating the very racial inequalities that they purport to oppose.

PART I

Counterrevolution in Historical and Theoretical Perspective

There is perhaps nothing more detrimental to an understanding of revolution than the common assumption that the revolutionary process has come to an end when liberation is achieved and the turmoil and the violence, inherent in all wars of independence, have come to an end.

Hannah Arendt, *On Revolution*[1]

In the pithy observation above, Hannah Arendt methodically lets the air out of the balloon of "revolution," pointing up that it invariably is a prelude to its antithesis: *counterrevolution*. Indeed, she points to the United States as a classic case where "the fever of constitution-making" that followed revolution, "far from expressing truly the revolutionary spirit of the country," was in fact "due to forces of reaction and either defeated the revolution or prevented its full development."[2]

In another illuminating passage, Arendt asserts that "the political scientist at least will know how to avoid the pitfall of the historian who tends to place his emphasis upon the first and violent state of rebellion and liberation, on the uprising against tyranny, to the detriment of the quieter second stage of revolution and constitution, because all the dramatic aspects of his story seem to be contained in the first stage and, perhaps, also because the turmoil of liberation has so frequently defeated the revolution."[3] Indeed, this rebuke to "the historian" is especially pertinent to left scholars who are enthralled with revolution but give short shrift to the messy and often contradictory aftermath of revolution.

However, the tug-of-war between revolution and counterrevolution is central to Marxist discourses. In an incisive essay published in *Logos* in 2011, Stephen Eric Bronner traces the concept of counterrevolution to Marx and Engels—specifically to Engels's *Revolution and Counter-Revolution in Germany* and to Marx's *Eighteenth Brumaire of Louis Napoleon*. In a passage that sheds as much light on Trump as on Napoleon, Bronner writes:

> Marx and Engels maintained that counter-revolution is embraced by the losers or those who feel they might become losers in dealing with the economic, political, and social forces comprising modernity. With its authoritarian nationalism, its preoccupation with prejudice and inequality, counter-revolution thus becomes the underside of the revolutionary struggle for cosmopolitanism, political liberty and social equality.[4]

In short, counterrevolution is built on the shards of revolution. The losers of revolution—in this case, the true believers and beneficiaries of white supremacy—do not fade quietly into the penumbra of history. Nor do they resign themselves to defeat. Over time, they retrench and mobilize to restore their power and privilege.

The restoration of power and privilege was not immediate. In *Black Reconstruction*, which runs over seven hundred pages, Du Bois shows that as soon as it became clear that the Union armies would not return fugitive slaves, Blacks declared a general strike against slavery using the same methods that they had used during the period of the fugitive slave. They ran away to the first place of safety and offered their services to the Federal Army. Note DuBois calling this "a general strike," deploying the language of labor's struggle against capitalism. "It was a general strike that involved directly in the end perhaps a half million people," Du Bois wrote. "They wanted to stop the economy of the plantation system, and to do that they left the plantations."[5]

Du Bois also documents, in fastidious detail, the myriad ways in which enslaved people struggled to claim their newfound freedom, despite the fact that "nine-tenths of the four million enslaved Blacks could neither read nor write, and [that] the overwhelming majority of them were isolated on country plantations."[6] In *Reconstruction* Eric Foner provides corroborating evidence of the agency with which slaves pursued freedom: "Like emancipation, the passage of the Reconstruction Act inspired Blacks with a millennial sense of living at the dawn of a new era. . . . Blacks found countless ways of pursuing aspirations for autonomy and equality, and seizing the opportunity to press for further change."[7]

Furthermore, in the immediate aftermath of the Civil War, there was an initial period of revolutionary transformation, building on the 1863 Emancipation Proclamation: not only the three Reconstruction Amendments to the Constitution, but also the 1866 Civil Rights Act, which declared that all citizens were equally protected by the law "without distinction of race or color, or previous condition of slavery or involuntary servitude." The 1866 act also proscribed discrimination in jobs and housing on the basis of race.

In a word, slavery was dead.

Not so fast! A portent of trouble was that the Civil Rights Act was passed over the veto of Andrew Johnson. The New York *Herald* reprimanded Johnson for forgetting that "we have passed through the fiery ordeal of a mighty revolution, and that the preexisting order of things is gone and can return no more—that a great work of reconstruction is before us, and that we cannot escape it."[8]

Lerone Bennett Jr., that much neglected public intellectual who was one of a left wing of writers at *Ebony* magazine, grappled with the wild oscillations of history in a 1981 issue of *Ebony*. He began with a sardonic depiction of Reconstruction:

Over.

It was, at long last, over and done with.

How could anyone doubt it? How could anyone fail to see that the race problem had been solved forever?

One man who had no doubt said, "All distinctions founded upon race and color have been forever abolished in the United States."

Another who saw things this way said the category of race has been forever abolished by law and that "there [were] no more colored people in this country."

Thus spoke the dreamers and prophets—and victims—in the first Reconstruction of the 1860s and 1870s.

It was precisely to dissipate any doubt about the constitutionality of the 1866 Civil Rights Act that Congress passed the Fourteenth Amendment two years later, followed by the Fifteenth Amendment in 1870. Thus were the final nails pounded into the coffin of slavery.

Or so it seemed.[9]

Only six years later, the disputed 1877 election led to the so-called Compromise of 1877—an unwritten pact that led to the withdrawal of the remaining federal troops from the South, marking the end of Reconstruction. W. E. B. DuBois wrote in his opus, *Black Reconstruction*: "The slave went free. Stood a brief moment in the sun. Then moved back again toward slavery." Note that Du Bois is careful in his diction. He did not say that Blacks moved back *to* slavery but rather *toward* slavery. He added pointedly: "A new slavery arose. . . . Democracy died save in the hearts of Black folk."[10]

Twenty years passed, marked by the rise of the Klan and the restoration of white supremacy in the South, before the coup de grace to Reconstruction was administered, this time by the Supreme Court in *Plessy v. Ferguson* (1896). The case riveted on Homer Plessy, an octoroon (in racist parlance), who refused to move from the "whites only" railcar.[11] With the *Plessy* ruling, "separate but equal" was given judicial sanction by the nation's highest court. This would remain frozen in law for seventy-five years, until the court ruled in *Brown v. Topeka Board of Education* that Justice Harlan, the sole dissenting vote in *Plessy*, was right all along, that "separate but equal" was in violation of the equal rights provision of our hallowed Constitution. The *Brown* decision paved the way for the dismantling of the Jim Crow system that was the stepchild of slavery.

Or so it seemed. Let us now begin our journey through the racial contradictions of the post–civil rights era, as the seeds of counterrevolution slowly but inexorably came to fruition. To paraphrase Du Bois, the Negro did not move back *to* Jim Crow, but rather one nail after another was pounded into the coffin of the civil rights revolution—stalling, eviscerating, and rolling back the hard-won gains of the epic struggle for racial equality.

CHAPTER ONE

NAILS IN THE COFFIN OF THE CIVIL RIGHTS REVOLUTION

We apparently expected that this social upheaval was going to be accomplished with peace, honesty and efficiency, and that the planters were going quietly to surrender the right to live on the labor of Black folk, after two hundred and fifty years of habitual exploitation.

W. E. B. Du Bois, *Black Reconstruction in America, 1860–1880*[1]

As with the Reconstruction Amendments a century earlier, the mere act of extending the full rights of citizenship to Blacks was met with massive resistance in the states of the old Confederacy. Leading politicians wasted no time in promulgating a Southern manifesto, endorsed in Congress by all the states in the former Confederacy. The manifesto assailed *Brown* as "an abuse of judicial power that trespassed upon states' rights."[2] These were fighting words, the language of Jim Crow all over again. Alas, the counterrevolution was in full swing, deploying the very logic and methods that had been deployed in the Civil War itself.

Nevertheless, *Brown* provided a crucial umbrella of legitimacy that helped to precipitate and sustain the budding civil rights movement. It was a grassroots movement by an oppressed people whose purpose was to restore rights so brutally suppressed. Yet it threw the entire society into crisis for a tumultuous decade! At times it assumed the semblance of a morality play: good struggling against manifest evil, ultimately reaching a denouement with the passage of landmark civil rights legislation in 1964 and 1965.

Almost forgotten from national memory is that the 1964 Civil Rights Act would have been filibustered, but for the assassination of President Kennedy. Remember too that the success of the civil rights movement owed little or nothing to the institutions of our putative democracy—state legislatures, courts, police, the two major political parties, and mass opinion all allied *against* the Black liberation movement. Granted, the movement had allies in all these domains, but to repeat, it was at bottom a grassroots movement of an oppressed minority and it ultimately succeeded out of conviction, perseverance, ingenuity, and sheer will. As with the abolition of slavery a century earlier, however, there was no restitution for generations of brutal oppression, once again exposing both the limits of passing laws and the false promise of "forty acres and a mule."

Indeed, it behooves us to pose the unexamined question: Was the so-called civil rights revolution a revolution in name only? Was this merely rhetorical flourish that provided a useful battle cry but that failed even in its most ardent iterations to address the fundamental issues of racial oppression? Yes, after two centuries the civil rights "revolution" eliminated dehumanizing Jim Crow practices in the South. Yes, at least formally it put an end to second-class citizenship. But think about it: the rights affirmed by the 1967 and 1968 Civil Rights Acts had been encoded in law by the 1866 Civil Rights Act and the Reconstruction Amendments. If this was progress, it was the progress of a people on a historical treadmill.[3]

Yet the passage of landmark civil rights legislation in the 1960s is widely regarded by scholars as the beginning of "the Second Reconstruction"—a term that C. Vann Woodward coined with a hopeful prognosis that "the second time around" (to invoke Lerone Bennett Jr.'s sardonic language) would lead the nation out of its racist morass. Or was the Second Reconstruction merely a ruse designed to appease the protestors and to serve white interests, as that inveterate "racial pessimist," Derrick Bell, contended? The ultimate question is whether the Second Reconstruction will end in shambles, as the First Reconstruction did a century earlier—in a tragic reversion to the status quo ante, save for some marginal gains that are celebrated only to obscure how far there is to go.

To state the obvious, the '64 and '65 Civil Rights Acts were momentous events, marking the end of the reign of terror in the South, disenfranchisement, and dehumanizing Jim Crow practices. And just as Blacks in 1866 had had a millennial sense of "living at the dawn of a new era," Blacks in 1968 had reason to believe that "the walls of segregation would come tumbling down." Indeed, after the landslide Democratic win in 1964, when Democrats swept all three branches of government, liberal pundits gleefully proclaimed: "Conservatism is dead."[4]

They could not have been more wrong. Only four years later, Richard Nixon was elected on the basis of a Southern strategy to bring the states of the former Confederacy into the ranks of the Republican Party. Looming in the background, George Wallace, the unapologetic champion of segregation, was gaining momentum and, as an ominous precursor to Donald Trump, was successfully appealing to white voters in Northern states. No sooner was Nixon elected to power than he nominated two outright segregationists to the Supreme Court.[5] Both were defeated in the Senate, which was still under the control of liberal Democrats, but it was only a matter of time before the Supreme Court would be packed by jurists nurtured by the Federalist Society and ideologically opposed to liberal rulings that sanctioned affirmative action.

My core argument is that the passage of landmark civil rights legislation in 1964 and 1965 did not mark the dawn of a new day and a Second Reconstruction, but on the contrary, it marked the apogee of the civil rights movement. It was "over," as Lerone Bennett Jr. had portended. And the ensuing half century has witnessed a relentless crusade to pound every last nail in the coffin of the civil rights revolution.

As Carol Anderson demonstrates in *White Rage*, Black gains are invariably short-lived. "The truth is that the hard-fought victories of the civil rights movement," she writes, "caused a reaction that stripped *Brown* of its power, severed the jugular of the Voting Rights Act, closed off access to higher education, poured crack cocaine into the inner cities, and locked up more black men proportionally that even apartheid-era South Africa."[6] Anderson quotes David Swinton, current chair of the Negro College Fund: "In virtually every area of life that counts, black people made strong progress in the 1960s, peaked in the '70s, and have been sliding back ever since."[7] The same refrain is found in Jason Hackworth's

Manufacturing Decline: "The reason that so many scholars placed *Black Reconstruction* on those reading lists is because it so neatly and presciently laid the foundation for understanding the paradoxical but repetitive pattern of racial progress followed by an angry reaction that often nullifies the progress made in the initial advance."[8]

The election of Barack Obama in 2008 provided a tentative interlude to four decades of backsliding on civil rights. Ironically, Obama's election exacerbated revanchist fervor to "take our country back." Isn't this what Mitch McConnell meant when he declared in October 2008, on the cusp of the midterm elections: "The single most important thing we want to achieve is for President Obama to be a one-term President."[9] A few days later, John Boehner minced no words when asked about his plans for the Obama agenda: "We're going to do everything—and I mean everything we can do—to kill it, stop it, slow it down, whatever we can."[10] "Kill it, stop it, slow it down"—precisely my point about the rhetoric and politics of counterrevolution.

What better indicator of the struggle between the forces of revolution and counterrevolution than the fierce tug of war that did not begin with Barack Obama's unexpected ascendency to the presidency, but was inadvertently exacerbated by it. Remember the unforgettable optic, on the eve of his election, when masses of exuberant followers assembled at Grant Park and Obama proclaimed: "This is our moment." He continued: "This is our time. Our time to turn the page on the policies of the past. Our time to bring new energy and new ideas to the challenges we face. Our time to offer a new direction for the country we love." In retrospect, this was the cusp between the past and an unanticipated future that was festering beneath the surface of electoral defeat.

Republicans lost no time in planning their comeback. According to a report by *Frontline*, as Democrats celebrated at inaugural balls across Washington, top GOP luminaries gathered at a swank Washington steakhouse, aptly called The Caucus Room. They looked shell-shocked and glum, according to those in attendance, but by the end of the night, they coalesced around a tough new strategy for taking on "the first Black president."[11] According to Newt Gingrich, the strategy going forward was to focus on jobs, spending, and the Tenth Amendment, emphasizing the autonomy of states' power. Norman Ornstein, a political scientist at the conservative American Enterprise Institute, reported that they figured out a way "to make the President's victories look messy and illegitimate." One wonders whether voter suppression was contemplated in the group's deliberations, since this evolved as a major tactic for assuring that the "red states" would never again lose their edge in the Electoral College.

Long story short, by the 2010 midterms, the Obama agenda was stopped in its tracks. And by 2016, the forces of counterrevolution were triumphant, thanks to an electoral system that the founders invented in order to defend slavery in the South.[12]

THE MAKING OF COUNTERREVOLUTION, NAIL BY NAIL

Long before the 1968 election, the Democratic Party was split by "an unholy alliance" between northern Democrats and southern Dixiecrats. The fissure became even more evident in the run-up to the 1968 election, when George Wallace surprised everyone by reaping significant support not only in the South, but in Democratic primaries in the North as well. In his 1969 book *The Emerging Republican Majority*, Kevin Phillips, a strategist in the Nixon campaign, declared that Nixon's election "bespoke the end of the New Deal Democratic hegemony and the beginning of a new era in American politics." The immediate cause was "Democratic voting streams quitting their party."[13] In effect, this amounted to white flight, not from urban neighborhoods and integrated schools but from a Democratic Party that committed the sin of abolishing Jim Crow and securing Blacks in the former Confederacy with the right to vote. Savvy politician that he was, Lyndon Johnson knew that the "solid South" would be lost to the Democratic Party. Of course, the reciprocal event was that the Republican Party assumed the mantle of "the party of segregation," as Thomas Edsall wrote in his 1992 book, *Chain Reaction: The Impact of Race, Rights, and Taxes on American Politics*.[14]

Alas, pronouncements of "the death of conservatism" were premature. After Nixon's election in 1968, Republicans went on to win five of the next six elections and seven of the ten elections until 2004, thus securing Republican control over the institutions of national power, including the Supreme Court. To curb defection among its traditional constituencies, the "New Democrats" under the leadership of Bill Clinton moved the party decidedly to the right. In 1994, responding to the moral panic over drugs and crime, Clinton endorsed the Violent Crime Control and Law Enforcement Act, which set the stage for mass incarceration.[15] The other shoe fell when Clinton affixed his signature to the 1996 Personal Responsibility and Work Opportunity Reconciliation Act, which ended welfare entitlements that dated back to the Depression. In a rare case of political courage, Clinton's two principal advisors resigned in protest.[16] Indeed, the very titles of these two bills betray their retrograde underpinnings.

It is commonplace to regard this oscillation from left to right as an inevitable swing of the political pendulum. However, in his essay "Notes on the Counter-Revolution," Stephen Eric Bronner presents a more incisive explanation: "The ongoing battle of opposing value systems was generated less by some abstract 'dialectic' than by a concrete and empirical conflict between the partisans of revolution and counterrevolution."[17] The challenge, then, is to identify the partisans of counterrevolution and to explain their political ascension.

Note, however, that the partisans of counterrevolution do not have to be preponderant to have a decisive impact on electoral politics. In 1991 Thomas and Mary Edsall observed: "The sea change in American presidential politics—the replacement of a liberal majority with a conservative majority—involved the conversion of a relatively small proportion of voters: the roughly five to ten percent of the electorate, made up primarily of white working-class voters empowered to give majority status to either political party."[18] This would eventually come to fruition with the 2016 election of Donald Trump.

Soon after Nixon's election in 1964, other nails were driven into the coffin. Given the rapidly shifting political currents, Nixon oscillated between opposing poles on civil rights. On the one hand, he nominated two outright segregationists to the Supreme Court. (Pound! Pound!) On the other hand, he appointed George Romney as secretary of HUD, whose declared mission was to integrate the suburbs, the very place to which whites had fled to escape the Black nemesis. When the predictable backlash erupted, Nixon reneged and eased Romney out of office. Integrated housing: another nail in the coffin.[19] (Pound!)

Another egregious flip-flop involved the Philadelphia Plan, which was the embryo of affirmative action policy. Affirmative action was actually the brainchild of liberals ensconced in Johnson's Department of Labor, but it was shelved after Humphrey's defeat. However, when Nixon was confronted with a raft of protests by Black workers at construction sites in New York, Detroit, and Chicago, he gave Arthur Fletcher, his Black assistant secretary of labor, and his boss George Shultz, the green light to resurrect the plan. In doing so, Nixon risked losing political capital in Congress when the plan was opposed, not by Republicans but by labor unions and Jewish organizations. Strangely, the plan received only equivocal support from civil rights leaders.

This was the strange career of the Philadelphia Plan: championed by Richard Nixon who was elected on the basis of his appeals to Southern racism, and opposed by Bayard Rustin, who was the principal organizer of the March on Washington. Rustin believed that the Philadelphia Plan was a cynical attempt by Nixon to break up the coalition of liberals, labor, and Jews, which had coalesced behind the successful march. This dubious theory was subsequently endorsed by a number of pundits, including Hugh Davis Graham, author of *The Civil Rights Era*.[20]

Let me suggest another explanation. In 1968, Nixon found himself torn between the forces of revolution and the forces of counterrevolution. Responding to the mounting protests against blatant discrimination in the construction trades, Nixon was persuaded to endorse the Philadelphia Plan championed by Arthur Fletcher, a Republican from Ohio who Nixon had appointed to serve as assistant secretary of labor in his incoming administration.[21] Fletcher regarded affirmative action as consistent with Republican precepts inasmuch as it relied on the free market, consisting of over 100 million jobs, to absorb Blacks broadly across the employment spectrum. Since the Philadelphia Plan was targeted for predominantly Democratic unions, it was not risky politically, or so it was assumed. However, when unions unleashed a firestorm of protest, Nixon quietly backed away from the policy that he had put into place.

Another turning point came when the Philadelphia Plan was challenged in the Supreme Court, where it was defended by Attorney General John Mitchell. After the court's favorable ruling, affirmative action mandates (the much maligned "goals and timetables") were extended to all government contractors. This included universities that were beneficiaries of governmental largesse. Now it was not lily white unions but erudite professors in lily white universities who used the weapon at their disposal—words—to pen erudite books that portrayed affirmative action as antithetical to democratic norms and a peril to academic freedom.[22] Given the fiery opposition in both public and scholarly discourses, Nixon again flip-flopped, and in the 1972 election he ran against the very "quotas" that he had put into effect. Another major nail in the coffin. (Pound!)

Excursus: The Strange Career of Affirmative Action

The breach over affirmative action not only shattered the liberal coalition that had coalesced in the March on Washington, but it also helped to resuscitate conservatism from its long slumber.

As Rustin knew all too well, affirmative action was divisive among unions that regarded their nepotistic hiring practices as a matter of racial privilege, especially when it came to jobs in construction and manufacturing.[23] For their part, Jewish leaders regarded affirmative action as reminiscent of the numerus clausus in Russia that restricted Jewish enrollment in universities. Furthermore, they regarded any form of "proportional representation" as a dangerous precedent, given their relatively small number in the population at large. By the 1980s, what had begun as an internal squabble within the liberal coalition emerged as a full-blown anti-affirmative-action crusade, now centered in the political Right. What explains this political metamorphosis?

In *Freedom Is Not Enough: The Opening of the American Workplace*, Nancy MacLean reveals how the rhetoric of compensatory treatment and the emerging political battles over affirmative action resurrected the conservative cause from the doldrums of Goldwater's defeat. For many years the Right struggled to find traction among die-hard Republicans.[24] By the early 1970s, conservative pundits realized they could reap political hay from white resentment over "quotas." Now it was conservative scholars who put their talents as wordsmiths to work. Writing in *Commentary* in 1972, Richard Herrnstein (later the coauthor with Charles Murray of *The Bell Curve*) railed against "the equalitarian orthodoxy."[25]

William Buckley, the founding editor of *The National Review*, discovered commonality with the new ideological pathways forged by the neocons at *Commentary*. According to MacLean, Buckley "observed the work of the neoconservatives with mounting admiration and excitement as Irving Kristol, for example, argued that conservatives were defending liberal institutions from liberals' own mounting complaints."[26]

Thus it passed that affirmative action provided conservatives with an issue that went beyond fighting Communism and championing free enterprise. At the same time, it dispelled suspicions that conservatives harbored a latent anti-Semitism or animus toward Blacks. With this ideological facelift, conservatives could now present themselves not as the enemy of equality but as the champion of colorblindness. Instead of opposition to Blacks and civil rights, they morphed into the champions of white males against "the New Equality" that, according to Robert Nisbet, was "the gravest single threat to liberty and social initiative."[27] Thus, with the help of the nascent neocons at *Commentary*, conservatives used the controversy over affirmative action to turn the tables on liberals and to develop an ideological blueprint for the restoration of conservatives to power.

By the 1980s, opposition to affirmative action had grown into a veritable crusade, waged by conservative pundits and publications with the complicity of right-wing foundations and think tanks. As in the case of the revolution that the partisans of counterrevolution sought to negate, the shifting political currents reached into the university and the ranks of social science. Charles Murray's 1984 book *Losing Ground* argued that the welfare state created the conditions that it purported to remedy: welfare dependency, non-work, family breakdown, rising crime, moral breakdown.[28] Thomas Sowell, Glenn Loury, and a cadre of Black conservatives, lavishly funded by foundations and ensconced in leading universities, put a Black face on "white sociology," vitiating claims that sociology had all along been driven by racism. Publication of *The Bell Curve* in 1994 marked the apex of the intellectual backlash, with the reinstatement of the scientific racism that supposedly had been relinquished to the trash heap nearly a century earlier. Nor was the backlash only about biology. As Adolph Reed wrote in *The Nation* in 1994: "We can trace Murray's legitimacy directly to the spinelessness, opportunism and racial bad faith of the liberals in the social-policy establishment. . . . Many of those objecting to Herrnstein and Murray's racism embrace positions that are almost indistinguishable, except for the resort to biology."[29]

If Thomas Sowell put a Black face on conservatism, William Julius Wilson put a Black face on racial liberalism. In his Godkin Lectures at Harvard in 1985, Daniel Patrick Moynihan could gloat: "The family report had been viewed as mistaken; the benign neglect memorandum was depicted as out-and-out racist. By mid-decade, however, various Black scholars were reaching similar conclusions, notably William Julius Wilson in his 1978 study, *The Declining Significance of Race.*" For his part, Moynihan was on record, as early as 1965, as opposed to compensatory treatment for Blacks, insisting that such policies had to be race neutral.[30] Once again, Wilson picked up the very ideological position for which Moynihan and white liberals had been pummeled. When he, too, came under attack, Wilson shifted his position to join those who argued that affirmative action should be class based. This position was congenial not only to many on the left but also to right-wing advocates who cast themselves as champions of the white working class.

In actuality, class-based affirmative action never had a chance of being enacted as policy, but it served as a red herring in the affirmative action debate. This explains why the idea of class-based affirmative action was embraced by the very conservatives who spearheaded the crusade against affirmative action: Clint Bolick, Dinesh D'Souza, Clarence Thomas, Charles Murray, Richard Herrnstein, and Newt Gingrich.[31] It was sheer political theater, as they feigned compassion for the working classes only to provide ideological cover for their assault on affirmative action.

According to MacLean, within less than a year of its proclamation, word spread that the Philadelphia Plan was to "die a quiet death."[32] In February 1973, Nixon appointed Peter Brennan, the New York City building-trades leader who organized the "hard-hat" demonstrations, as secretary of labor, thus driving another nail in the coffin of the civil rights movement. (Pound!)

The Republican Party's Ideological Facelift

The sheer force of the civil rights revolution, reinforced by the rise of Black militancy in the 1970s, made overt racism politically unacceptable.

It was replaced with a system of code words and dog whistles. Speaking with rare candor in an anonymous interview in 1981, Lee Atwater—Reagan's campaign consultant—explained the evolution of the Southern strategy:

> You start out in 1954 by saying, "Nigger, nigger, nigger." By 1968 you can't say "nigger"—that hurts you. Backfires. So you say stuff like, states' rights and all that stuff. You're getting so abstract now [that] you're talking about cutting taxes, and all these things you're talking about are totally economic things and a byproduct of them is [that] Blacks get hurt worse than whites. And subconsciously maybe that is part of it. I'm not saying that. But I'm saying that if it is getting that abstract, and that coded, that we are doing away with the racial problem one way or the other. You follow me—because obviously sitting around saying, "We want to cut this," is much more an abstract than even the busing thing, and a hell of a lot more abstract than "Nigger, nigger."[33]

These rhetorical artifices allowed conservatives to tap white resentment not by assailing Blacks directly but by championing small government, states' rights, and lower taxes.

Thus, the electoral success of Republicans during the post–civil rights era was the result of not only racial backlash. It also reflected the inroads that conservative tenets had made with voters with conservative proclivities who wavered in their loyalty to the Democratic Party. Though Republicans inherited the dubious mantle of "the party of segregation," more was involved than white backlash. "Wallace defined a new right-wing populism," Thomas and Mary Edsall wrote, "capitalizing on voter reaction to the emergence of racial, cultural, and moral liberalism."[34]

The Logic of Revanchism

Logically and politically, the partisans of counterrevolution were compelled to begin where the revolution had begun—with the civil rights movement. Thus, conservative intellectuals and strategists seized upon the mounting popular opposition to the racial liberalism that culminated with the passage of civil rights legislation in the 1960s. As we have seen, a second line of attack was on affirmative action, which stoked racial grievance inasmuch as Blacks were regarded as receiving "preference" over whites. A third line of attack was on "welfare"—that is to say, Aid for Dependent Children (AFDC). The strategy that activists deployed was to racialize welfare—to pretend that it existed as a sop to Blacks, who, in their racist imaginary, preferred welfare to work. This strategy was highly effective in mobilizing white resentment against welfare, despite the fact that two-thirds of AFDC recipients were white. The assonance between "welfare" and "the welfare state" was exploited to the hilt, in that these three strategies were ultimately dress rehearsals for a larger assault on the welfare state itself.

Welfare had come under withering attack over several decades, no doubt heightened by the success of the welfare rights movement in expanding the welfare rolls during the late '60s and '70s. In the '80s Ronald Reagan stoked white grievance with his riff about "the welfare queen" with eighty names, thirty addresses, and twelve Social Security cards who drove around Chicago's South Side in a Cadillac.[35]

For all the political wrangling, AFDC was never a very costly program. Its benefits went primarily to children and their mothers and consisted of a rent supplement and a meager living allowance. Between 1970 and 1993, total federal and state spending on AFDC benefits increased from $15.5 billion to $22.3 billion (adjusted for inflation). Even though the number of recipients increased by 91 percent, costs increased by only 44 percent because the average monthly AFDC benefit per family shrank by almost half. The final blow came in 1996, when Bill Clinton, casting himself as a New Democrat, affixed his signature to the Personal Responsibility and Work Opportunity Act, annulling welfare entitlements that had been in place since the New Deal.[36] Another cruel nail in the coffin of the civil rights movement. (Pound!) And an opening salvo in a crusade against the welfare state itself.

RACE AND NEOLIBERALISM

In the foregoing pages, I have recounted the plethora of factors that have stalled, rolled back, eviscerated, and ultimately defeated the civil rights revolution that culminated with the passage of landmark legislation in 1964 and 1965. Along with that litany of factors, we should also consider the larger transformations in American society that not only undercut the gains of the civil rights movement but also introduced other barriers that were not directly aimed at Blacks but fell on them disproportionately. These not only eroded past gains but also diminished future opportunity. This was the advent of neoliberalism, rooted in major transformations in the global economy that, five or ten steps removed, placed other formidable obstacles on the road to economic mobility. Only in hindsight is it clear that Bill Clinton, the archetypal New Democrat, represented a transitional period in what crystallized into neoliberalism.[37]

Let me make two related points about race and neoliberalism. First, race and racism were used, with political cunning, to epitomize all that is wrong with the welfare state, to whip up antagonism toward the "big government" that gave us the New Deal and the Great Society, and to impart new legitimacy to "states' rights," which was the ideological linchpin of the Civil War and a catalyst of the civil rights movement. Second, the policies enacted under the emergent neoliberal regime have had particularly devastating effects on African Americans. So much the better, as Lee Atwater stated with unusual candor, since this tapped the lode of submerged racism and gave credence to the lie that liberal programs were designed to help Blacks at the expense of everybody else. Indeed, Glenn Beck denounced universal healthcare, universal college, and green jobs as "stealth reparations" for African Americans.[38]

Downsizing of Government and Outsourcing of Government Services
The public sector has long been the staple of the Black middle class. This evolved partly because wages were lower in the public sector before the emergence of public-sector unions; partly because, in the era of affirmative action, the government could more easily control its own employment practices than those in the private sector; and partly because it was useful to put a Black face on such governmental functions as corrections and social services, in sharp contrast to the uniformed services, which remained a bastion of white privilege.

Today 21.2 percent of all Black workers are public employees, compared with 16.3 percent of non-Black workers.[39] Moreover, "the fact that Blacks are disproportionately represented in government employment makes the entire public sector vulnerable to attack, not just because billionaires like the Koch brothers back Tea Party politicians, but because huge sections of the white public are prepared to withhold solidarity for racial reasons," as Glen Ford asserted in a radio commentary.[40] Furthermore, racist stereotypes feed the image of government workers as inefficient and unproductive and thereby use racism to justify the privatization of government services.[41]

Free Trade

During the debate over NAFTA (North American Free Trade Agreement), the eccentric third party candidate Ross Perot proclaimed that he could hear the "giant sucking sound" of jobs going from the United States to Mexico and other low-wage nations. His prophecy came true. Under NAFTA, the United States strategically agreed to trade off its ageing and uncompetitive industrial plants for greater access to markets for U.S. exports, ranging from high technology and aviation to agricultural products, to intellectual property and mass culture. The sucking sounds that we heard after the passage of the NAFTA—the hemorrhaging of blue-collar jobs and the downward pressure on wages—are race neutral but they had disproportionate impact on Blacks. Just when Blacks had finally secured a foothold in such industries as textiles, automobiles, and steel, millions of these jobs were exported to low-wage counties.

Neoliberal Immigration Policy

Immigration is commonly regarded as a project of the political Left, presumably because the Left is more sympathetic to the struggles of immigrants. Though true, the bigger picture is that the champions of mass immigration in the post–civil rights period were not liberals but free-market economists (now tagged as "neoliberals") who contended that increased immigration was a panacea for a variety of economic ills. A notable example is Julian Simon, who in 1988 published the book *The Economic Consequences of Immigration* and two years later followed up with an article in *The Public Interest*, entitled "The Case for Greatly Increased Immigration." In them, Simon made the following arguments:

1. The nation stood to gain technologically through the addition of "top scientific talent." (Never mind that from the standpoint of the sending countries, this amounted to a brain drain.)

2. Immigration was necessary to satisfy business's demand for labor, given the declining birth rates that had sunk even below replacement levels. (One wonders if the legions of Blacks without jobs were ever part of the calculus.)

3. Immigrants helped to pay for the social security pensions of the burgeoning number of retirees. To wit, a 2005 article in the *New York Times* reported that in 2002 illegal immigrants had paid $6.4 billion in Social Security taxes for benefits they would never receive.[42]

4. Immigration boosted the image of the United States abroad. (Read: immigrants fit constructively into the global economy, not to speak of foreign policy agendas.)

Granted, there were some strident voices on the Right, like Peter Brimelow, whose book *Alien Nation* was an anti-immigrant screed in the worst nativist tradition. In contrast, Simon's book advanced a respectable economic case for mass immigration and received rhapsodic reviews in the *National Review*, *Forbes*, *Business Week*, *The Spectator*, and *Barron's National Business and Fiscal Weekly*.

Other cheerleaders of "greatly increased immigration" contended that immigration lowered inflation (never mind that it does this by depressing wages). Still others argued that immigrants lowered the deficit by propping up domestic manufacturing and generating economic activity through "enclave economies" (never mind that this amounts the creation of a sub-proletariat of immigrant workers). And still others exulted that immigrants provided the energy to renew the fading American spirit of enterprise and innovation (never mind that this amounts to disinvestment in Black labor, whose family roots go back to the beginning of the nation). Where are the avatars of "greatly increased immigration" when it comes to protecting these immigrants from nativist calumny? Is it that they do not want to own up to the role that they play in relying on immigrants for capitalist growth, without being held to account for the negative externalities that immigration has on wages generally?

Excursus: The (Virtually) Untold Story of the 1965 Immigration Act

The 1965 Immigration and Nationality Act eliminated the national-origins quotas that were instituted in 1924. Given its timing—1965—there is a tendency to assume that this reform was a facet of the civil rights era. However, the legislation was not advanced by Black leaders, or for that matter, by ethnic groups seeking to promote immigration. What then was its source? Who were the actors or advocacy groups who put immigration reform on the heels of passage of the 1964 and 1965 Civil Rights Acts?

The answer to this question is hidden in plain sight: in the official title of the Hart-Celler Immigration Act. In 1924, when the national-origins provision was enacted, Emmanuel Celler was a young congressman from a predominantly Jewish and Italian district in Brooklyn, New York. That year Congress approved a sweeping overhaul of immigration policy. Not only did the legislation drastically cut the volume of immigration, but it was particularly targeted for Eastern and Southern Europeans (read: Jews and Italians). Not only that, but it pegged the quotas to the extent that groups were represented in the 1880 census, before the great wave of immigration disproportionately from Eastern and Southern Europe. Celler was in the forefront of those who opposed the bill as discriminatory against Jews and Italians. For decades, Jewish defense organizations periodically waged a battle to revoke these national-origins quotas, but to no avail. As fate would have it, Celler was chairman of the Judiciary Committee in the Senate, where he steered the civil rights bills through Congress. In 1965 he also seized the opportunity to finally revoke the national-origins quotas.

Of course, Celler did not do this alone. Despite the historical impact of the 1965 Immigration Act, the full story of its passage is rarely mentioned, much less celebrated. However, this momentous event is copiously documented in Mae Ngai's book *Impossible Subjects: Illegal Aliens and the Making of Modern America*.[43] According to Ngai, leaders of the American Jewish Congress brought together a group of prominent Jewish historians, sociologists, and demographers who made a case for abolishing the national-origins quota system established in 1924. The group included Oscar Handlin, the preeminent historian of immigration, and his protégé, Arthur Mann. These scholars made a case for the 1965 Immigration Act that abolished the national-origins quotas. When the act was debated in Congress, skeptical senators from Southern states asked whether the act would open up the floodgates of immigration to people the world over. They were informed by leading experts that their fears were unwarranted insofar as the family preferences embedded in immigration policy would assure that immigration flows would correspond, more or less, to the representation of ethnic groups at the present time.

As it turned out, the great majority of immigrant arrivals under the 1965 act were people of color: mostly from Latin America, Asia, and the Caribbean. Ironically, this was an unintentional consequence of the act. Its purpose had not been to diversify immigration policy but rather to eliminate the discriminatory national-origins quotas in the 1924 Immigration Act.[44] However, the 1965 act drastically transformed the peopling of the United States for generations.

Gentrification

Cities across the nation are not undergoing gentrification because yuppies have discovered the charms of city life. Rather, the gentrification and revitalization of American cities reflect seismic shifts in the global economy, congruent with the ambitions of politicians and developers. A byproduct, however, has been the reclamation of Black neighborhoods in major American cities previously abandoned by white flight to the suburbs. No surprise that results from the 2010 census indicated a substantial decline of Blacks in cities across the nation, such as Detroit, Chicago, Oakland, Cleveland, Boston, New York, and Atlanta.[45]

Nor is this because Blacks have belatedly discovered "the brass ring" of the suburbs, as William Frey, a demographer at the Brookings Institute, has suggested.[46] In a 2011 op-ed in the *New York Times*, Thomas Sugrue offered a more incisive explanation: "Those Blacks heading outward from Detroit aren't moving to all suburbs equally. Rather, they move into places with older houses, rundown shopping districts and declining tax revenues." Sugrue aptly terms this "secondhand suburbia," a far cry from the situation when whites fled urban neighborhoods for a dream house in thriving suburban communities with rising real estate values.[47]

Racial Cleansing

Worse even than gentrification is the perverse effect of HOPE VI, a policy initiative of Bill Clinton and his HUD secretary, Henry Cisneros. Begun in 1992, its ostensible purpose was to revitalize the worst public housing in the United States. HOPE is an acronym for "housing opportunity for people everywhere," an Orwellian construct for a policy that demolished over 100,000 units of public housing in the first ten years of program funding.[48] In Chicago, entire public housing communities were obliterated, over the rage and tears of their occupants and with the deafening silence of Barack Obama and the complicity of Valerie Jarrett.[49] In other cities like Atlanta, the public housing that was demolished had been occupied by stable working-class families but sat on real estate that was ripe for development. Against their intentions, urban sociologists have been complicit in the systematic displacement of African Americans from neighborhoods and cities where they had deep roots. As James Baldwin famously declared in the 1960s, "urban renewal" is another name for "Negro removal."[50]

The neoliberal city has accelerated the destruction of public housing. Its residents invariably find refuge in other poor and segregated communities. The startling failure of programs under the specious logic of "deconcentrating poverty," is copiously documented in Edward Goetz's 2003 study, *Clearing the Way: Deconcentrating the Poor*. As Goetz writes in his concluding sentence: "The scattering of poor people, in itself, accomplishes little."[51] However, as suggested by the title of his book, it "clears the way" for capitalist plunder, all in the name of the "urban revitalization."

Schooling

What does schooling have to do with neoliberalism? A great deal. In the eyes of the new Malthusians, the neoliberal city could be ever more beatific, and real estate ever more valuable, if we could eliminate the poor Blacks who are regarded as a vestigial drag on the body politic, as opposed to immigrants who are regarded as bringing energy, vitality, and economic activity to declining neighborhoods. Good schools are essential for attracting young, affluent buyers to gentrifying neighborhoods. Despite its moniker, the program No Child Left Behind has provided a ruse for closing down "failing schools," this time over the rage and tears of families who are then dispersed to other neighborhoods. In this way the charter school movement amounts to a piecemeal privatization of public education and fits perfectly within the neoliberal agenda.[52]

Mass Incarceration

"The carceral state," as Loic Wacquant calls it, currently involves the incarceration of some 2.3 million people, two-thirds of whom are Black and Latinx men. More than 7 million Americans are behind bars, on probation, or on parole. Few analysts have connected the dots between mass incarceration and gentrification since the pacification of ghetto neighborhoods is a precondition for white home buyers and renters.[53] This is also the logic behind aggressive policing, "weed and seed policies" (the "community policing" initiated under Clinton), stop-and-frisk policies, and the targeting of minority males for marijuana arrests. Harry Levine has documented that between 1997 and 2007 the New York City police targeted minority neighborhoods and arrested over 400,000 males for possessing small amounts of marijuana.[54] The end result of the carceral state, with its mandatory sentencing and three-strike provisions, has been the expulsion of a class of "marked men" who are condemned to joblessness and poverty.

Mass incarceration has had devastating effects on families, as Michelle Alexander demonstrates, condemning another generation of Black children to growing up in poverty.[55] Many states deny the franchise to felons, an ostensibly race-neutral mechanism that, like the poll tax and literacy tests of yore, disfranchise large numbers of Black voters.

Voter Suppression

The 1965 Voting Rights Act is celebrated as the "crown jewel of the civil rights movement." It was the last and most important bulwark of the Jim Crow system to fall, since restoration of the right to vote was crucial for guaranteeing all the other rights of citizenship, especially due process and equal rights. Indeed, it was the unprecedented outpouring of Black voters that secured the election of Barack Obama in 2008 (only 43 percent of whites nationally voted for Obama). This sent shock waves through the Republican Party, which responded by revving up efforts to suppress the Black vote.

According to Scott Keeter, director of survey research at the Pew Research Center, the shifting demographics of Middle America are "a ticking time bomb for Republicans."[56] This explains why "eight of eleven states in the former Confederacy" have passed restrictive voting laws since the 2010 election," according to Ari Berman. Nor is this only a Southern phenomenon. According to the Brennan Center of Social Justice, since the 2010 elections, twenty-three states have adopted new voting restrictions, such as ID laws. As in the era of Jim Crow, they artfully depended on ruses that are neutral on their face but discriminatory in practice.[57] Nearly 200,000 Floridians, approximately 26,000 of them Black, were declared ineligible to vote in 2012. States like Ohio and Wisconsin initiated a policy of "voter purging" that ostensibly removes the names of ineligible voters, but wrongly removes many eligible voters as well. Indeed, this practice was a factor in Gore's loss to Bush in 2000.[58] Kareem Crayton, a professor of law at UNC-Chapel Hill, has stated: "After Reconstruction, we saw efforts by conservative whites in Southern state legislatures to cut back on opportunities for Black Americans to cast a ballot. It's hard to dismiss the theory that what we're seeing today is a replay of that scenario."[59]

Neoliberalism is a racist project. Not only does it rely upon racism for its justification and implementation, but its burden falls heavily on Blacks, exacerbating the racial divide on which it prospers.

In closing, let us pivot back to Lerone Bennett's prescient meditation on the Second Reconstruction, written in 1981:

> Is history repeating itself?
>
> Are we helpless pawns in some mad historical game?
>
> Are we destined to relive the agonies of our ancestors? . . .
>
> The same story began unfolding in precisely the same way precisely 100 years later in the 1960s.
>
> Once again, Blacks and their White allies went to the barricades. Once again, breaches were made in the Great White Wall. Once again, there were voting rights bills and public accommodations and Black sheriffs and mayors and even a Black U.S. senator. And then—in the 1970s and 1980s—the same forces that dug the grave of the first Reconstruction—a massive White backlash and a massive defection by White liberals, the economic interests of powerful industrialists, growing unease over welfare and taxation for social purposes, a national economic crisis, an

ambiguous and ambivalent new president, and a new and conservative Supreme Court—began to dig the grave of the Second. Whatever the explanation, the unfolding drama of "the second time around," the same old racial track has provoked no end of discussion in Black America where more and more people are saying, with different degrees of sophistication, "We have seen this movie before."[60]

CHAPTER TWO

HOW DANIEL PATRICK MOYNIHAN DERAILED THE CIVIL RIGHTS REVOLUTION

It's disheartening, disappointing that it seems like some of the gains that
we made as we came along and as we were thinking of our children . . .
and we find that we are fighting for some of the same things. True, we've
made progress along the way, but when you look at things and where
we should be as far as race is concerned, economics and other things of
that nature, I feel that we've gone backwards.

> Pricilla Harris Wallace, graduate of Howard School of
> Social Work, on President Johnson's address at Howard
> University, June 4, 1965, "To Fulfill These Rights"[1]

The civil rights revolution came to a triumphant climax with the passage
of the 1964 and 1965 Civil Rights Acts that ended legal segregation and
the disfranchisement of African Americans in the South. In *The Moynihan Report and The Politics of Controversy*, Lee Rainwater and William L. Yancey wrote: "The year 1965 may be known in history as the
time when the civil rights movement discovered, in the sense of becoming
explicitly aware, that abolishing legal racism would not produce Negro
equality."[2] Indeed, this was very much on the minds of movement leaders.
As Martin Luther King put it: "What good is it to be able to be allowed
to eat in a restaurant if you can't afford a hamburger," a refrain that was
repeated, with minor variations, by movement leaders.[3]

It is widely assumed that the civil rights movement was a victim of its own success in that it achieved its legislative goals. Indeed, in the aftermath of the controversy unleashed by his report *The Negro Family*, Daniel Patrick Moynihan would claim that "the civil-rights movement had no program for going beyond the traditional and relatively easy issues of segregation and discrimination."[4] However, this is a patently false statement, and as I will show, a deliberate evasion. Even before the passage of the Civil Rights Acts of 1964 and 1965, movement leaders were anticipating a second phase of the struggle, one that shifted from "liberty" to "equality." To pay for the proverbial hamburger meant gaining access to jobs that paid a living wage. Indeed, it boils down to a simple proposition: If, as people say, "the family is the cornerstone of our society," then a job that pays a living wage is the cornerstone of the family.

BEYOND CIVIL RIGHTS

By 1965 movement leaders not only contemplated a second phase of the civil rights movement but were evolving a discourse and a corresponding plan of action around the idea of "compensatory treatment" with respect to jobs and education. As early as October 1963, the issue of compensation was debated in no less a public forum than the *New York Times Magazine*. The debate centered on whether there should be "'compensation' for Negroes." Arguing for compensation was Whitney Young, executive director of the National Urban League. Already on the defensive, Young wrote: "The Urban League is asking for a special effort, not for special privileges. This effort has been described as 'preferential treatment,' 'indemnification,' 'special consideration,' 'compensatory action.' These are 'scare' phrases that obscure the meaning of the proposal and go against the grain of our native sense of fair play. . . . What we ask now is for a brief period there be a deliberate and massive effort to include the Negro citizen in the mainstream of American life." Arguing against compensation was Kyle Haselden, editor of *Christian Century* and author of *The Racial Problems in Christian Perspective*. Haselden contended that "our goal should be parity, not preferment." And he struck the chord that would pervade anti-affirmative-action discourse down to the present: "Compensation for Negroes is a subtle but pernicious form of racism."[5]

The mere suggestion of compensation sent shock waves through an unexpected venue: the editors of *Commentary* magazine, renowned in the 1960s as a preeminent journal of liberal thought and a haven for New York intellectuals. In retrospect, by the 1960s, *Commentary* was slowly morphing into an incubus for a new political paradigm: neoconservatism. To the *Commentary* editors and circle of writers (dubbed "the family"), the mere mention of "compensation" aroused the specter of "quotas," a reminder of the numerus clausus in Russia that restricted Jewish access to colleges and the professions. Jewish leaders also harbored memory of the limits on Jewish enrollment during the 1920s in elite colleges in the United States, including Harvard and Columbia.

Memory of discriminatory quotas also stretched back to the national-origins quotas enacted in 1924, which were targeted against Eastern European Jews, along with Italians and other "races" from Southern and Eastern Europe. For decades, Jewish defense groups lobbied to repeal these quotas, which they regarded as a flagrant violation of democratic norms and a dangerous precedent. As detailed in chapter 1, the movement to abolish the national-origins quotas finally succeeded with the passage of the 1965 Immigration Act, thanks to the support of Emmanuel Celler and a coalition of Jewish organizations and prominent scholars, most notably Oscar Handlin.[6]

Quotas in any shape or form were anathema, all the more so because Jews are an overrepresented minority with respect to college admissions. In 1975 Nathan Glazer, a frequent contributor to *Commentary*, wrote the first book-length polemic against quotas. Entitled *Affirmative Discrimination*, the book is memorable for one incendiary passage, that affirmative action was reminiscent of the Nuremberg laws.[7] Clearly, this was a wake-up call that affirmative action was antithetical to Jewish interests.

Concerns over the new direction of the civil rights movement led *Commentary* to sponsor a roundtable discussion on "liberalism and the Negro" at the Town Hall in New York City. Norman Podhoretz, *Commentary*'s editor-in-chief, introduced the roundtable by noting that liberals were now divided into two schools: traditional liberals, who sought to integrate "deserving Negroes one by one into white society," and "a new school of liberal (or perhaps it should be called radical) thought" based on the premise that "the rights and privileges of an individual rest upon the status attained by the group to which he belongs." Behind this elliptical language was the specter of quotas. Finally, Podhoretz laid his cards on the table:

> This school of thought insists that radical measures are now needed to overcome the Negro's inherited disabilities. Whitney Young of the National Urban League, for example, has recently spoken of a domestic Marshall Plan, a crash program which he says need last only ten years, in order to bring the Negro community to a point where it can *begin* to compete on equal terms with the white world. Other Negro leaders have similarly talked about 10 percent quotas in hiring, housing, and so on. Negroes, they say, ought to be represented in all areas of American life according to their proportion in the population, and where they are not so represented, one is entitled to draw an inference of discrimination. The slogan "preferential treatment for Negroes" is the most controversial one that has come up in this discussion.[8]

Never mind that the Anti-Defamation League also protested the under-representation of Jews in the boardrooms of major corporations and called for remedial action.

Commentary brought its heavyweights to the roundtable: Nathan Glazer, Sidney Hook, Gunnar Myrdal, and James Baldwin (who had published several of his early essays in *Commentary*). Glazer, Hook, and Myrdal declared their blanket opposition to any system of racial preference. Glazer touted the success of New York's Fair Employment Practices Law, implying that racial justice could be achieved within the same liberal framework that worked for other groups. Hook argued that by lowering the standards for Negroes, preference was patronizing and, in effect, treated Blacks as second-class citizens. Myrdal cautioned that preference amounted to tokenism and that what was needed was a program to lift *all poor people* out of poverty.

James Baldwin stood alone, parrying the arguments thrust at him with wit and resolve. When Hook gloated over the expansion of ethical principles in American society, Baldwin retorted:

What strikes me here is that you are an American talking about American society and I am an American talking about American society—both of us very concerned with it—and yet your version of American society is really very difficult for me to recognize. My experience in it has simply not been yours.[9]

Indeed, the day's proceedings corroborated Podhoretz's initial observation of "a widening split between the Negro movement and the white liberal community." In effect, Podhoretz drew a line in the sand, warning that if movement leaders were moving in the direction of "quotas," they would lose the support of Jewish liberals.

"THE WHOLE HOG"

Fast forward to 1965 and the passage of the Voting Rights Act, remembered for Lyndon Johnson's historic speech before a special session of Congress, culminating with the president proclaiming, in his Southern drawl, "And we shall overcome." The speech was ghostwritten by Richard Goodwin, who also gave the Great Society its name. In his autobiography, Goodwin recounts being summoned to Johnson's office and being told: "You did a good job on that voting rights. A fine job." Johnson continued: "Now, voting rights are important, but it's only the tail on the pig, when we ought to be going for the whole hog. . . . We've got the biggest pulpit in the world up here, and we ought to use it to do a little preaching. Why don't you see what you can do. You're my regular alter ego."[10]

Goodwin was tasked with ghostwriting the commencement address that Johnson was to deliver at Howard University on June 5, 1965. Through a mysterious set of circumstances, Goodwin was matched with a second ghostwriter—Daniel Patrick Moynihan, who held the position of deputy secretary of labor for policy planning and research. Only weeks before, Moynihan had completed a report on the Negro family, which his boss, George Schultz, had sent over to Bill Moyers in the White House. Goodwin, LBJ's principal speechwriter, an archliberal, was assigned to collaborate with Moynihan, a nascent neoconservative, on the Howard address. According to Godfrey Hodgson, Moynihan's biographer, "there is some dispute about Moynihan's precise part in the drafting of the Howard speech."[11] However, certain passages are vintage Goodwin, while other passages could only have been written by Moynihan. Indeed, like the two-headed monster of *Sesame Street*, Goodwin and Moynihan were like two heads on one body, in querulous opposition with each other.

According to James Patterson, Moynihan was "a gregarious, ambitious, and persistent fellow who had crafted good connections with influential presidential aides."[12] By Moynihan's own account, he used his connection with Bill Moyers to elbow his way into serving as Goodwin's collaborator for the Howard address. Moynihan essentially hijacked Goodwin's language and intentions and shifted the discourse away from "equality as a fact and as a result" to a disquisition on "the Negro family."

Aptly entitled "To Fulfill These Rights," the speech was conceived as a prelude to a conference of scholars, leaders, and government officials that would develop a blueprint for the next phase of the civil rights revolution. This was the speech where LBJ famously intoned that "freedom is not enough." He went on to say:

> You do not take a person who, for years, has been hobbled by chains and liberate him, bring him up to the starting line of a race and then say, "You are free to compete with all the others," and still justly believe that you have been completely fair. Thus it is not enough to open the gates of opportunity. All our citizens must have the ability to walk through those gates.

Johnson's oratory then went a critical step further:

> This is the next and more profound stage of the battle for civil rights. We seek not just freedom but opportunity—not just legal equity but human ability—not just equality as a right and a theory but equality as a fact and a result.[13]

These last words—"not just equality as a right and a theory but equality as a fact and a result"—could only have been written by Goodwin, since they invoke the logic and language of reparations or compensatory programs to address past wrongs. Johnson further declared that "equality" would be the hallmark of "the next and more profound stage of the battle for civil rights." Goodwin had given LBJ what he asked for: "the whole hog."

Alas, at this exact juncture, Johnson's speech took an abrupt detour away from "equal results" and lapsed into a disquisition on "the Negro family." Think about it: what is the connective tissue between "equality as a fact and as a result" and "the Negro family"? Such a non sequitur requires some deft rhetoric. On cue, Johnson appended a caveat to his ringing declaration for "the next and more profound stage of the battle for civil rights":

> Equal opportunity is essential, but not enough. Men and women of all races are born with the same range of abilities. But ability is not just the product of birth. Ability is stretched or stunted by the family you live with, and the neighborhoods you live in, by the school you go to and the poverty or the richness of your surroundings. It is the product of a hundred unseen forces playing upon the infant, the child, and the man.[14]

With this sleight of hand, the focus is shifted away from the powerful societal institutions that produce and reproduce racial inequality to "the family you live with."

FOLLOW THE ENDNOTES

What possessed Daniel Patrick Moynihan, whose PhD was in international relations, to conduct a study of "the Negro family" from his remote perch in the Department of Labor? Where did he turn up the intellectual fodder for such a study? Deep Throat's famous advice was to "follow the money." The academic equivalent is to "follow the endnotes."

Note 3 of the Moynihan Report is especially telling: "For a view that present Negro demands go beyond this traditional position, see Nathan Glazer, "Negroes and Jews: The New Challenge to Pluralism," *Commentary*, December 1964." In this article, Glazer says flat-out that Black demands for preferential hiring and the rhetoric of equal results constitute a threat "to the kind of society in which Jews succeeded and which Jewish liberalism considers desirable."[15] Notes 7 and 60 then refer to *Beyond the Melting Pot*, published in 1963. Although Glazer and Moynihan are listed as coauthors, in the preface we learn that Glazer was the sole author of the chapters "The Negroes," "The Puerto Ricans," "The Jews," and "The Italians." Moynihan was the author of the chapter "The Irish" and the brief conclusion.[16]

Glazer's chapter "The Negroes" warrants close scrutiny. Glazer asks why schools that were "adequate enough" for children of other groups in the past "seem nevertheless inadequate for the present wave of children?" To which he answers:

> There is little question where the major part of the answer must be found: in the home and family and community. . . . It is there that the heritage of two hundred years of slavery and a hundred years of discrimination is concentrated; and it is there that we find the serious obstacles to the ability to make use of a free educational system to advance into higher occupations and to eliminate the massive problems that afflict colored Americans and the city.[17]

Ergo, the problems of contemporary Blacks mired in poverty are byproducts of past racism dating back to slavery—ravages that have so damaged Blacks that their children are unable to take advantage of schools that in the past had provided ladders of opportunity for Jews and other immigrants. Thus, with another sleight of hand, past racism is invoked as a smokescreen for avoiding the extent to which racism was still embedded in all major institutions—in the North as well as the South and, most deleteriously, in the realm of education and jobs.[18]

Let me be clear: my point is not that Moynihan was guilty of any malfeasance in heavily relying on his coauthor and friend, Nathan Glazer. Indeed, Moynihan was scrupulous in citing his sources. What is striking is how much of his report relies on this single source.[19] Clearly, Glazer was the "invisible hand" behind the Moynihan Report. Indeed, Glazer says as much in a 2015 interview for a special issue of *Education Next*, published by the Hoover Institution, to mark the fiftieth anniversary of the Moynihan Report:

Moynihan collaborated with me on the book *Beyond the Melting Pot* in the early 1960s, an experience that may have done a good deal to orient him to family problems and family structure, which I emphasized to him in explaining the idea of the book. I was at that time strongly influenced by the culture-personality school of anthropology, which placed great weight on early family influences.[20]

There is other evidence that Glazer's pet theory about the dysfunctional Black family was the basis for the Moynihan Report. Notes 12, 13, and 14 refer to Glazer's introduction to the 1963 edition of Stanley Elkins's controversial book, *Slavery*, in which Elkins compares slavery to the concentration camps in terms of the psychic damage inflicted upon its victims.[21] Glazer cites the prevalent depiction of the slave in the South as "childlike, irresponsible, incapable of thought or foresight, lazy, ignorant, totally dependent upon his master, happy."[22] However, the stereotype and the factual claim are blurred, and the reader is left to wonder if Glazer is implying, albeit with scholarly circumspection, that the cultural legacy of slavery and the damage it inflicted on "the Black psyche" are part of the reason that Black children do poorly in school today.[23] In 1960, Glazer published an article in *Commentary* under the title "Is 'Integration' Possible in the New York Schools?" Without citing any evidence, he provides this grim depiction of Negro and Puerto Rican children:

> Very large numbers come from homes in which they receive no care, are not fed properly, are perhaps abused physically and psychologically. The school may be a haven—but more likely it is another area in which a depressed and miserable existence is reflected in apathy, outrageous behavior, resistance.

Glazer then cites a recent editorial in the Pittsburgh *Courier* arguing that instead of school integration, it would be better "to make the education of Negro children, in the de facto schools, as good as possible."[24]

Notes 18, 19, and 20 of the Moynihan Report then cite E. Franklin Frazier's *The Negro Family in the United States*. As it turned out, Nathan Glazer was in the process of publishing "a revised and abridged edition" of Frazier's 1939 book, which was based on Frazier's 1932 dissertation, "The Negro Family in Chicago." In his foreword, Glazer avers that Frazier's book "has lost nothing in immediacy and relevance."[25] However, Glazer utterly misrepresents Frazier's study and selects passages that serve his argument concerning the dysfunctional Black family.

According to his biographer, Anthony Platt, Frazier sought to correct the bias of existing studies that, in Frazier's words, "have most often dealt with the pathological side of family life and have become the basis of unwarranted generalization, concerning the character of the whole group."[26] Indeed, Platt takes direct aim at Moynihan: "Although he [Frazier] regarded instabilities in family life as a tremendous impediment to social and racial equality, he found it almost impossible to separate family from other institutions, and certainly he did not subscribe to the view that disorganized family life was the chief handicap of the Black community, no matter how much Burgess, Moynihan, and others attributed this view to him."[27]

Thus, instead of envisioning "the next and more profound stage" in the liberation process, Moynihan reverted to a discredited discourse on the Black family to support his preposterous idea that we must *first* repair the torn fabric of "the Negro family." James Farmer, co-founder and national director of the Congress of Racial Equality, responded with exasperation: "We are sick unto death of being analyzed, mesmerized, bought, sold, and slobbered over while the same evils that are the ingredients of our oppression go unattended."[28]

THE ARTIFICE OF SEMANTIC INFILTRATION

What we see at work here is a remarkable display of "semantic infiltration," a term that Moynihan attributed to "the world of diplomacy."[29] It is an Orwellian appropriation of the language of one's political opponents for the purpose of blurring distinctions and molding it to one's own political ends. For example, Moynihan invoked the language of "special effort," "equal results," and "the next and more profound stage of the battle for civil rights"—all of which are mentioned in the early pages of the Moynihan Report—only to shift the focus to "the establishment of a stable Negro family structure."[30]

When semantic infiltration is done right, the audience may not realize that a rhetorical shill game has been played on them. At Johnson's
direction, Goodwin shared an advance draft of the Howard speech with
Martin Luther King, Roy Wilkins, Whitney Young, and A. Philip Ran-
dolph. In his autobiography, Goodwin writes that all of them were en-
thusiastic, though he notes, tongue in cheek, that Stokely Carmichael,
Rap Brown, and Malcolm X were not on his calling list.[31] Johnson would
later resent that the same movement leaders who sang his praises for
the Howard speech turned against him after the Moynihan Report was
leaked to the press.

The Howard address also elicited contradictory judgments from political pundits. The *New York Times* editorialized, "President Johnson has
addressed himself boldly to what is unquestionably the most basic and
also the most complicated phase of the civil rights struggle—the need for
translating newly reinforced legal rights into genuine equality."[32] On the
other hand, Mary McGrory of the *Washington Star* gave the speech a
very different spin: "President Johnson suggested that the time had come
for them [Blacks] to come to grips with their own worst problem, 'the
breakdown of Negro family life.'"[33] Such is the muddle sown by the two-
headed monster!

It was Goodwin who proposed following up the Howard address
with a conference under the same title: "To Fulfill These Rights." Its mandate was to develop a blueprint for the next phase of the civil rights
revolution. However, after the brouhaha over the Moynihan Report, the
conference was postponed until the fall, and two game-changing events
happened in the hiatus. One was the Watts "riot" in Los Angeles between
August 11 and 16. The disorder was triggered by an act of police brutality, which brought the seething resentments of the Black community to
the surface in a spasm of violence.

The other game-changer was that Moynihan's report on "the Negro
family" unleashed a storm of controversy after it was leaked to the
press.[34] No longer were there calls for an immense public works program or a "domestic Marshall Plan."[35] The explosive backlash in public
opinion was exemplified by the headline in the *Wall Street Journal* on
August 16, the last day of the "riot." Its headline blared: "Family Life

Breakdown in Negro Slums Sows Seeds of Race Violence—Husbandless Homes Spawn Young Hoodlums, Impede Reforms, Sociologists Say." It then quoted leading sociologists and "a just released government study" that included a gamut of statistics on how family disorganization engendered pathology and disorder.

Two days later Rowland Evans and Robert Novak, two prominent conservative journalists, weighed in with their inside view of how Moynihan came to write the report. Of course, there was no mention of the rampant segregation and occupational apartheid that condemned Blacks to the fringes of the job market even in burgeoning economies like Los Angeles. According to Evans and Novak, Moynihan wondered why the plight of Blacks was getting worse at a time of declining unemployment.[36] Moynihan's answer to his own quandary was predictable: the breakdown of the Negro family.

Political insiders let it be known that it was Moynihan who leaked his report to Bill Moyers, over the head of his boss, Secretary of Labor W. Willard Wirtz, who was fearful that the report "would become grist for the racist propaganda mills."[37] One is left to wonder why this did not dawn on Moynihan. Or was it that he put his interests and political ambitions ahead of blaming the victim?

In any event, the political repercussions were profound. According to Robert Dallek, LBJ's biographer, "though Johnson was far from abandoning his civil rights campaign, he now approached the issue of Black rights with greater caution than had been the case in the first two years of his term. He wanted the discussion of Black rights, and particularly of affirmative action to advance Black opportunity, temporarily put aside."[38] In his memoir, Goodwin writes that the conference To Fulfill These Rights, when it finally occurred, was "a total and irretrievable failure."[39]

There you have it: the death knell of the "the next and more profound stage in the battle for civil rights." Liberty shorn of equality, as though the two are not intrinsic to each other! Moynihan had succeeded in derailing the civil rights movement. Even as he was pilloried by a legion of critics—scholars, civil rights leaders, and Black and liberal commentators—this only shifted the discourse away from any consideration of compensatory programs in hiring and education. For his part, Moynihan bathed in the limelight and was catapulted from obscurity to prominence, leading to an illustrious career in politics.

LIBERAL BAD FAITH

Clearly, Moynihan did damage to the struggle for racial justice at this critical moment in its history when, for an instant, it seemed like the movement was on the cusp of a critical next stage in the liberation struggle.

As I commented in chapter 1, the passage of landmark civil rights laws in 1964 and 1965 was the high-water mark not only of the civil rights movement but of liberalism itself. The first devastating blow came with the election of Richard Nixon in 1968, based on a "Southern strategy" that appealed to a mounting white backlash in the North as well as the South. The seeds for counterrevolution had been planted. Over the next half century, this counterrevolution would gain momentum and succeed in stunting and rolling back many of the gains of the civil rights movement.[40]

We cannot change the course of history, and as Moynihan conceded, this was a "moment lost." Nevertheless, it behooves us to make sense of "the two heads" at war with each other in President Johnson's Howard address.

First, there was a hidden agenda behind the Moynihan report on the Negro family. Like Glazer, who represented a viewpoint that was gathering steam among "the family" at *Commentary* magazine, Moynihan was a steadfast critic of "affirmative action." Again, we can rely on Moynihan's own words, never uttered in his report but on full display in a long article for the *Atlantic Monthly* in August 1968. The article is titled "The New Racialism," and after a treatise on how liberals abandoned their traditional opposition to decentralized government, the narrative focuses on Ocean Hill–Brownsville in New York City, where school decentralization had devolved into a contentious battle between Blacks and Jews. Finally, Moynihan laid his cards on the table:

> Let me be blunt. If ethnic quotas are to be imposed on American universities and similarly quasi-public institutions, it is Jews who will be almost driven out. . . . If ethnic quotas should come to Harvard (surely they

won't!), something like seven out of eight Jewish undergraduates would have to leave, and I would imagine it to be a higher proportion in the graduate schools.[41]

This language amounts to sheer fearmongering. Nobody, not even the most devoted proponents of affirmative action, ever contemplated a system of proportionate representation that would place a ceiling of 3 percent on Jews, commensurate with their proportion in the population at large. Indeed, in an early section of the report, "The Demand for Equality," Moynihan notes the semantic shift whereby "equality of opportunity now has a different meaning for Negroes than it does for whites." And here he quotes none other than Nathan Glazer:

> The demand for economic equality is now not the demand for equal opportunities for the equally qualified: it is now the demand for equality of economic results . . . The demand for equality in education . . . has also become a demand for equality of results, of outcomes.[42]

It would appear that this contrived moral panic was the driving force behind the report: the fear that "the demand for equality of results" was antithetical to Jewish interests.

The problem with memory is that it is selective and often self-serving. The call for "compensatory treatment" was not comparable to the numerus clausus in Russia or the quotas against Jews in elite colleges in the 1920s. It was not aimed at overrepresented groups, least of all Jews, but only meant to provide opportunity to the descendants of enslaved people who have been excluded from whole industries and job sectors, as well as institutions of higher learning, for all of American history. To treat affirmative action as "the new racialism" was pure casuistry. Furthermore, it was unethical to whip up Jewish fears in order to undercut affirmative action.

Given that Moynihan was a traditional liberal who had previously supported the civil rights movement, he felt compelled to justify his defection from this next stage in the battle for civil rights. He did this by concealing his deeds in a smokescreen of self-righteousness, once again on the pages of *Commentary* magazine. I refer here to an article in the February 1967 issue, under the title "The President and the Negro: The Moment Lost." In his recapitulation of history, Moynihan discloses that he was the one who sought "the next and more profound stage" in the civil rights struggle, which was to repair the damaged Black family that was a roadblock to racial progress. He then heaps blame for "the moment lost" on the very groups who were wounded by his political machinations:

> The moment came when, as it were, the nation had the resources, and the leadership, and the will to make a *total* as against a partial commitment to the cause of Negro equality. It did not do so. But it was not Northern conservatives or Southern segregationists who stood in the way. For that one brief moment their opposition would not have prevailed. This time the opposition emanated from the supposed proponents of such a commitment: from Negro leaders unable to comprehend their opportunity; from civil-rights militants, Negro and white, caught up in a frenzy of arrogance and nihilism; and from white liberals unwilling to expend a jot of prestige to do a difficult but dangerous job that had to be done, and could have been done. But was not.[43]

Moynihan then engages in another shameless display of semantic infiltration. Nowhere in his fifteen thousand words of self-exoneration is the name of Richard Goodwin mentioned. Nor for that matter does Moynihan reveal that he had a hand in the ghostwriting of Johnson's speech. After all, it was the *President* who advocated "the next and more profound stage of the battle for civil rights" and "not just equality as a right and a theory, but equality as a fact and a result." Leaving Moynihan to shed false tears that six months later "the initiative was in ruins."

After a break in the text, Moynihan asks: Why? What went wrong? He offers this self-serving answer: The civil rights movement "allowed the question of developing a program to be superseded by a preposterous and fruitless controversy over an anonymous Department of Labor report which had been the original precipitant of the Howard speech." A report that he finally acknowledges "was written by me." After which he reverts to his refrain regarding the grave dysfunctions of the Negro family, capped off with this tearful bromide: "A broken family is broken; a deserted wife is alone; an abandoned child needs help." All leading to a proposal for a national family plan, like those in Europe and Canada. And like the one that, to his credit, he would later prevail on President Nixon to back, though it never came to fruition.

In fairness to Moynihan, his concept of policy making sprang from a conviction that, as a matter of political expediency, policy had to be colorblind. He enunciated this with clarity at a symposium sponsored by *Daedalus* in 1965. Asked by Everett Hughes, the eminent sociologist, whether more might be accomplished by addressing the issue of poverty than by targeting programs for "the Negro," Moynihan proffered this retort: "I will answer the question by saying that in order to do anything about Negro Americans on the scale that our data would indicate, we have to declare that we are doing it for *everybody*." Though in the very next sentence he conceded that "the problem of the Negro American *is* now a special one, and is not just an intense case of the problem of all poor people."[44] In the jargon of social science, this is the hotly debated issue of whether government should pursue "race-specific" or "universal" public policy. This is a legitimate issue for debate, and Moynihan cannot be faulted for arguing for "universal" public policy.

Moynihan's fatal error is that he pretended that movement leaders had no program for that "next and more profound stage," even as he used the Howard address in a subversive attack on affirmative action. Instead of engaging the issue and debating it in candor, he used "the Negro family" as a red herring to shift the focus of analysis from affirmative action. In doing so, he unleashed a specious debate that vitiated all discussion of compensatory programs. And in this final act of Machiavellian guile, he blamed his critics for the imbroglio that he himself had caused.

THROUGH THE REARVIEW MIRROR OF HISTORY

We can make better sense of "the moment lost" by examining the destinies of the cast of characters in this societal drama.

Soon after Nixon's election in 1968, Moynihan was appointed counselor to the president for urban affairs. No longer was "the next stage in the battle for civil rights" on his policy agenda. On the contrary, in his famous memo to President Nixon in 1969, Moynihan urged a period of "benign neglect." Here are Moynihan's exact words:

> The time may have come when the issue of race could benefit from a period of "benign neglect." The subject has been too much talked about. The forum has been too much taken over to hysterics, paranoids, and boodlers on all sides. We need a period in which Negro progress continues and racial rhetoric fades.[45]

Stated in plain English, Negroes got their rights with the passage of landmark civil rights legislation in 1964 and 1965, but they were on their own in the pursuit of equality.

After narrowly edging out Bella Abzug in the 1972 primary, Moynihan was elected senator from New York, where he came to be known as "the philosopher-king of the Senate." In a 2010 article in *The American Spectator*, Fred Iklé revealed that he was the diplomat who introduced the term *semantic infiltration* to Moynihan. With reference to Moynihan, Iklé went on to say that "a philosopher-king understands that infiltrating misleading words can gain an unwarranted political advantage," as was demonstrably the case with Moynihan's rhetorical theft.[46]

Richard Goodwin had resigned his position as speechwriter in 1965, resisting LBJ's arm-twisting to remain on the job, though in 1968 he had been drawn back into politics to write speeches for Robert Kennedy and Eugene McCarthy. Devastated by the assassination of Robert Kennedy and disillusioned by LBJ's escalation of the war in Vietnam, Goodwin had retreated to a small house in Maine, where he worked as a freelance writer of books, articles, and a play. Much of his energy was spent in ardent opposition to the relentless escalation of the Vietnam War. In his 1988 memoir, *Remembering America*, Goodwin bemoans the nation's retreat from the noble idealism of the sixties, "preferring instead to fortify the barriers—of race, of class, of income—against which the fair expectations and 'inalienable rights' of millions are dashed."[47] His bracketing "inalienable rights" in quotes conveys the cynicism he had so long resisted with a rare combination of acumen and rhetorical elegance.

While Goodwin confronted the demons that imperiled American democracy, Nathan Glazer continued to wage battle against the apparition of quotas. In a cover story for *The Nation* in 1982, Earl Shorris, author of *Jews without Mercy*, wrote: "Nathan Glazer, the chief neoconservative theoretician in the fight against affirmative action programs, led in the argument that what is good for the Blacks is no longer good for the Jews."[48] To the consternation of his erstwhile allies at *Commentary*, in 1998 Glazer announced that he had "changed his mind" on affirmative action, and in 2002 he signed an amicus brief defending the University of Michigan's admissions policies.[49] Of course, Glazer's mea culpa came after the damage was done and affirmative action had been essentially gutted, thanks to a discourse that Glazer did so much to propagate.

In a strange twist of history, the ghosts of "compensatory treatment" came back to life under circumstances that defy the imagination. The reasons are complicated, but in 1969, Richard Nixon resurrected the Philadelphia Plan, which was the brainchild of faceless bureaucrats in Johnson's Department of Labor.[50] The aim of the plan, shelved after Humphrey's defeat, was to integrate the lily-white construction trades in Philadelphia and other cities. As I commented earlier, Nixon's embrace of the Philadelphia Plan was adamantly opposed by unions and Jewish organizations, and even by Bayard Rustin, who regarded it as a devious plan to shatter the liberal coalition that had coalesced in the 1963 March on Washington.

Why Nixon and the Republicans in Congress supported the Philadelphia Plan is the subject of much speculation. In his history *The Civil Rights Era*, Hugh Davis Graham gives credence to Rustin's theory that this was a devious attempt by Nixon to rupture the liberal coalition.[51] However, Dean Kotlowski rejects this "theory" in his study *Nixon's Civil Rights*. He writes: "There is no evidence of presidential interest in dividing the Democrats during July 1969, when Nixon first defended the plan before congressional leaders."[52]

There is another side to the story. The "father of affirmative action" was Arthur Fletcher, a Black Republican from Washington State who, like Moynihan before him, was an assistant to the secretary of labor. Fletcher won the backing of his boss, George Schultz, and Nixon himself, precisely because the Philadelphia Plan was consistent with Republican tenets: it envisioned no new government programs, no make-work schemes, no major public expenditures. On the contrary, it looked to the private sector to lead the nation out of its racial morass at a time when there were noisy, headline-grabbing protests at construction sites in cities across the nation, including Chicago, Philadelphia, and New York. John Mitchell—another unsung hero of affirmative action—vigorously and successfully defended the plan in the federal courts, at which time it was extended to all government contractors. This was the inception of affirmative action as we came to know it. However, as both Graham and Kotlowski acknowledged, once opposition mounted and affirmative action became a political liability, Nixon flip-flopped and attacked the very "quotas" that he had put into place.[53]

Alas, *Commentary's* worst nightmare had come to pass. However, this was only act 2 in this implausible drama. LBJ's appointment of Thurgood Marshall to the Supreme Court in 1967 marked the beginning of the end of liberal domination of the Supreme Court. Republicans controlled the White House in thirty-two of the next forty years and appointed nine justices to the Supreme Court, the youngest of whom had been nurtured by the Federalist Society and reflected its adamant opposition to affirmative action. Once the balance on the court switched in favor of Republicans during Reagan's tenure, affirmative action was eviscerated in a series of decisions, essentially holding that affirmative action was, as Moynihan had asserted in 1969, "the new Racialism." Speaking of semantic infiltration, these justices piously held that affirmative action violated the Fourteenth Amendment, whose original intent was to protect the rights of emancipated slaves.

As discussed above, the earliest organized opposition to affirmative action occurred when it was only in its embryonic stage, and it came from liberals, not conservatives. At the event at Town Hall in 1964, Norman Podhoretz declared, in so many words, that if the move to "equality" entailed compensatory programs for Negroes, this would cause a breach between Jews and Blacks. Which is precisely what happened. According to Benjamin Balint, who was an assistant editor at *Commentary* between 2001 and 2004: "Nearly every month now, another major *Commentary* piece on the subject thumped down: 'Negro Militants, Jewish Liberals, and the Unions' (Tom Brooks); 'Integration and the Negro Mood' (Harold Isaacs); 'The Negro and the Democratic Coalition' (Samuel Lubell); 'The Negro and the New York Schools' (Midge Decter); 'Negroes and Jews: The New Challenge to Pluralism' (Nathan Glazer); 'The President and the Negro' (Pat Moynihan)."[54] According to Balint, "*Commentary* launched a steady barrage on affirmative action right through the 1990s."[55]

The squabble over affirmative action was only the beginning of a dalliance between *Commentary* and conservatism. According to MacLean, by 1968 Norman Podhoretz and Irving Kristol schmoozed regularly with William Buckley, editor of *The National Review*, and collaborated in awakening senescent conservatism with an overdue facelift.[56] No longer would conservatives present themselves as belligerent to Blacks, Jews, workers, and other liberal constituencies. Rather they would recast conservatism as the champion of all these groups against the transgressions of the Left, and affirmative action in particular. "Ironically it was Irish Catholic Daniel Patrick Moynihan," writes MacLean, "who sounded the alarm most powerfully for a new conservative Jewish identity politics that marched under the banner of color-blindness."[57]

By the 1980s opposition to affirmative action mushroomed into a veritable crusade at the forefront of political debate. Thus, we are left with the irony that Jewish defection from liberalism helped to give rise to the New Right, which eventually triumphed electorally, changed the balance on the Supreme Court, and resulted in an exorcism of the demon that *Commentary*'s "family" most feared: affirmative action.

CHAPTER THREE

THE LIFE AND DEATH OF AFFIRMATIVE ACTION

The white liberal believes something should be done, but not too soon
and not here. He is all negation, the white liberal: now is not the time,
this is not the place, the weapon you have is too large or too small. . . .
He wants results without risks, freedom without danger, love without
hate. He affirms tomorrow, denies yesterday, and evades today.

Lerone Bennett Jr., "Tea and Sympathy:
Liberals and Other White Hopes"[1]

As a youthful radical, Nathan Glazer wanted to change the world. Sadly,
he will be remembered for his perfidy in leading the assault against affirmative action policy.

In chapter 2, I argued that Nathan Glazer was the "invisible hand"
that guided Daniel Patrick Moynihan in his Machiavellian attempt
to undercut the "new direction" of the civil rights movement. Having
achieved their legislative objectives with the passage of the 1964 and
1965 Civil Rights Acts, movement leaders shifted their focus from "liberty" to "equality" and were demanding "compensatory treatment" in
jobs and education. By the 1970s, the worst fears of the cognoscenti who
Norman Podhoretz had convened in February 1964 to ponder "the crisis

in liberalism" had materialized. Compensatory treatment had morphed into affirmative action, with mandates that extended to most large employers in the public and private sectors alike.

In the debates leading up to passage of the 1964 Civil Rights Act, Hubert Humphrey, then senator from Minnesota, had assured opponents that Title VII's proscription of employment discrimination would not lead to quotas. Nevertheless, implementing affirmative action often entailed setting numerical goals for including underrepresented minorities. In the 1978 *Bakke* case, the Supreme Court ruled that the medical school at the University of California, Davis, had violated the equal protection clause of the Fourteenth Amendment by setting aside sixteen of one hundred admissions for minority applicants. However, a majority on the Supreme Court ruled that race could be one factor among others, and the ruling was considered a victory for affirmative action.

This was the context in which Nathan Glazer emerged as the earliest and most influential critic of affirmative action. More than any other single person, he shaped the intellectual discourse and fueled the mounting popular backlash against affirmative action. However, three decades later, to the consternation of his allies at *Commentary*, Glazer declared that he had "changed his mind" on affirmative action. This was heralded in an article by James Traub in the *New York Times Magazine*, under the title "Nathan Glazer Changes His Mind, Again."[2]

It goes without saying that no single person with a pen in hand is responsible for the gutting of affirmative action. My point is that affirmative action did not die a natural death but was the casualty of a political crusade to roll it back and ultimately gut it. Nathan Glazer laid the foundation for this evolving anti-affirmative-action discourse. And three decades later, after the damage was done, he was unable to put the genie back into the bottle, despite admitting that his key assumptions had been mistaken.

Glazer's first volley came with a paper published in the December 1964 issue of *Commentary* under the title "Negroes and Jews: The New Challenge to Pluralism." What was the new challenge to pluralism? According to Glazer, in cities like New York, Blacks were demanding greater access to neighborhoods, schools, and jobs that were the social and economic anchor of distinctly Jewish communities. To quote Glazer:

> The force of present-day Negro demands is that the subcommunity, because it either protects privileges or creates inequality, *has no right to exist*. This is why these new demands pose quite a challenge to the Jewish community, or to any sub-community.[3]

Note that this position contradicts one of Glazer's favorite tenets: in our society all rights attach to the individual, not the group. Glazer reasoned as follows:

> [Jews] are not protected against demands for entry on equal footing into other institutions which are the true seats of Jewish exclusiveness—the Jewish business, for example, the Jewish union, or the Jewish (or largely Jewish) neighborhood and school. Thus Jews find their interests and those of formally less liberal neighbors becoming similar: they both have an interest in maintaining an area restricted to their own kind; an interest in managing the friendship and educational experiences of their children; an interest in passing on advantages in money and skills to them.[4]

"Maintaining an area restricted to their own kind." Alas, Glazer had unwittingly embraced the logic and language of apartheid, which meant "apartness" in South Africa. Furthermore, New York City was experiencing a large migration of Blacks from the South, and movement leaders were demanding greater access to neighborhoods, schools, and jobs. Jews were dominant in the public sector, as teachers, social workers, and functionaries in an array of departments within New York City's civil service. A similar pattern existed among the Irish, who were concentrated in the uniformed services as police and firemen and, to this day, put up fierce barriers to the inclusion of Blacks. To large extent, New York City was a patchwork of ethnic neighborhoods, with Blacks assigned by default to live in several large "ghettos."

Upon reflection, the notion of "the Jewish business," "the Jewish union," or "the Jewish school or neighborhood" is fraught with specious and even dangerous assumptions. It is a violation of democratic norms to suppose that particular groups have a unique claim on institutions within the public domain. Indeed, Jewish defense groups like the Anti-Defamation League (ADL) have vigorously challenged any such claims as patently discriminatory.

Glazer came under criticism from Herbert Hill, the long-standing Jewish labor director of the NAACP, who was a champion of Black labor rights. Hill wrote: "Ironically, the goals and methods of the Black struggle to which Glazer pointed with disapproval characterized the history of many Jewish organizations in their earlier efforts to realize Jewish aspirations."[5] For example, in the 1940s the ADL vigorously fought housing covenants that restricted Jewish access to suburban developments. It also fought against social clubs that discriminated against ethnic outsiders, as well as restrictive quotas in college admissions. As Joseph Bensman wryly put it: "All groups tear down the barriers ahead of them and erect barriers behind them."[6]

In a series of articles during the 1960s and 1970s, Glazer continued to inveigh against the specter of affirmative action. A pet argument was that colorblindness was a defining characteristic of American democracy and of liberalism in general. Glazer cited the 1964 Civil Rights Act as a case in point: it proscribed discrimination against *anyone* on the basis of race, color, religion, sex, or national origin. For Glazer, affirmative action was the antithesis of colorblindness: it used group classifications to extend preference or benefits to underrepresented minorities.

Advocates of affirmative action, however, held that college admissions have never been colorblind. Though white ethnics experienced prejudice and discrimination, they nevertheless reaped the benefits of white privilege. This was Ira Katznelson's core argument in his 2006 book *When Affirmative Action Was White*.[7] For defenders of affirmative action, what was at stake was not a "quota system" based on "group representation" but rather a necessary corrective, and a meager one at that, for centuries of racial exclusion, including exclusion from hallowed institutions of higher learning.

In 1970, a second edition of Glazer and Moynihan's *Beyond the Melting Pot* was published. This presented Glazer with an occasion for a mea culpa concerning one passage that had given him "considerable pain." In the first edition he had written:

> It is not possible for Negroes to view themselves as other ethnic groups view themselves because—and this is the key to much in the Negro world—the Negro is only an American, and nothing else. He has no values and culture to guard and protect. He insists that the white world deal with his problems, because . . . he is so much the product of America.[8]

Though Glazer recanted his assertion that Negroes have "no values and culture to guard and protect," he went on to explain in the second edition that he had only meant that Blacks are "so completely American in origin" that unlike other groups of foreign origin, "they had no strong incentives to create schools to preserve a foreign language, hospitals and old-age homes to give comfort to those raised in a foreign culture, or even to develop retail stores to serve a distinctively foreign market."[9] This apologia only makes matters worse. Not only do Blacks have self-help traditions similar to white ethnics, including the development of social and cultural institutions, but unlike other groups, Blacks had to deplete scarce resources in a long and arduous struggle for elementary civil rights. Glazer's apologia only reveals the extent to which he sees the world through a narrowly Jewish optic.

Glazer was not alone in regarding Blacks as lacking a culture and identity all their own. In *An American Dilemma*, Gunnar Myrdal described Blacks as "white men with Black skin."[10] Ironically, this was a liberal tenet that was intended as a compliment! Its intent was to convey that but for the happenstance of color, Blacks were fully American. But this is not a tenable argument either, since it erases all that *is* unique in Black history and culture, whose roots go back centuries before the wave of immigrants from eastern and southern Europe at the turn of the twentieth century.

Worse than a gaffe is Glazer's lapse into "sociological racism" in *Beyond the Melting Pot*.[11] Two examples will suffice.

The core argument in *Beyond the Melting Pot* is that ethnic groups have defied the dreaded melting pot. To be sure, their cultures and communities are not static. As Glazer acknowledges, "Italian Americans might share precious little with Italians in Italy, but in America they were a distinctive group that maintained itself, was identifiable, and gave something to those who identified with it." In short, "ethnicity is a real and felt basis of political and social action."[12]

That may seem both obvious and innocuous, but it leads to a deeply problematic line of inquiry. According to Glazer, by its very nature pluralism leads to "the validating of some degree of discrimination—difficult to call simply racist—if it was not for the purpose of defending something positive rather than simply excluding someone because of his race."[13] The esteemed authors of Beyond the Melting Pot called this "positive discrimination" and defined it as "the effort to bring together people of distinctive backgrounds or interests or potential interests for some socially valued end."[14] By this logic, it was not out of any racial animus that Blacks were excluded from "Jewish neighborhoods" in Forest Hills, Queens, or Borough Park, Brooklyn. However, it was of little consolation to Blacks and others to be told that their exclusion from housing, schools, or jobs did not stem from racial animus, but only from a quintessential human penchant to favor one's "own kind."

There is irony in the fact that Glazer coined positive discrimination to legitimate behavior whose purpose was to defend ethnic boundaries. In some nations—England and India, for example—the term positive discrimination is applied to affirmative action, signifying that it has positive intentions and consequences. Thus, we are left with the irony that Glazer has no hesitation in defending "positive discrimination" that benefits ethnic groups, but he takes umbrage at "positive discrimination" that delivers justice to the victims of American apartheid.

Glazer's most egregious lapse into "sociological racism" is so enmeshed with conventional wisdom that it easily escapes notice. With an air of innocence, in his chapter "The Negroes," Glazer writes:

And yet one cannot help asking: why were schools that were indifferent to the problems of the children of other groups, forty and fifty years ago, adequate enough for them, but seem nevertheless inadequate for the present wave of children?

His answer:

> There is little question where the major part of the answer must be found:
> in the home and family and community—not in its overt values which . . .
> are positive in relation to education, but in its conditions and circum-
> stances. It is there that the heritage of two hundred years of slavery and
> a hundred years of discrimination is concentrated; and it is there that we
> find the serious obstacles to the ability to make use of a free educational
> system to advance into higher occupations and to eliminate the massive
> problems that afflict colored Americans and the city.[15]

It is hard to imagine a more startling lack of "the sociological imagination," to use the term coined by C. Wright Mills. This is the language and
logic that Moynihan parroted in his screed on the Negro family, which
did so much to derail the civil rights movement from its "next step in the
liberation project."

Glazer's personal crusade against affirmative action culminated with
Affirmative Discrimination: Ethnic Inequality and Public Polity published in 1975. This was the first book-length polemic against affirmative action, and it came at the time that Glazer enjoyed a reputation as a
leading public intellectual with impeccable liberal credentials—"one of
Harvard's adornments," as Martin Marty described Glazer in his review
of *Affirmative Discrimination* in the *Christian Century*. Another reviewer
commented: "Because of his influence, it [*Affirmative Discrimination*]
may well stimulate policy revision at the highest levels of our government and courts."[16]

Glazer's core argument was that ethnic groups in America were free
to maintain themselves on a voluntary basis without any constraints im-
posed by the state. This policy of "salutary neglect," however, was imperiled by the emergence of "a new ethnic pattern," whereby the state
recorded the ethnic affiliation of its citizens for the purpose of identifying
racial disparities in terms of jobs, housing, schools, and other institutional settings. For Glazer, this constituted a dangerous breach of the
social contract. "We have not yet reached the degraded condition of the
Nuremberg laws," he wrote, "but undoubtedly we will have to create a

new law of personal ethnic and racial status to define just who is eligible for these benefits, to replace the laws we have banned to determine who should be subject to discrimination."[17]

Needless to say, the mere mention of the Nuremberg Laws by this prominent *Commentary* intellectual was enough to raise a red flag that affirmative action was fraught with danger. Unfortunately, Glazer forgets that the Nuremberg Laws were themselves modeled after laws and practices in the Jim Crow South.[18] Still worse, he betrays the memory of the victims of Nazi genocide by using their unfathomable tragedy to defeat proposals designed not to persecute a racial group but rather to counter the effects of our nation's version of the Nuremberg Laws.

It behooves us to ask how this upwardly mobile son of a poor immigrant worker with socialist proclivities emerged in the vanguard of the movement to gut affirmative action? Let us delve into his personal biography for clues to what led Glazer to cast aside his liberal proclivities and to spearhead the crusade against affirmative action.

"FROM SOCIALISM TO SOCIOLOGY"

This was the witty title that Glazer chose for an autobiographical essay in a volume on prominent sociologists.[19] He provides graphic details about his political education, acknowledging that he was a socialist "not by conversion but by descent." His father, a garment worker who operated a sewing machine, faithfully voted for Norman Thomas and, as a member of the International Ladies Garment Workers Union, fought against Communist control of the union. Glazer describes his upbringing as one of calculated compromises: "socialist, but not too socialist; Orthodox, but not too Orthodox; friendly to Palestine, but not a Zionist; Yiddish-speaking, but not too Yiddishist."[20] To that litany of antinomies, we can add that Glazer repudiated racism, but disparaged affirmative action.

There is another contradiction that we can glean from Glazer's biographical account. In his journey from socialism to sociology, Glazer helped to advance the theory that Jewish success in America derived from a uniquely Jewish reverence for learning. Yet in his biographical account, he discloses that he and his six siblings "were not expected to go to college."[21] As the youngest of seven children, he was under less pressure to contribute to family earnings, and he enrolled in City College of New York (CCNY) in 1940. There he gravitated to Avukah, a student Zionist organization, which Glazer describes as a group of "intellectual socialist Zionists"— just the right mix of religion, politics, and intellectuality. And as we know from Joseph Dorman's documentary *Arguing the World*, Glazer became a denizen of fabled Alcove 1, the political hotbed that produced the four acolytes featured in Dorman's film: Daniel Bell, Irving Howe, Irving Kristol, and Nathan Glazer.[22] Other denizens included Seymour Martin Lipset and Philip Selznick, who later were instrumental in helping Glazer secure a position in Berkeley's Sociology Department in 1962.

These biographical details shed light on Glazer's ascent from immigrant poverty to the heights of academe. First off, when Glazer enrolled at CCNY, it was tuition free. There he forged a network of friends who would provide indispensable help throughout his career. According to Glazer's own account, it was Daniel Bell who helped him get his first job as a research assistant at the American Jewish Committee in 1944, which in turn led to a job at the *Contemporary Jewish Record*, which later morphed into *Commentary* magazine. This was the network that put our unemployed neophyte, with a talent for writing, on the road to success.

For years Glazer oscillated between his job at *Commentary* and his doctoral studies at Columbia. His first book, *American Judaism*, was based on lectures he gave at the University of Chicago in 1955 at the invitation of Daniel Boorstin, a leading social historian. In 1957 another old-school tie came into play. Seymour Martin Lipset, Glazer's companion on the subway to CCNY, resigned from the staff of a research project on Communism in American life. Glazer then used this topic for his doctoral dissertation and eventually published it as a book entitled *The Social Basis of American Communism*.[23]

Glazer received his PhD in 1962, at the ripe age of thirty-nine. After a year in Japan, he took a position, with the help of Daniel Patrick Moynihan—whom he had met through Irving Kristol—at the Housing and Home Finance Agency in Washington. His career path seemed to lack clear direction. Glazer had contributed to David Riesman's *The Lonely Crowd* and had stints as a visiting professor at Berkeley, Bennington, and Smith, but at the age of forty, he still had no regular academic position.

In Glazer's own words: "I was not sure what I would do after *Beyond the Melting Pot*. From an academic journeyman spending a year teaching at one institution after another I had become a wandering semiacademic grantsman, collecting small grants to write one book after another."[24]

Another crony from Alcove 1 came to the rescue. Through Irving Kristol, Glazer met Lewis Feuer, who helped him secure a position at Berkeley, where two other of his CCNY cronies, Seymour Martin Lipset and Philip Selznick, were on the sociology faculty. This was 1963, the same year that *Beyond the Melting Pot* was published. Decades later Glazer would succeed Kristol as co-editor, with Daniel Bell, of *The Public Interest*. Let me be clear: none of this calls into question Glazer's merit as a scholar or public intellectual. It is only to say that the old boys' network proved indispensable as Glazer navigated from an unemployed college graduate through a series of career transitions. According to James Traub, "In 1969, Moynihan helped Glazer secure a teaching position at Harvard that was one of five created by the Ford Foundation to focus intellectual energy on the problems of the city."[25]

Why is this litany of events salient to this chapter? Because at the same time that Nathan Glazer was a strident adversary of affirmative action, he was himself a textbook case of the wiles and guiles that translate into "preference." It is difficult to avoid the conclusion that affirmative action is treated as problematic or unfair only when it is extended to striving minorities.

GLAZER'S SECOND THOUGHTS

In 1987, two decades after Glazer had left Berkeley and, with Moynihan's help, had secured a position at Harvard's School of Education, Glazer published a second edition of *Affirmative Discrimination*. In the opening paragraph he writes, "Remarkably little has changed to affect the contours of the issue as it was laid out here in 1975." Yet, he concedes, "One fear and one hope failed to be realized in the dozen [intervening] years.[26]

The fear had been that "affirmative action would spread beyond the initial groups targeted for government concern to include others." In retrospect, however, Glazer concedes that his fear that affirmative action would usher in a system of "proportionate representation" were greatly exaggerated. By conjuring up memory of the numerus clausus in Russia or the Nuremberg Laws in Nazi Germany, Glazer chose to obscure the difference between a racial classification aimed *against* denigrated minorities and a racial classification that sought *remedy* for centuries of slavery and Jim Crow. Now that Glazer conceded that this "fear" was unwarranted—which is to say, that affirmative action was not detrimental to Jewish interests—he was free to give it his grudging endorsement.

The hope that failed to materialize, according to Glazer, was that "the progress of Blacks would continue and obviate such measures." His "sin" was that he was too optimistic. However, an honest reckoning would require that Glazer examine the intellectual and political assumptions on which this optimism was predicated. Why did he fail to see what was evident to movement leaders in 1964—that passing a law proscribing discrimination in employment was not enough? That racism in labor markets was entrenched and unabated, partly because Title VII lacked effective enforcement mechanisms. If these truths were not transparent to Glazer in 1964, certainly they were self-evident when he published the second edition of *Affirmative Discrimination* in 1975. At bottom, Glazer's optimism was a sunny cover for opposing a policy that was anathema to "the family" at *Commentary*.

Alas, in 1997 a proclamation swept across the land: "we are all multiculturalists now."[27] So held Nathan Glazer, the erstwhile apostle of pluralism, now bemoaning "the failure of assimilation" to integrate Blacks into the mainstream of American society. Glazer now conceded affirmative action was warranted in order to salvage American democracy from its patent failure to solve the race problem.

Despite his erstwhile allegiance to pluralism, Glazer conceded that most ethnic groups were in fact assimilating, as indicated by soaring rates of intermarriage across ethnic lines. Even among Jews, the rate of intermarriage had reached 50 percent or more.[28] Despite the hopes of the multiculturalists, Asians and Latinos—at least those with light skin— were assimilating rapidly into the American mainstream. Indeed, post-1965 immigrants were assimilating more rapidly and more completely than the immigrants of Glazer's generation half a century earlier.

In 1999 James Traub published an article in the *New York Times Magazine* titled "Nathan Glazer Changes His Mind, Again."[29] He began on a sardonic note: "Nathan Glazer has had more thoughts in his lifetime than most people have had thoughts." However, Traub shrewdly observed, *We Are All Multiculturalists Now* only appears to be about ethnicity. It is really about race and the urgency of addressing the unfinished racial agenda.

Ironically, the very group that Glazer had portrayed in 1963 as having "no culture of their own that is worthy of protection" is now providing much of the cultural and political ferment for multiculturalism and conspicuously resisting the melting pot. Glazer might have gone even further to see that hip-hop culture has not only invigorated identity and cultural distinctiveness among Blacks but has had a transformative influence on youth culture generally. With slight exaggeration, instead of Blacks becoming "more like us" in terms of assimilation, they have made the rest of us, or at least our children, "more like them." Put another way, Blacks provide vivid proof that assimilation can be a two-way street.

However, there is a sinister flip side to Glazer's mantra that "we are all multiculturalists now." Rather than celebrating multiculturalism, he is doing the opposite: he regards multiculturalism as reflecting "the price America is paying for its inability or unwillingness to incorporate into its society African Americans, in the same way and to the same degree it has incorporated so many groups."[30] Glazer cites statistics indicating that Black economic progress had been stalled since the 1970s. And instead of his previous optimism in thinking that Blacks would follow in the footsteps of other immigrants, Glazer seems to be conceding that we need multiculturalism to salve the enduring scars of racism.

In a review sardonically titled "Let Them Eat Multiculturalism," historian Barry Goldberg brings to light all that is disingenuous in Glazer's feigned acceptance of multiculturalism:

> [Glazer] is still opposed to any state action to lessen racial separation and subordination. He remains convinced that anything less than "color blind" social policy and legal reasoning is, even when not "reverse

discrimination," bound to fail. . . . The book is a morbid symptom of our political culture's ability to live with racial inequality. Glazer is certainly chastened. His faith in our common destiny across the color line has been weakened. But, unwilling to make a material and psychological investment in building a racially egalitarian democratic society, Glazer offers a relatively low-cost solution for white Americans repelled by Black rage and political mobilization: Let them eat multiculturalism![31]

Thus has Glazer forsaken the socialist impulses of his youth. Instead he gives us a faux confession that he was wrong in expecting that the civil rights revolution would lead to more rapid progress. However, as Goldberg shows, Glazer spurns governmental action to promote integration, insisting that "the forces that will produce the changes we are looking for are individual and voluntaristic, rather than governmental and authoritative."[32] Glazer is consistent with the conservative position enunciated in his 1988 book *The Limits of Social Policy*. He is once again offering academic legitimation for abandoning the struggle for racial equality. His answer: Let them eat multiculturalism.

A POSTSCRIPT

Pat Moynihan, famous as a raconteur, tells a good story about *Beyond the Melting Pot*:

> Murray Kempton, a dear friend, was going to review the book in the *Herald Tribune*. And lo and behold, he froze at the typewriter, and four days and several bottles of whiskey later, he explained that there was not going to be a review. He said, "What am I going to say about a book that goes on for 300 pages complaining that Negroes are not Jews?"[33]

This anecdote points up the fatal flaw in Nathan Glazer's prolific scholarship: he viewed Blacks through a narrow Jewish optic that distorted his perspective of Blacks and Jews alike.

CHAPTER FOUR

THE COMEBACK OF THE CULTURE OF POVERTY

For more than 40 years, social scientists investigating the causes of poverty have tended to treat cultural explanations like Lord Voldemort: That Which Must Not Be Named. The reticence was a legacy of the ugly battles that erupted after Daniel Patrick Moynihan, then an assistant labor secretary in the Johnson administration, introduced the idea of a "culture of poverty" to the public in a startling 1965 report. Although Moynihan didn't coin the phrase (that distinction belongs to the anthropologist Oscar Lewis), his description of the urban Black family as caught in an inescapable "tangle of pathology" of unmarried mothers and welfare dependency was seen as attributing self-perpetuating moral deficiencies to Black people, as if blaming them for their own misfortune.

Patricia Cohen, *New York Times*[1]

"'Culture of Poverty' Makes a Comeback." So read the headline of Patricia Cohen's front-page article in the October 17, 2010, *New York Times*. The article was prompted by a recent issue of the *Annals of the American Academy of Political and Social Science* under the title "Reconsidering Culture and Poverty."[2] In their introductory essay, the editors,

Mario Luis Small, David J. Harding, and Michèle Lamont had struck a
triumphant note:

> Culture is back on the poverty research agenda. Over the past decade,
> sociologists, demographers, and even economists have begun asking ques-
> tions about the role of culture in many aspects of poverty and even explic-
> itly explaining the behavior of the low-income population in reference to
> cultural factors.[3]

Cohen uncritically accepted two myths woven by William Julius Wilson, the prominent Harvard sociologist, and repeated by his acolytes:
first, that Moynihan was clobbered for bringing to light compromising
facts about Black families, and second, that this torrent of criticism con-
strained a generation of social scientists from investigating the relation
between culture and poverty, for fear of being pilloried for "blaming the
victim." These two myths spawned a third, patently self-serving myth:
thanks to intrepid scholars who reject political correctness, it is now per-
missible to consider the role that culture plays in the production and
reproduction of racial inequalities.

These myths contend that for four decades academia has abetted a
censorial form of anti-racism that prevented serious research into the
persistence of poverty among Black Americans. If only, or so the myth-
makers insist, we stopped worrying about offending people, we could
acknowledge that there is something amiss in Black culture—not, as the
politically correct would have it, the politics of class—and that this re-
pressed or unstated factor explains racial inequality.

Notwithstanding the election of Barack Obama, the last forty years
have been a period of racial backlash. The three pillars of anti-racist public policy—affirmative action, school integration, and racial districting
(to prevent the dilution of the Black vote)—have all been eviscerated,
thanks in large part to rulings of a Supreme Court packed with conservative justices. Indeed, the comeback of the culture of poverty, albeit in new
rhetorical guise, signifies a reversion to the status quo ante: the discourses
and policy agenda that existed before the Black protest movement forced
the nation to confront its collective responsibility for two centuries of

slavery and a century of Jim Crow—racism that pervaded all major institutions of our society, North and South. Such momentous issues are brushed away as a new generation of sociologists delves into myopic examination of a small sphere where culture makes some measurable difference. They are determined to prove that "culture matters."

It is indisputable that the publication of Moynihan's report on "the Negro family" evoked a torrent of criticism and that Moynihan was thrown on the defensive.[4] I remember seeing him on *Meet the Press* in late 1965, pleading for understanding:

> I was trying to show that unemployment statistics, which are so dull, and you read so many of them, and you don't know what they may mean, and they're hard to believe—that unemployment ended up nonetheless with orphaned children, with abandoned mothers, with men living furtive lives without even an address, that unemployment had flesh and blood and it could bleed. That's all I was trying to do.[5]

Perhaps. However, it is grossly inaccurate to say, as Wilson does in the *Annals*, that Moynihan came under fire for bringing to light facts that "could be construed as unflattering or stigmatizing to people of color."[6] Or that Moynihan was prescient, in that the proportion of Black children born outside marriage has doubled from one-quarter in 1965 to one-half today.

The problem from the beginning was not Moynihan's publication of what were actually well-established facts, but rather his distorted interpretation of these facts. Moynihan made the fatal error of inverting cause and effect. Although he acknowledged that past racism and unemployment undermined Black families, he held that the pathology in "the Negro American family" had not only assumed a life of its own but was the *primary* determinant of the litany of problems that beset lower-class Blacks. To quote from chapter 4 of the Moynihan Report: "Once or twice removed, [the weakness of family structure] will be found to be the principal source of most of the aberrant, inadequate, or anti-social behavior that did not establish, but now serves to perpetuate the cycle of poverty and deprivation."[7] The next chapter adds an even more inflated claim:

"At this point the present tangle of pathology is capable of perpetuating itself without assistance from the white world." And then the zinger: "The cycle can be broken only if these distortions are set right."[8]

This last statement had dire implications for public policy, especially when placed in historical context. With his report on the Negro family, Moynihan had shifted the conceptual framework that underlay policy making. Instead of attacking racist barriers, he suggested that legislation focus on the putative defects of "the" Black family. In the report's concluding chapter, "The Case for National Action," Moynihan called for "a national effort" to strengthen the Negro family, though he offered no specific policy recommendations for accomplishing that end, as Herbert Gans attested in a 1965 article in *Commonweal*.[9] Not only did Moynihan leave a vacuum that could be filled with a politics that blamed Blacks for their own troubles, but he also tacked on a startling addendum:

> After [the repair of the Black family], how this group of Americans chooses to run its affairs, take advantage of its opportunities, or fail to do so, is none of the nation's business.[10]

The Moynihan Report elicited fierce condemnation not because it brought to light troubles within Black families but because it threatened to derail the Black liberation movement in its pursuit of equality. In one palpable example of that derailment, a 1966 White House conference called "To Fulfill These Rights"—which was designed to chart the next phase of the protest movement—was overshadowed by preoccupation with the Moynihan Report and the ensuing controversy.

Far from having a chilling effect on research and analysis about culture in relationship to poverty, the debate over the Moynihan Report spawned a canon of critical scholarship. For the first time, scholars came to terms with the economic underpinning of the nuclear family, which is damaged when breadwinners are unemployed for long periods of time. The same was true of white families during the Depression.

No longer was the nuclear family, with its patriarchal foundations, the unquestioned societal norm. The blatantly tendentious language that pervaded the Moynihan Report—"broken homes" and "illegitimate births"—was purged from the professional lexicon. More important, feminist scholars compelled us to reassess single parenting. In her 1973 study *All Our Kin*, Carol Stack showed how poor single mothers develop a domestic network consisting of that indispensable grandmother along with grandfathers, uncles, aunts, cousins, and a patchwork of neighbors and friends who provide mutual assistance with child-rearing and the other exigencies of life.[11] By comparison, the prototypical nuclear family, sequestered in a suburban house, surrounded by hedges and cut off from neighbors, removed from the pulsating vitality of poor urban neighborhoods, looks rather bleak! A Black friend once commented, "I didn't know that Blacks had weak families until I got to college."

Moynihan's harshest critics did not deny the manifest troubles in Black families. Nor did they deny that the culture of poor people is often markedly at variance with the cultural norms and practices in more privileged sectors of society. How could it be otherwise? The key point of contention was whether, under conditions of prolonged poverty, those cultural adaptations "assume a life of their own" and are passed down from parents to children through normal processes of cultural transmission. In other words, the imbroglio over the Moynihan Report was never about whether culture matters but about whether culture is or ever can be an independent and self-sustaining factor in the production and reproduction of poverty.

Many scholars have challenged the notion of culture as an independent, causal factor in generating poverty, but none more effectively than Elliot Liebow in his 1967 study, *Tally's Corner*.[12] Liebow's subjects were men who had neither regular jobs nor stable families and took refuge on the street corner, where they devised "a shadow system of values" to shield themselves from a profound sense of personal failure.

Liebow did not deny culture—indeed, he documented it in scrupulous detail. However, he insisted that the street-corner man was not a carrier of an independent cultural tradition. To be sure, there were obvious similarities between parents and children, but Liebow held that these were not the product of cultural transmission but rather reflected the fact that "the son goes out and independently experiences the same failures, in the same areas, and for much the same reasons as his father."[13] Thus, it is not their culture that needs to be changed, but rather a political economy that fails to provide jobs that pay a living wage to millions of the nation's poor, along with a system of occupational apartheid that has excluded a whole people from entire job sectors throughout American history.

Liebow is not alone. Although left scholars insist that poverty is rooted in political economy, it is preposterous to accuse them of disregarding culture. For example, the anthropologist Oscar Lewis, who first deployed the term, was an avowed socialist, and the culture of poverty entered popular discourse through the ideas of another socialist, Michael Harrington, in his 1962 book, *The Other America*.[14] Both men prioritized structural explanations of poverty. They argued that the despair and coping mechanisms associated with the *culture* of poverty were anchored in *conditions* of poverty, and that the only remedy for the culture of poverty was the elimination of poverty itself.

The claim that the furor over the Moynihan Report stymied research on lower-class culture for four decades is patently false. What was the massive underclass discourse of the 1980s if not old wine in new bottles— that is, Moynihan's cultural arguments repackaged for a new generation of scholars and pundits?

As with the culture of poverty, the conception of the underclass had liberal origins. In his 1962 book *Challenge to Affluence*, Gunnar Myrdal borrowed a Swedish term for the lower class, *underklassen*, to refer to people who languished in poverty even during periods of economic growth and prosperity.[15] This term entered popular discourse with the 1982 publication of Ken Auletta's *The Underclass*, based on a series in *The New Yorker*.[16]

Then, between 1986 and 1988, there was an outpouring of articles in *U.S. News and World Report*, *The Atlantic Monthly*, *Fortune*, *Newsweek*, *Reader's Digest*, and *Time*, all providing graphic and frightening portrayals of pathology and disorder in the nation's ghettos. The image was of poverty feeding on itself, with the implication that cultural pathology was not just a byproduct of poverty but was itself a cause of pathological behavior. This was the explicit claim of a 1987 *Fortune* article by Myron Magnet:

What primarily defines [the underclass] is not so much their poverty or race as their behavior—their chronic lawlessness, drug use, out-of-wedlock births, nonwork, welfare dependency and school failure. "Underclass" describes a state of mind and a way of life. It is at least as much cultural as an economic condition.[17]

Social science lagged behind journalism, but by the late '80s, with the backing of charitable foundations, a cottage industry of technocratic studies appeared, documenting the size and social constitution of the underclass. In his 1991 article "The Underclass Myth," Adolph Reed noted the reinstatement of the culture-of-poverty theory during the Reagan-Bush era. The pendulum had swung so far to "culture" that Reed was pleading for a restoration of "structure":

We should insist on returning the focus of the discussion of the production and reproduction of poverty to examination of its sources in the operations of the American political and economic system. Specifically, the discussion should focus on such phenomena as the logic of deindustrialization, models of urban redevelopment driven by real-estate speculation, the general intensification of polarization of wealth, income, and opportunity in American society, the ways in which race and gender figure into those dynamics, and, not least, the role of public policy in reproducing and legitimating them.

Reed ended on a note of personal exasperation: "I want the record to show that I do not want to hear another word about drugs or crime without hearing in the same breath about decent jobs, adequate housing, and egalitarian education."[18]

Yet here we are, three decades later, with a special issue of a prestigious journal, the *Annals*, launched with fanfare and a congressional briefing, bombastically claiming that "culture is back on the policy agenda," as though it had not been there all along. Even as the editors take up this "long-abandoned topic," however, they are careful to distance themselves from culture-of-poverty theorists who were accused of "blaming the victim," and they scoff at the idea that the poor "might cease to be poor if they changed their culture." Indeed, readers are assured that "none of the three editors of this volume happens to fall on the right of the political spectrum." Alas, the culture of poverty has not made a comeback after all. The new culturalists have learned from the mistakes of the past, and only want to study culture in the context of poverty—that is, in the selective and limited ways that culture matters in the lives of the poor.

True to form, the rest of the *Annals* issue was a compendium of studies informed by this "more sophisticated" conception of culture. One study is titled "How Black and Latino Service Workers Make Decisions about Making Referrals." Another explores how poor men define "a good job." Another examines the "repertoire of infidelity" among low-income men.

The problem is less with the questions asked than with the ones left unexamined. The editors and authors are careful to bracket their inquiries with appropriate obeisance to the ultimate grounding of culture in social structure. But their research objectives, methodology, data collection, and analysis are all riveted on the role of culture. Is obeisance enough? If the cultural practices under examination are merely links in a chain of causation and are ultimately rooted in poverty and joblessness, why are *these* not the object of inquiry? Why aren't we talking about the calamity of another generation of Black youth who, excluded from job markets, are left to languish on the margins, until they cross the line of legality and are swept up by the criminal justice system and consigned to unconscionable years in prison, where they find work for less than a dollar an hour, if paid at all? Upon release they are "marked men," unable to find employment or to assume such quotidian roles as those of husband or father.

Enter the sociologist, to record the agony of the dispossessed. Does it really matter how they define a "good job" when they have virtually no prospect of finding one? Does it matter how they approach procreation, how they juggle "doubt, duty, and destiny" when they are denied the jobs that are the sine qua non of parenthood? Or is it that sociologists are asking the wrong questions? Do the answers bring us any closer to comprehending why this nation has millions of racial outcasts who are consigned to a social death?

Obeisance is not enough. The *Annals* issue caps off with an article by William Julius Wilson, "Why Both Social Structure and Culture Matter in a Holistic Analysis of Inner-City Poverty." Wilson purports to show "not only the independent contributions of social structure and culture, but also how they interact to shape different group outcomes that embody racial inequality." At first blush this is an unassailable line of inquiry. But what is Wilson getting at with his prosaic language about "the interaction of structure and culture"? The answer is found several pages later: "One of the effects of living in a racially segregated, poor neighborhood is the exposure to cultural traits that may not be conducive to facilitating social mobility."[19] This is tantamount to blaming Blacks for the racism of employers and other gatekeepers.

Like Moynihan before him, Wilson inverts cause and effect. He thinks that Black youth are not socially mobile *because* of their cultural proclivities—"sexual conquests, hanging out on the street after school, party drugs, and hip-hop music." But a far more convincing explanation is that these youth are encircled by structural barriers and consequently resort to these cultural defenses, as Douglas Glasgow argued in his neglected 1981 book, *The Black Underclass*.[20] Liebow had it right when he stripped away surface appearances and put culture in its proper social and existential context:

> If, in the course of concealing his failure, or of concealing his fear of even trying, [the streetcorner man] pretends—through the device of public fictions—that he does not want these things in the first place and claims he has all along been responding to a different set of rules and prizes, we do not do him or ourselves any good by accepting this claim at face value.[21]

It makes little sense to draw comparisons—as Wilson does—between the culture of a pariah class and that of mainstream youth, putting aside the facts that white suburban youth also strut around in saggy pants, listen to hip-hop music, and are far more prone to drug use than are their ghetto counterparts. Wilson's theoretical postulates about "deconcentrating poverty" have also led him to support the demolition of public housing across the nation. Is this how cultural change takes place—with dynamite, the destruction of poor communities, and the dispersal of its residents? Or do we have to transform the ghetto itself, not by reconstructing the identities of its people but through a wholesale commitment to eliminating poverty and joblessness?

Although he violates his own axiom about the integral relationship between culture and social structure, Wilson injects what might be called the "culturalist caveat." In a section on "the relative importance of structure and culture," he concedes that "structural factors are likely to play a far greater role than cultural factors in bringing about rapid neighborhood change." But what structural changes does he have in mind? Despite the fact that Wilson's signature issue for many years was jobs, jobs, jobs, since his cultural turn, there has been little mention of jobs. Affirmative action is apparently off the table, and there is no policy redress for the nation's four million "disconnected youth" who are out of school and out of work.

Instead, Wilson places all his bets on education—specifically, the Harlem Children's Zone (HCZ), a schooling and social services organization predicated on the idea that the challenge is to "take the ghetto out of the child," much as earlier missionaries and educators sought to "take the Indian out of the child." Wilson trumpets HCZ's "spectacular" results, citing a study by Harvard economists Will Dobbie and Roland Fryer that purports to show that HCZ students are closing the achievement gap with students in public schools.[22] However, these findings are based on a single class and a single test in a single year. Also, the measure of progress was scoring at grade level in math and reading. As critics have pointed out, grade-level work is a weak predictor of future academic success. Furthermore, thanks to "score inflation"—not only prepping students for the test but also lowering the score required for achieving grade level—marks were up throughout New York on the 2007 exam, the one that Dobbie and Fryer analyzed.

Never mind, the die is cast. With Wilson's backing, the Obama administration made HCZ the model for twenty Promise Neighborhoods across the nation.[23] At best, however, HCZ is a showcase project that, even multiplied twenty times, is no remedy for the deep and widening income gap between Blacks and others. At worst, the Obama administration used it to camouflage its utter failure to address issues of racism and poverty.

The new culturalists can bemoan the supposed erasure of culture from poverty research in the wake of the Moynihan Report, but far more troubling is that nearly five decades have witnessed the erasure of racism and poverty from political discourse, both inside and outside the academy. The *Annals* issue makes virtually no mention of institutionalized racism. To be sure, there is much discussion of poverty, but not as a historical or structural phenomenon. Instead we are presented with reductionist manifestations of poverty that obscure its larger constellation.

Thus there is no thought of restoring the safety net. Or resurrecting affirmative action. Or once again constructing public housing as the housing of last resort. Or decriminalizing drugs and rescinding mandatory sentencing. Or enforcing anti-discrimination laws with the same vigor that police exercise in targeting Black and Latino youth for marijuana possession. Or creating jobs programs for disconnected youth and for the chronically unemployed. Against this background, the ballyhooed "restoration" of culture to poverty discourse can mean only one thing: an evasion of the persistent racial and economic inequalities that shift the blame to the victim.

The methodological reductionism that is the hallmark of the new culturalists is a betrayal of the sociological imagination, which C. Wright Mills defined as an exploration of the intersection between history and biography. Instead, the new culturalists give us biography shorn of history, and culture ripped from its moorings in social structure. Against their intentions, they end up providing erudite justification for retrograde public policy, less through acts of commission than through their silences and opacities.

PART II

Deconstructing Victim-Blaming Discourses

> Like most things in life, our practice of blame is susceptible to the vices of being done from the wrong sort of motive, in the wrong degree, in the wrong way, or with the wrong sort of object.
>
> Miranda Fricker, "What Is the Point of Blame?"[1]

To her observation above about the ethics of blame, moral philosopher Miranda Fricker adds that "blame is easily abused and misused." Our concern here is with a paradoxical and perverse *misuse* of blame: where the object of blame is not the perpetrators of injustice, but rather their victims! This practice has become known as "blaming the victim."

We can see in a flash how this sinister use of "blame" is pertinent to matters of race. With a rhetorical sleight of hand, it is not the slave owner or the overseer that is blameworthy, nor an entrenched system of chattel slavery that existed for over two centuries, nor generations of whites to this day who directly or indirectly benefited from slavery, but rather, through a corrupt twist of logic, their victims—the very people who supplied cheap labor on which the American empire was built! What better example of "the wrong sort of motive, in the wrong degree, in the wrong way, or with the wrong sort of object."

It is all the more telling that the phrase "blaming the victim" did not enter the sociological lexicon until 1971, thanks to William Ryan, a sociologist, who penned a book entitled *Blaming the Victim*. This neologism requires that we twist our minds like pretzels to make sense of the maddening incongruity of blaming victims for their own victimization![2]

Ryan's coinage of "blaming the victim" had a particular historical context associated with the shifting racial politics of the post-segregation era. As we saw in part I, the mobilization of Black insurgency during the 1950s and 1960s marked the beginning of the end of the Jim Crow system, which was a stepchild of slavery. It reached a triumphant climax with the passage of landmark legislation in 1964 and 1965.

However, only two months after passage of the 1965 Voting Rights Act, a "riot" exploded in the Watts neighborhood of Los Angeles. It raged for five days, and ended with thirty-four deaths and over three thousand arrests, not to speak of $40 million of property damage.

The Watts rebellion engendered a radically new conception of racial conflict, signified by the publication in 1971 of a book by Robert Fogelson entitled *Violence as Protest: A Study of Riots and Ghettos*.[3] His title provided timely recognition that violence can be a manifestation of protest and a legitimate expression of the seething resentments of an oppressed people. This was echoed as well in the rebellions in Newark in 1967, Chicago in 1966, Detroit in 1967, and a spate of uprisings unleashed by the assassination of Martin Luther King on April 4, 1968.

As Elizabeth Hinton has recently written, "the term 'riot' is a misnomer," emanating from the rhetoric of politicians, the media, and social scientists, and leading the public, then and now, to view these incidents as "devoid of any political motivation or content." On the other hand, "rebellion served as a message to the nation that the civil rights of the mid-1960s, the equal-opportunity and self-help programs of the War on Poverty, and ongoing nonviolent protest were inadequate to solving the problem of racial inequality and its countless manifestations and consequences. Something else was needed.[4]

Clearly, these urban uprisings were in startling contrast to the orderly marches and nonviolence of the civil rights movement. They were fueled by the heightened politics of Black militancy, the Black Panthers, and the Black power movement. These ideological shifts conveyed a powerful message "from the bottom" that it is not enough to pass laws that belatedly extend rights of citizenship that were supposedly secured by the Reconstruction Amendments passed in the wake of the Civil War. A mobilized Black movement was demanding steps to counter white supremacy and systemic racism. Simply stated, the Watts rebellion signaled a transition of the Black protest movement from "liberation" to "equality."

In 1967, as "cities were burning," President Johnson appointed a commission with the prosaic title the National Advisory Commission on Civil Disorders. It is memorable for two bold declarations: (1) "Our nation is moving toward two societies, one Black, one white—separate and unequal." And (2) "What white Americans have never fully understood—but what the Negro can never forget—is that white society is deeply implicated in the ghetto. White institutions created it, white institutions maintain it, and white society condones it."[5]

Even before the blunt admonitions of the Kerner Commission—indeed, even before the "turn" to violent protest—there were signs that liberal support for the civil rights movement was waning. In 1963, Murray Friedman, a historian at Temple University, published a piece in the *Atlantic Monthly* contending that "the liberal white is increasingly uneasy about the nature and consequences of the Negro revolt." He continued: "After school desegregation came to Northern cities, white liberals realized that the Negro was not just an abstraction, and not just a Southern problem." And he concluded with this salvo: "In a final analysis, a liberal, white, middle-class society wants to have change, but without trouble."[6]

In 1994, Friedman published a book entitled *What Went Wrong? The Creation and Collapse of the Black-Jewish Alliance.*[7] As mentioned above, even as the civil rights acts were wending their way through Congress, Black leaders were planning for a next phase in the movement that would pry open barriers to jobs and education that had excluded Blacks for centuries. However, both union leaders and Jewish leaders at *Commentary* magazine were fearful that Black demands for jobs and education would come at their expense. Indeed, there was vehement opposition to affirmative action long before the term was coined. As Friedman prophesized, the "liberal coalition" of Blacks, Jews, and union leaders who participated in the 1963 March on Washington was falling apart.

Another ominous change in the political landscape involved the resuscitation of conservatives from a long period of somnolence. The sheer force of the civil rights upheaval had squelched criticism from white conservatives. However, in 1969—the year of Richard Nixon's ascendency to the White House—Edward Banfield published an incendiary piece entitled "Rioting Mainly for Fun and Profit." The title speaks volumes, and the article was published in the *Public Interest*, the voice of a new political formation of "neocons" who unapologetically defected from liberal dogma.[8]

Alas, at the very moment when the Black movement had achieved its policy objectives with the passage of landmark civil rights legislation, the movement was losing the support of liberals and faced the increased hostility of both neocons and a resuscitated political right. As Friedman shrewdly noted in his 1963 article in the *Atlantic Monthly*, the passage of the two Civil Rights Acts did not signify the triumph of the civil rights movement, but rather its last hurrah.[9]

Martin Luther King was well aware of the ominous shift in the political winds. In 1963, even before the passage of the Civil Rights Acts, he published a book aptly titled *Why We Can't Wait*. In it, King provides this account of his appearance with Roy Wilkins on *Meet the Press*:

> There were the usual questions about how much more the Negro wants, but there seemed to be a new undercurrent of implications related to the sturdy strength of our movement. Without the courtly complexities, we were, in effect, being asked if we could be trusted to hold back the surging tides of discontent so that those on shore would not be made too uncomfortable by the buffeting and onrushing waves. Some of the questions implied that our leadership would be judged in accordance with our capacity to "keep the Negro from going too far." The quotes are mine, but I think the phrase mirrors the thinking of the panelists as well as of many other white Americans.[10]

Two years later, King published *Where Do We Go From Here: Chaos or Community?* Again, his subtitle conveyed his apprehension that the movement was in danger of dissolution. And he struck precisely the chord that is the thematic of this book:

> The inevitable counterrevolution that succeeds every period of progress is taking place. Failing to understand this as a normal process of development, some Negroes are falling into unjustified pessimism and despair. Focusing on the ultimate goal, and discovering it still distant, they declare no progress has been made.[11]

The book included a thirty-five-page chapter titled "Racism and the White Backlash." He chose his words carefully:

> The step backward has a new name today. It is called the "white backlash." But the white backlash is nothing new. . . . The white backlash is an expression of the same vacillations, the same search for rationalizations, the same lack of commitment that has always characterized white Americans on the issue of race.[12]

In 1966, Kevin Phillips, a prominent pundit, wrote a prescient book titled *The Emerging Republican Majority*. This was only two years after Barry Goldwater's devastating defeat (Johnson won 486 votes in the Electoral College, compared to 52 votes for Goldwater.) Pundits crowed that "conservatism was dead." However, Phillips's prognostication was realized two years later when Richard Nixon defeated Vice President Humphrey in a landslide, predicated on a "Southern strategy" that lured Southerners to defect from the Democratic Party. In another portentous turn of events, George Wallace was making inroads into blue-collar districts in the North. Remember, all of these fateful political realignments were put into motion by the fact that African Americans had secured their rights, including the right to vote.

The result was that the unholy alliance between Northern liberals and Southern Dixiecrats was shattered, as Southerners defected en masse to the Republican Party, thus obviating its claim as "the party of Lincoln." Almost overnight, the Republican Party morphed into "the party of segregation." When Lyndon Johnson signed the Voting Rights Act, he predicted the end of "the Solid South" for at least a generation.[13] Indeed,

Republicans went on to control the White House in twenty-eight of the next forty-two years. The only exceptions were two Southerners: Jimmy Carter in 1978 and Bill Clinton in 1994 and 1998. Furthermore, conservatives gradually staged a takeover of the Supreme Court, thanks to the machinations of the Federalist Society. To invoke Hannah Arendt again, the political tables had turned as the forces of revolution yielded to the forces of counterrevolution.

Let us now examine the emergence and significance of the blaming-the-victim rhetoric within the political context outlined above. "Blaming the victim" emerged as a new rhetoric for blunting and rolling back the hard-won gains of the civil rights movement. The thrust of the Black liberation movement was to drive a wedge in the walls of segregation that had excluded Blacks from access to jobs and education through all of American history. In a repeat of history, learned scholars and jurists artfully developed new logics and discourses that shifted responsibility and blame onto Blacks themselves. Blacks had won their rights, but as will be seen in the coming chapters, in one way or another barriers were erected to undermine and frustrate Black aspirations. And in a cruel replay of Reconstruction, the euphoria of the Civil Rights Acts gradually gave way to painful realization that the walls of segregation were not going to come tumbling down.

Let William Ryan speak for himself about the pernicious logic of blaming the victim:

> The generic process of Blaming the Victim is applied to almost every American problem. The miserable health care of the poor is explained away on the grounds that the victim has poor motivation and lacks health information. . . . The problems of slum housing are traced to the characteristics of tenants who are labeled as "Southern rural migrants" not yet "acculturated to life in the big city. The "multiproblem" poor, it is claimed, suffer the psychological effects of impoverishment, the "culture of poverty," and the deviant value system of the lower classes; consequently, though unwittingly, they cause their own troubles. . . . The growing number of families receiving welfare are fallaciously linked together with the increased number of illegitimate children as twin results

of promiscuity and sexual abandon among members of the lower orders. Every important social problem—crime, mental illness, civil disorder, unemployment—has been analyzed within the framework of the victim-blaming ideology.[14]

As Ryan goes on to say, blaming the victim is different from old-fashioned racism that categorically defined Blacks as biologically inferior or morally unfit. In this respect, blaming the victim is not retrograde but rather has its foundation in liberal thought and practice. In effect, Blacks are not maligned so much as they are pitied.

If Blacks are their own worst enemy, or as Jim Sleeper penned, if Blacks "participate in their own victimization,"[15] there is no warrant for a war on poverty. Nor a mandate to enforce laws against discrimination in jobs, education, and housing.[16] Nor reason to endorse affirmative action for Blacks.[17] Through the optic of victim-blamers, the moniker of "institutionalized racism" is "a nonsense phrase."[18] And the idea of "reparations" is dismissed as preposterous—not only unrealistic but also a dead end, as Adolph Reed has forcefully argued.[19]

William Julius Wilson unwittingly contributed to blaming-the-victim rhetoric with his 1978 book *The Declining Significance of Race*.[20] Wilson held that the post–civil rights era was one of relative tolerance, which witnessed the advance of middle-class Blacks in a wide array of occupations. On the other hand, true to the rhetoric of blaming the victim, Wilson held that lower-class Blacks lacked the education and skills to climb the ladder of success. Instead of arguing for programs and policies that would counter the massive discrimination against Blacks in jobs, education, and housing, Wilson picked up the other end of the stick and argued, virtually echoing Booker T. Washington, that Blacks had to cultivate the habits and skills to compete for jobs in the marketplace. In a second book, purportedly on his policy agenda, Wilson floated the idea of a program modeled after the WPA during the Depression, a far cry from attacking the occupational apartheid that categorically excluded Blacks from coveted jobs.[21]

Wilson's ill-titled book was published at a time when "civil rights fatigue" had set in and the Democratic Party shifted its priorities away from the Black struggle. For example, President Clinton signed both the crime bill that fueled mass incarceration and the bill dismantling welfare that had provided a safety net for Blacks and poor people generally. Furthermore, Clinton backed away from support of affirmative action with his tepid refrain to "mend not end" affirmative action.[22] As the saying goes, "With friends like this, who needs enemies?"

An even more blatant form of victim blaming came from Dinesh D'Souza in his 1995 book, *The End of Racism*. D'Souza proclaimed that racism is a residue of the past and that the troubles of Blacks spring from their own pathologies, which pervade Black culture and communities. According to D'Souza, if only Blacks got their values right and renounced their "oppositional culture," they too could "build the civilization resources of a people whose culture is frequently unsuited to the requirements of the modern world."[23] As we will see in chapter 6, D'Souza's language is a throwback to the 1912 project of Booker T. Washington and Robert E. Park to "educate the primitive."

In 1999 a new discourse emerged by prominent race scholars who broke the good news: we are on the cusp of "a post-racial society."[24] The exponents of this position presented no new facts, but rather were swayed by their conviction that "race" was an atavism from a premodern era and should be discarded altogether from sociological discourse. The race-is-over crowd was vindicated by the election of Barack Obama in 2008 and 2012. However, with Donald Trump's elevation to power in 2016, the ardent contentions of the post-racial crowd were put to rest.

Ryan's theoretical perspective is also instructive for what the rhetoric of blaming-the-victim does *not* do. Ryan writes: "We are persuaded to ignore the obvious: the continued blatant discrimination against the Negro. . . . Almost all our make-believe liberal programs aimed at correcting our urban problems are off target; they are designed either to change the poor man or to cool him out."[25]

Finally, Ryan directs his fire at Daniel Patrick Moynihan and his derogatory portrayal of "the Black family." To quote Ryan: "If the Negro family produces young men *incapable* of achieving equality, let's deal with that first before we go on to the task of challenging the pervasive racism that informs and shapes and distorts every social institution."[26]

In the final analysis, the blaming-the-poor rhetoric conveniently exonerates American society of responsibility for the perpetual crisis that besets Blacks and defeats their aspirations.

In *The Cult of True Victimhood*, Alyson Cole underscores Ryan's point and asserts, "Victim blaming is a uniquely liberal ideology that, unlike crude racism, entraps those most inclined to be sympathetic and committed to helping the disadvantaged."[27] Cole further argues: "Blaming the victim provides an ingenious middle ground: the middle-class liberal may leave the system that benefits him intact while still seeming to care for those it victimizes." Thus, "they get to 'absolve' themselves of their 'sins' of complicity in injustice."[28]

As Cole points out, victim-blaming theories usually focus on poor African Americans and trace their putative pathologies to the "heritage of slavery." As a consequence, Moynihan, along with scores of race scholars, escape responsibility and blame for the current struggles of African Americans by affixing responsibility and blame on defunct ancestors.

In the following essays, I examine a series of victim-blaming discourses that effectively blame Blacks themselves for their racial inequalities. Tears flow for the struggles of the descendants of slavery. However, little or no attention is directed at the powerful institutions that are complicit in the production and reproduction of racism.

To paraphrase James Baldwin, we cannot use the crimes of the past to gloss over the crimes of the present. Put simply, we must stop blaming the victim and invoking a specious rhetoric to avoid confronting our own complicity in the enduring legacy of slavery.

CHAPTER FIVE

SOCIAL SCIENCE AND THE OCCLUSION OF POLITICAL ECONOMY

In propaganda gainst the Negro since emancipation in this land, we
face one of the most stupendous efforts the world ever saw to discredit
human beings, an effort involving universities, history, science, social life
and religion.

W. E. B. Du Bois, *Black Reconstruction*[1]

One could say then, as a general rule, that white misunderstanding, mis-
representation, evasion, and self-deception on matters related to race are
among the most pervasive mental phenomena of the past few hundred
years, a cognitive and moral economy psychically required for conquest,
colonization, and enslavement.

Charles W. Mills, *The Racial Contract*[2]

Social science has long bathed in self-congratulation for its repudiation of
scientific racism—the various doctrines that traced racial hierarchy to the
genes. However, no sooner were these theories thrown into the proverbial
trash bin than another theory sprung up that explained racial hierarchy
in terms of *culture*. According to this view, groups that languish on the
bottom do so because they are saddled with aberrant or dysfunctional
value systems that impede their social and economic mobility.

Though projected as a new theory, on closer examination the focus on culture in relation to race and racial hierarchy was a throwback to ideas that held currency even before the ascent of social Darwinism and biological determinism in the late nineteenth century. When Europe colonized Africa in the seventeenth century, the distinction between "the civilized European" and "the savage African" was invented to provide justification for colonialism. The English who settled North America and the Dutch who settled the Cape of Good Hope shared a conception of "savagery" that they applied to the native people they encountered. In his comparative study *White Supremacy*, George Fredrickson wrote:

> These beliefs were not yet racist in the nineteenth-century sense of the term because they were not based on an explicit doctrine of genetic or biological inequality; but they could provide an equivalent basis for considering some categories of human beings inferior to others in ways that made it legitimate to treat them differently from Europeans.[3]

Two theoretical abstractions were contrived to divide the human race into superior and inferior categories. The first was the distinction between "Christian" and "heathen." The second, between "civilized" and "savage." This, of course, is the obsolete nomenclature of seventeenth-century Europe. However, to my ear it has disturbing resonance with the present-day characterization of the poor and downtrodden as culturally and morally inferior.

"Sloth" and "immorality" are the terms that recur in early-twentieth-century discourse on poverty. Although contemporary social science has purged itself of such patently value-laden terminology, in devious ways social science discourses continue to posit culture and morality as explanations of why the poor languish in poverty. How different are we, really, from our forebears who invoked heathenism and savagery to legitimate racial hierarchy? Indeed, I was tempted to entitle this chapter "Heathenism and Savagery in the Inner City."

If this seems far-fetched, consider Dinesh D'Souza's book *The End of Racism*.[4] According to D'Souza, racism has its origins in the superiority of Western civilization. Europeans were obsessed with the conspicuous "civilization gap" between themselves and the primitive peoples who were destined to become their colonial subjects. D'Souza concedes that social Darwinism and the entire biological paradigm were a monumental blunder. Instead, he wants to bring us back to an earlier paradigm that traced racial inequality to differences in "civilization."[5]

Yet D'Souza is not a crude cultural determinist. He acknowledges that "cultures frequently change in response to the restrictions and opportunities generated by particular circumstances." Here he embraces the work of recent theorists—some of them with liberal and even left stripes—who argue that Blacks have developed an "oppositional culture," one that D'Souza concedes "emerged out of the crucible of racism and historical oppression directed specifically at Blacks." According to D'Souza, this oppositional culture manifests itself as sheer pathology, and in recent decades there has been "a breakdown of civilization within the African American community," evident in high rates of crime, illegitimacy, drugs, welfare dependency, and other pathologies. This "civilizational crisis," according to D'Souza, "points to deficiencies not of biology but of culture."[6]

Consistent with his diagnosis, D'Souza calls upon Blacks to undergo a "civilizational renewal." To this end, he proposes a series of public policies that would encourage and enforce civility and personal responsibility among the reprobate classes. In terms reminiscent of Booker T. Washington, D'Souza ends his book with an exhortation to Blacks to become "the truest and noblest exemplars of Western civilization."[7]

Although liberals have had a field day skewering D'Souza for his contention that the end of racism is upon us, my contention is that his basic position, which traces ethnic inequality to differences in culture, is *not* fundamentally at odds with prevailing thought in the social sciences. D'Souza only echoes in bald terms propositions that are advanced, with more circumspection, by leading social scientists.

For example, D'Souza's book is peppered with citations to a large canon of empirical studies that have probed the culture and morality of poor minorities. His transgression is not in advancing a new theory, but rather in carrying this theory to its logical conclusion with ruthless consistency. After all, if the problem with Blacks is located in their moral and cultural decadence, then does it not follow that their deliverance lies in their moral and cultural rehabilitation? Is this not the message we heard even from the 1995 Million Man March? And repeated in 2015 at its twentieth anniversary march? Never mind that a year earlier, with the publication of *The Bell Curve*, we witnessed the recrudescence of theories purporting the intellectual inferiority of races, theories that we thought had been thoroughly discredited. Alas, social science had gone full circle!

Despite these oscillations, a new liberal orthodoxy had evolved that affirmed the primacy of environment over genes and was wedded to the idea that race is "socially constructed." No longer was race regarded as fixed and immutable. There was hope, especially among Blacks, that the walls of racism would come falling down.

However, the dominant liberal paradigm had at least two fateful flaws that permitted the evolution of a new brand of racism, one that was tailored to the racial realities of the post-segregation era.

The first flaw was to conceptualize and define racism in terms of attitudes rather than conditions.[8] It was of course recognized that Blacks and whites differed in their life chances and living standards, but these differences were assumed to stem from racial prejudice—that is, from the distorted and malicious beliefs that whites had about Blacks. Theoretical reductionism combined with methodological reductionism to produce scores of studies that sought to measure the extent and sources of prejudice in individuals, all with the ultimate aim of devising strategies for disabusing bigots of their benighted beliefs.[9]

Here, alas, was an incredible inversion of "white social science." The prevailing paradigm was centered on a praxis that ministered to the oppressor rather than to the oppressed! The thrust of social research and social policy was directed not at improving conditions for Blacks but rather at reforming attitudes among whites. Liberation for Blacks would have to wait for whites to undergo a therapeutic transformation.

A second flaw in the liberal paradigm stemmed from the ambiguity surrounding the claim that racial differences can be traced not to genes but to "environment." Rarely was *environment* construed in terms of structures of oppression that denied Blacks elementary rights of citizenship and subjected them to systematic abuse by all major institutions, including institutions of higher learning. Instead, *environment* was construed as pertaining to the deprivations of Blacks themselves, conditions that perpetuated poverty from one generation to the next.

Once again, a flawed theoretical premise inspired the proliferation of a voluminous body of research: scores of ethnographic studies scoured every aspect of Black families, neighborhoods, and communities in a misdirected search for the factors that explained Black underachievement. Though it was not their intention, these studies yielded a portrait of social disorganization and cultural pathology that in effect located the sources of Black poverty and marginality within the Black community itself.[10] Ironically, the same liberal sociology that had relinquished scientific racism to the trash bin of history found itself resurrecting a victim-blaming paradigm that merely substituted culture for genes!

This refurbished paradigm has engendered a series of victim-blaming discourses. In a regrettable betrayal of the sociological imagination, as originally enunciated by C. Wright Mills, mainstream sociology has resorted to reductive strategies that shift the focus of analysis and blame away from societal institutions and instead place it on the doorstep of oppressed minorities and their defective cultures.

To wit: In the 1950s, the buzzword was *cultural deprivation*. The liberal position, reiterated in scores of studies, was that the academic underachievement of minority children had its sources not in their genes but in the cultural deprivations associated with their homes, neighborhoods, and communities. The remedy, then, was to provide these culturally bereft children with the cultural materials and experiences that accounted for the academic success of their middle-class counterparts.[11]

In the 1960s and 1970s, *culture of poverty* entered the sociological lexicon. Oscar Lewis, who coined the term, argued that as a reaction and adaptation to their circumstances, the poor develop a distinctive "way of life" that is passed down from one generation to the next. In yet another leap of faith, Lewis held that children steeped in the culture of poverty would be unprepared to take advantage of opportunities even if they were to arise. The implication of this model was that poverty and racial disadvantage had become self-perpetuating. Writing in 1965, Daniel Patrick Moynihan held that Black pathology "is capable of perpetuating itself without the assistance from the white world."[12]

In the 1980s, the term *underclass* dominated academic discourse. Originally coined by Gunnar Myrdal to refer to groups that remain mired in poverty even during periods of economic expansion and declining unemployment, the term was now used to suggest that this subaltern class was not only materially deprived but lived outside the prevailing normative order as well. One writer put it this way:

> Disproportionately Black and Hispanic, they are still a minority within these minorities. What primarily defines them is not so much their poverty or race as their behavior—their chronic lawlessness, drug use, out-of-wedlock births, nonwork, welfare dependency, and school failure. "Underclass" describes a state of mind and a way of life. It is at least as much cultural as an economic condition.[13]

In the 1990s, yet another voguish stigma came onstream, this time with a leftist twist. It was held that the poor develop an "oppositional culture." In this view, behavior that is conventionally regarded as aberrant is actually a form of "resistance" to hierarchy and domination. Unlike earlier models, "resistance theorists" placed the cultural responses of the poor in a context of political economy. Nevertheless, they share the core assumption that oppositional culture and practices are not only a product of marginality but play an active role in driving the poor deeper into poverty. In this way, or so resistance theorists believed, the poor become implicated in the social reproduction of inequality.[14]

In 2016 Orlando Patterson stoked controversy when he blamed hip-hop culture for the problems of ghetto youth. Patterson is a professor at Harvard University renowned for his 1982 book *Slavery and Social Death*, which portrays the dehumanization of slavery. One wonders why Patterson succumbed to a microscopic analysis of young black men who fall prey to "a cool-pose culture" consisting of "hanging out on the street after school, shopping and dressing sharply, sexual conquests, party drugs, hip-hop music and culture."[15] His brief extended to sociologists

who are putatively so riveted on socioeconomic factors and social structure that they fail to take culture seriously. In advancing this position,
Patterson loses sight of C. Wright Mills's conception of "the sociological
imagination" as the relationship between history and biology, between
personal experience and societal structures. Instead, he lapses into a fatal
reductionism that utterly fails to shed light on the conditions and context
that shape the behavior that he piously condemns.

Note that all these discourses have been challenged by critics for
blaming the victim by shifting responsibility for social inequality away
from societal institutions onto the poor themselves. However, as the suc-
cession of theoretical positions suggests, no sooner is the head of this
theoretical dragon severed than it regenerates another. The nomenclature
changes, but the core assumption is the same: cultural deficiencies explain
how and why the poor languish in poverty.

In so many words, the implication is that these latter-day heathens
and savages fail to comport themselves according to the norms of "civil
society"—the very society that, with callous incivility, places a stigma
of inferiority on its ethnic minorities; casts them into isolated ghettos,
barrios, and ethnic slums; denies them access to jobs and opportunities
that would provide channels of mobility, and then judges them for not
playing according to the rules of a system that victimizes them. And as a
crowning irony, it castigates them for not displaying the cultural virtues
and living by the moral codes that are presumed to govern the lives of
their oppressors.[16]

Despite their claim of value neutrality, social scientists are implicated
in the legitimation of institutionalized racism. With grants from government and foundations, they are commissioned to penetrate the interior of
the nation's ghettos and barrios, armed with the tools of their respective
disciplines, to ferret out the reasons that these pariahs are not exemplars
of middle-class virtues. With inculcated myopia, these field studies record
the manifest reality: social disorganization, cultural pathology, and patterns of self-destructive and antisocial behavior. These men and women
of science mean no harm. On the contrary, like the missionaries who
once voyaged to distant colonies, they want to lift the downtrodden to a
higher plane. Against their intentions, they unwittingly placed a stamp of

scientific legitimacy on the idea that the groups on the bottom are condemned by their own cultural and moral deficiencies.

It is not my intention to substitute the myopia of the person who cannot see the forest for the trees with the myopia of the person who sees
only forest and cannot discern the complex process of reproduction that
occurs within. It is easily demonstrable that the culture of the poor differs
in important respects from the culture of the middle classes. Nor can it
be denied that the poor, out of stark necessity, develop cultural responses
and defenses that are dysfunctional in relation to such mainstream institutions as schools and job markets. None of these caveats, however, warrants the claim that there is a *causal* relation between culture and poverty.

The problem, fundamentally, has to do with the reification of culture.
Reification occurs whenever culture is treated as a thing unto itself, di-
vorced from the material and social conditions in which it is anchored.
In principle, there is little disagreement with this proposition: culture-of-
poverty theorists acknowledge that the cultural patterns of the poor are
"adaptive" to the situations in which the poor find themselves and thus
are ultimately rooted in social structure.

However, a further theoretical claim is made, and this is where controversy begins. It is held that once culture comes into existence, it takes on
"a life of its own." This problematic assumption leads to the supposition
that the culture of poverty exists as an independent and self-sustaining
culture, one that not only constitutes a distinctive way of life but also is
capable of reproducing itself from one generation to the next. This is the
"cycle of poverty" often cited in the social science literature. Reforming
the culture of poverty is thus the key to breaking this vicious cycle.

But does culture really take on "a life of its own"? This is the core
assumption that deserves critical scrutiny. Granted, in terms of surface
appearances, culture seems to have a life of its own. To repeat, we can
readily observe the poor living by values and codes of behavior that are
divergent from those of middle-class society, and this has received docu-
mentation by scores of ethnographic studies. However, the counterargu-
ment, advanced by critics of the culture of poverty, is that what looks
like a shared culture is, on closer examination, similar responses of discrete actors to the exigencies and circumstances that define and limit their

choices. This is not culture pursued for its own sake or prized for its intrinsic worth. Properly defined, it is not a culture at all, but only defensive and reactive responses to structures of inequality as they impinge on the personal sphere of life. If it is a culture at all, it is a culture of last resort.

Elliott Liebow had it right in *Tally's Corner*. Generally speaking, his subjects were streetcorner men who did not hold steady jobs, maintain monogamous relationships, or function as parents for their children. Nevertheless, Liebow rejected the idea that they had different values with respect to work and family or that their behavior signified a distinctive subculture:

> The streetcorner man does not appear as a carrier of an independent cultural tradition. His behavior appears not so much as a way of realizing the distinctive goals and values of his own subculture, or of conforming to its models, but rather as his way of trying to achieve many of the goals and values of the larger society, of failing to do this, and of concealing his failure from others and from himself as best he can.[17]

Liebow also offers this eloquent rebuttal to the claim that the poverty subculture is self-perpetuating:

> Many similarities between the lower-class Negro father and son (or mother and daughter) do not result from "cultural transmission" but from the fact that the son goes out and independently experiences the same failures, in the same areas, and for much the same reasons as his father.[18]

In short, it is not culture but racial and class hierarchy that is reproduced from one generation to the next.

Put another way, the culture of poor and marginalized groups does not exist in a vacuum. Rather, it is in constant and dynamic interaction with the matrix of political, economic, and social factors in which it is embedded. The "sin of reification" occurs whenever this culture is abstracted from this larger matrix and assigned independent causal significance.[19] Does culture matter? Yes, but only in conjunction with the material and social factors in which it is anchored and on which it depends for its sustenance.

Like a flower cut away from its stem, culture stripped away from the structures on which it depends rapidly loses its resilience and, all too soon, its vitality. This is no less true for the privileged than it is for the unprivileged. Take a corporate executive—white, male, and affluent—who is a casualty of downsizing and unable to find a comparable job. How long does it take before he experiences a commensurate diminution of status and self-esteem? Before his marriage is strained to the breaking point? Before he takes refuge in whatever figurative "street corner" is relevant to his status and circumstances? What then can we expect of the racial pariahs who are cast to the fringes of society, where survival, much less self-respect, is a daily challenge? Shall we administer a psychological test? Shall we summon the ethnographer to record their cultural flailing as they pitifully attempt to salvage shreds of their tattered self?

On the other hand, if we scrupulously observe the injunction against abstracting culture from political economy, then we must also reject a praxis that would address culture alone, without addressing the matrix of political, economic, and social factors in which culture is embedded. Melioristic reform that addresses symptoms but neglects underlying causes is doomed to failure. This refrain is echoed by Gerald Berreman, a prominent anthropologist:

> If I were asked, "What practical inference, if any is to be drawn from the comparative study of inherited inequality—of ascriptive social ranking?" I would say it is this: There is no way to reform such institutions; the only solution is their dissolution.[20]

Abram Kardiner and Lionel Ovesey—the authors of a 1951 study entitled *The Mark of Oppression*—came to the same blunt conclusion: "There is only one way that the products of oppression can be dissolved, and that is to stop the oppression."[21]

In the final analysis, the reification of culture not only constitutes bad theory, but it also leads to ineffectual social policy. Its net effect is to shift the onus of moral and political responsibility for social change away from powerful institutions that could make a difference onto the individuals who are rendered powerless by these very institutions.

We social scientists need to take off our political blinders and refuse to place a stamp of scientific legitimacy on victim-blaming discourses. This requires that we subject the sociological enterprise to the critical eye that C. Wright Mills brought to *The Power Elite*.[22] This begins with elite universities whose imprimatur alone launches careers, opens up doors to prestigious publishing houses and the op-ed pages of leading newspapers, and helps secure grants from foundations and government agencies. Grants, in turn, allow these entrepreneurs to form "schools" and "dream teams" that propagate their pet theories to fledgling scholars. It is an open secret that the academic wheel is greased with money, which means that the people and interests who control the purse strings are the engineers of knowledge production. As Mills acknowledges, the referee system for grants, like the referee system for journals, functions to enforce ideological conformity by rejecting submissions that go too far in challenging the prevailing wisdom. Then there are the professional associations that often resemble fraternal associations, replete with a "rewardocracy" that dispenses honorific titles, awards, and sinecures that invest hegemony with an indispensable aura of legitimacy.

To be sure, dissident viewpoints are tolerated in the academy, if only because they sustain the myth of the liberal university as a bastion of freedom that thrives on diversity and dissent. The ultimate issue pertains to power in its various dimensions. Which viewpoints prevail? Which receive material support? Which are canonized? Above all, which are influential in terms of politics and public policy?

In their provocative intervention on race and reflexivity, Mustafa Emirbayer and Matthew Desmond warn of "the scholastic unconscious" and compare scholars to fish in water who "remain less than fully aware of how their thinking *as scholars* carries with it unexplored assumptions that distort their perceptions of the racial order."[23] This is an astute observation that raises a penetrating question: whether sociologists, against their intentions, have practiced a *white* sociology, reflecting the experiences, interests, and sensibilities of whites. Alas, there is much political work to be done before sociology lives up to its emancipatory promise.

Sociology has two other glaring omissions that I address in the chapters that follow: (1) the marginalization of Marxism from the sociological canon on race, and (2) the occlusion of Black sociologists from the sociological canon and the revelatory scholarship of W. E. B. Du Bois in particular. Fortunately, this has been significantly remedied by Aldon Morris's groundbreaking study *The Scholar Denied*.[24] As will be seen, Du Bois not only broke with the obscurantist abstractions of Chicago sociology, but he also pioneered the foundations of scientific sociology as we know it.

CHAPTER SIX

EDUCATION AS A FALSE PANACEA

From Tuskegee to the Harlem Children's Zone

Social studies served to conceal the arbitrary, unjust, and oppressive nature of Black subordination in the South.

James D. Anderson, *The Education of Blacks in the South, 1860–1935*[1]

In recent years, there has been much controversy surrounding the Harlem Children's Zone as a model for the future of education. . . . To date, HCZ has an endowment of $175 million and revenue of $75 million. Stanley Druckenmiller, a former hedge fund manager and college friend of Canada, who has given over $100 million since 2006, donated most of the funds. In comparison, each federally designated promise zone receives about a quarter, if that, of HCZ's endowment over multiple years.

Denzell Jobson, "Is the Harlem Children's Zone Accomplishing Its Goal?"[2]

"THE EDUCATION OF PRIMITIVE MAN"

In 1912, Robert Ezra Park—then a publicist and ghostwriter for Booker T. Washington—planned a conference at Tuskegee under the title "The Education of Primitive Man." The conference had bold ambitions. Some 3,700 people were invited, and the U.S. Department of State extended an invitation to all governments that had "Negro possessions."

Park sounded the keynote for the conference by posing a question: "How far is it possible by means of education to abridge the apprenticeship of the younger to the older races, or at least to make it less cruel and inhuman than it now frequently is?"[3]

With that invocation, Park echoed the ideas of Herbert Spencer, the British sociologist who, according to historian Daniel Breslau, was "the most influential source of 19th-century sociology in the United States."[4] Spencer and the Spencerians held that the social hierarchy was the result of natural differences in intellectual endowment. In short, biology was destiny. By the beginning of the twentieth century, however, reformers came to regard education as a means of promoting individual development and alleviating social problems.[5] Park reflected this reformist impulse in his belief that education is the institutional mechanism for uplifting "the primitive to the level of 'civilized man.'" Indeed, the scholars who flocked to the Tuskegee conference represented an updated version of the missionaries who brought religion to the heathen, thus placing a salve on the cruelties of colonialism, both domestic and foreign.

There is no clearer articulation of this viewpoint than Booker T. Washington's elegy in his 1901 autobiography, *Up from Slavery*. Washington averred: "Notwithstanding the cruelty and moral wrong of slavery, the ten million Negroes inhabiting this country, who themselves or whose ancestors went through the school of American slavery, are in a stronger and more hopeful condition, materially, intellectually, morally, and religiously, than is true of an equal number of Black people in any other portion of the globe."[6] So there we have it: slavery was a "school" to uplift and civilize the benighted descendants of slavery.

Though Washington is renowned as an apostle of "industrial education," Tuskegee was not a trade school.[7] Its stated mission was to "complete the education begun under slavery" through the cultivation of discipline and work habits.[8] As James Anderson documents in *The Education of Blacks in the South, 1860–1935*, the industrialists and philanthropists who promoted and financed the Hampton-Tuskegee model sought to fit Blacks "into the southern agricultural economy as wage laborers, sharecroppers, and domestic workers."[9] Not only did the three million Blacks liberated from slavery provide indispensable labor for the Southern economy, but as one industrialist quoted by Anderson added, Negroes would "protect the South's economy against the onslaught of unionized labor."[10]

Enter Robert Ezra Park, the organizer of the Tuskegee conference "The Education of Primitive Man." By a twist of fate, Park had an encounter with W. I. Thomas, the leading light at the University of Chicago, who delivered a paper titled "Education and Cultural Traits."[11] According to the Tuskegee student newspaper, "Professor Thomas revived the old question of the fitness of the Negro as a race to acquire the culture of the white man and participate in the white man's civilization, but he did it in a novel and surprisingly witty manner."[12] Long story short, Park and Thomas struck up a friendship and with Thomas's support, Park secured a position at the University of Chicago in 1914 at the ripe age of fifty. Initially he was a part-time assistant lecturer (in today's parlance, an adjunct), but he quickly secured a full-time position and eventually emerged as "the father of the Chicago school of race relations." According to John Stanfield in *Philanthropy and Jim Crow in American Social Science*, "Booker T. Washington, through his sponsorship of Robert E. Park, was a founder of the celebrated Chicago school of race relations."[13]

Park's strange career raises an intriguing question: to what extent did Park carry Washington's worldview with him, as intellectual baggage, as he morphed from a reporter to a speechwriter and publicist for Booker T. Washington, and finally, to a professor at the University of Chicago who spun theories concerning universal laws as they pertain to race?

Park retained his loyalty to Washington. In an autobiographical note found after his death at the age of eighty, Park had written: "I probably learned more about human nature and society, in the South under Booker Washington, than I learned elsewhere in all my previous studies." Park stipulated that he was not interested in the Negro problem "as it is ordinarily conceived." Rather he ruminated about "the historical process by which civilization, not merely here but elsewhere, has evolved, drawing into the circle of its influence an ever widening circle of races and peoples."[14] Soon after securing a position at the University of Chicago, Park collaborated with Ernest Burgess, in writing one of the first textbooks in sociology, *Introduction to the Science of Sociology*.[15] It was a voluminous compendium of existing knowledge that ran 1,040 pages, much of it centered on race. Dubbed "the Green Bible" for its green cover, it served as the authoritative source that inculcated the first two generations of race scholars.

The main thrust of the Green Bible was to apply Darwin's theory of evolution to the realm of human society. "Social Darwinism," as it came to be called, held that the laws of evolution, including competition and natural selection, could be observed in the emergence of racial hierarchies, extending on a continuum ranging from "backward races" to "advanced races." Essentially, social Darwinism amounted to a racial theory of human evolution. Park once wrote with chilling equanimity, "Races and cultures die—it has always been so—but civilization lives on."[16]

Spencerism was already approaching obsolescence by the time the *Introduction to the Science of Sociology* was published in 1921. Even so, the Green Bible retained its authority until it went out of print in 1943. A year later, Gunnar Myrdal published his opus, *An American Dilemma*, funded by the Carnegie Foundation, which marked a paradigm shift in race knowledge.[17]

In retrospect, it may be tempting to regard Robert Park and the first generation of Chicago sociologists as merely "men of their time" who reflected prevailing discourses. This does not withstand scrutiny, however. The founding of the nation's first department of sociology in 1892 did not signify the advent of new epistemologies. Far from it. The "science" that these sociologists claimed in the title of the Green Bible was laden with the prescientific twaddle of Spencerism. As Andrew Abbott writes in *Department and Discipline: Chicago Sociology at One Hundred*, "From the 1940s onward much of sociology came to think of itself as a science, uninterested in what it defined as a prescientific past."[18] By the 1940s, Park and Burgess had come to be disdained by their own colleagues as wallowing in "the most absurd heights of obscurantist abstraction."[19]

Abbott also gives passing reference to Albion Small's "open-mouthed admiration of Marx." Indeed, this comment is pregnant with significance. Like other early sociologists, Small was the son of a minister and the founder of the University of Chicago's Department of Sociology in 1892, when the progressive movement made inroads into the previously cloistered atmosphere of the university. In 1896, he published an article in the nascent *American Journal of Sociology* under the title "Scholarship and Social Agitation." Small cataloged the burning issues of the times—child labor, the right to strike, compulsory arbitration, progressive taxation, municipal ownership of utilities—and declared that "scholars are shirkers unless they grapple with these problems."[20]

A few years later, when a young firebrand on the faculty, Edward Bemis, was summarily fired, Small did an about-face and declared that "although I hope to take up reform movements years hence, I am now going off in my lectures into transcendental philosophy so as to be as far as possible from these reform movements and thus establish the scientific character of my department."[21] Clearly, the fledgling Department of Sociology was under pressure to avoid the stain of Marxism.

At the very time that Park and Burgess were wallowing in "the most absurd heights of obscurantist abstraction," there was a rival body of research and knowledge production on race that anteceded Chicago sociology by half a century, and to this day is generally ignored in the mainstream of American social science. I am alluding, of course, to the pioneering research of Karl Marx, which was ignored or disparaged by the illuminati who gave birth to Chicago sociology. Marxism was regarded as heresy and banished from respectable sociological discourse. Indeed, it is reasonable to conclude that the hidden agenda of the Green Bible was to provide an alternative to Marxism.

This hidden agenda is documented in a 1974 book, *The Sociologists of the Chair: A Radical Analysis of the Formative Years of North American Sociology (1883–1922)*. This obscure study is rarely cited by historians. Its authors, Herman Schwendinger and Julia R. Schwendinger, offer a penetrating critique of both Spencerian thought and its Marxist alternative. According to Schwendinger and Schwendinger, "The founders of American sociology adopted Darwinian ideas in order to buttress their own racist and imperial doctrines."[22] The flip side of this proposition is that the founders of sociology chose to ignore the fact that "Marx had developed a materialist strategy for analyzing historical relations *before* the rise of American sociology."[23] This is a stunning revelation in that the emergent Chicago school of race relations not only propagated racist epistemologies, but it deliberately turned a blind eye to the politically inconvenient truths of an epistemological precursor.

Consider this striking example: in 1846, fifteen years before the Civil War, Marx wrote, "Without slavery there would be no cotton, without cotton there would be no modern industry."[24] In a single sentence, Marx summed up the relationship of slavery to the emerging industrial economies in both the United States and England, dependent as they were on abundant and cheap cotton for their burgeoning textile industries. Implicit, too, was a theory of race and racism, which turned the prevailing conception of slavery on its head. In the Marxist schema, slavery did not exist because of some preexisting racial animus. Rather, racism was invented and propagated in order to provide moral justification for slavery. This elaborate system of falsification and delusion was necessary in order to make sense of the existence of two centuries of slavery in a nation whose founding covenant proclaimed that "all men are created equal."

Stacked against Marx's revelatory scholarship, the contentions of *Introduction to the Science of Sociology* were pretentious obfuscation. Simply stated, the men and women who founded the Chicago school of race relations had a choice between Spencer and Marx, and they chose Spencer!

There is another occlusion in the historiography of Chicago sociology that has only recently been brought to light, thanks to the assiduous scholarship of Aldon Morris, in *The Scholar Denied: W. E. B. Du Bois and the Birth of Modern Sociology*. According to the hegemonic narrative, Chicago sociology "produced the major theories, concepts, and pathbreaking textbook that guided the emerging field for decades." However, Morris demonstrates that it is W. E. B. Du Bois who not only exposed the shibboleths of establishment sociology, but was the unacclaimed founder of scientific sociology.[25] Morris even proffers evidence that "Park knew about Du Bois's pioneering studies but failed to accord them the scholarly credit they merited."[26]

Let us examine the facets of Du Bois's biography that prefigure his trajectory into social science. Du Bois grew up in one of the few Black families in Barrington, Massachusetts. After high school, he enrolled in Fisk University, a historically Black university, and then went on to graduate school at Harvard, where he was the first African American to earn a PhD. His prize-winning dissertation was titled "The Suppression of the African Slave Trade to the United States of America." With a scholarship from the Slater Foundation, he went on to study political science at the University of Berlin, which at the time was the center of cutting-edge scholarship in the nascent social sciences. To his surprise, in Germany he was treated as a social equal of whites. He later wrote in his autobiography, "I found myself on the outside of the American world, looking in."[27] In Berlin he was also trained in statistics and quantitative analysis, which at the time were regarded as fundamental to sociology's ambition to gain recognition as a science.

In 1896 Du Bois secured a one-year position at the University of Pennsylvania, which sought to subsidize a study of the influx of Blacks in Philadelphia. Du Bois energetically pursued this opportunity, with exemplary results. As Morris comments: *The Philadelphia Negro* "contained analysis in what would become major subfields of modern American sociology, including stratification, class, race, gender, work and occupations, crime, demography and population, institutions, religion, and leisure."[28] Nor did Du Bois avoid investigating social disorganization, including crime, which he argued was "largely rooted in social conditions rather than in biological and social degeneracy, as white social scientists usually claimed."[29] *The Philadelphia Negro* pioneered empirical methods of inquiry that, according the Morris, produced "the first classic of American scientific sociology."[30]

Nevertheless, the barriers to employment at a white university were insurmountable, and in 1897 Du Bois accepted a position at Atlanta University, described as "a historically Black institution of higher learning, located in the heart of Atlanta's black community." He taught courses in history and economics for thirteen years, "making a name in social science, letters, literature, and activism while pioneering the first scientific school of American sociology." Du Bois attracted other Black sociologists who collaborated in the development of the Atlanta school of sociology. According to Schwendinger and Schwendinger, under Du Bois's leadership, Black scholars launched studies on an immense range of topics: "Negro mortality, urbanization, the effort of Negroes for their own social betterment, Negroes in business, college-bred Negroes, the Negro common school, the Negro artisan, the Negro church, and Negro crime."[31] As Du Bois wrote, "There was no study of the race problem in America . . . which did not depend in some degree upon the investigations made at Atlanta University."[32]

Indeed, despite little or no external funding, this prodigious scholarship was unmatched anywhere in American academe—with the exception of "the Tuskegee machine," a term that reflects the control that Booker T. Washington exercised over the flow of philanthropy."[33] In addition to the "Atlanta papers," there was a series of "Atlanta conferences," where the intellectual and practical implications of each year's research could be debated. Clearly, the Atlanta school of sociology was animated by a shared sense of mission, buttressed by an optimistic faith that "science" might bring to light the causes and remedies of the Black plight.

Yet the Atlanta papers and conferences failed to capture the attention of white sociologists. Du Bois commented sardonically in 1909:

> So far as the American world of science and letters was concerned, we never "belonged"; we remained unrecognized in learned societies and academic groups. We rated merely as Negroes studying Negroes, and after all, what had Negroes to do with America or science?[34]

Nevertheless, as Morris observed, the fruits of the Du Bois–Atlanta school gained influence through "subterranean routes before bursting into mainstream recognition a century later."[35]

Though Chicago sociology shunned Marxism and bathed in Spencerism, there were other discourses emerging that challenged the stale orthodoxies in the *Introduction to the Science of Sociology*. Du Bois was attuned to the work of Franz Boas, the anthropologist who challenged social Darwinism and its biological theories of race. Instead, Boas held that mankind progresses from lower to higher levels of civilization, predicated not on biology but on culture. As Howard Winant writes in his survey "The Dark Side of the Force: One Hundred Years of the Sociology of Race," this "culturalist turn" replaced the social Darwinist and Spencerian theories of evolutionism and yet still explained the apparently intractable nature of race.[36] In short, Boas's new paradigm amounted to evolutionism without biology!

This progressive precept had its detractors who were not prepared to give up cherished assumptions. Among the old guard was the philosopher John Dewey, another University of Chicago acolyte. As Thomas Fallace has shown, Dewey subscribed to a "linear historicism" by which cultures progressed on a continuum from the primitive to the civilized. Like Park and Thomas, Dewey conceded that the outcome was not destined by biology but held that "primitive man" was a circumstance of history and "non-Western cultures represented earlier, more primitive stages of life that had been surpassed by more advanced, superior societies."[37]

Left unanswered was the question of whether "culture is destiny." Park clung to the assumption that "primitive man" could leapfrog over stages in the evolution, from savagery to civilization.[38] He wrestled with this question in a 1918 essay "Education in its Relation to the Conflict and Fusion of Cultures." Park wrote that "the Negro, when he landed in the United States, left behind him almost everything but his dark complexion and his tropical temperament," which he described as "a genial, sunny, and social disposition."[39] He added that "temperament determines what things the individual and the group will be interested in; what elements of the general culture, to which they have access, they will assimilate; what, to state it pedagogically, they will learn."[40] Thus, Park's verdict was that unlike the European races, Blacks were unassimilable, steeped in both romanticized charms and deeply ingrained deficits of primitiveness.

Yet Park is also remembered for vigorously recruiting Black students to the doctoral program in sociology at the University of Chicago. Taken at face value, this indicated an equalitarian streak and Park's belief that these Black students, some of whom had been educated at Howard University, would go on to propagate the theoretical claims of the race-relations cycle to students enrolled at segregated Black colleges.

Writing in 1993, Stanford Lyman showed how leading social theorists, from Robert Park to Gunnar Myrdal to Talcott Parsons, used an evolutionary teleology to avoid the issue of civil rights. Instead they advanced theoretical models that projected racial improvement as an ineluctable evolutionary process of societal change. Lyman wrote sardonically,

"Since the time for teleological redemption is ever long, Blacks might consign their civil and egalitarian future to faith in the ultimate fulfillment of the inclusive cycle's promise."[41] He ended with a blanket indictment of sociology for its failure to confront its complicity in perpetuating white supremacy: "Sociology . . . has been part of the problem and not part of the solution."[42]

TUSKEGEE NORTH: THE HARLEM CHILDREN'S ZONE

My purpose now is to take a perilous leap across the time dimension in order to explore the subtle but illuminating parallels between Robert Ezra Park and William Julius Wilson, as well as the parallels between Tuskegee and the Harlem Children's Zone (HCZ).

HCZ is an elaborate program of charter schools and community programs that was the centerpiece of Barack Obama's urban policy.[43] In drawing comparisons between Tuskegee and "Tuskegee North," I am not oblivious to the glaring differences between the two, beginning with the fact that Tuskegee prepared Blacks for subordinate jobs in a segregated regional economy, whereas HCZ's declared mission is to prepare Black students, through education, to climb the ladder of success.

Arguably, William Julius Wilson and the Harlem Children's Zone are to "the Second Reconstruction" (the post–civil rights era) what Robert Ezra Park and Tuskegee were to the First Reconstruction (the aftermath of the Civil War). Is education once again being used to divert attention away from the urgent problems that are not being addressed, in a nation still riven by the legacy of slavery?

Turning this proposition on its head, are we still invoking "education" as the panacea for addressing the deep and persistent inequalities that beg for other remedies? To paraphrase Franz Fanon, do we still use the *products* of oppression to justify oppression? Or concoct victim-blaming discourses that shift blame to powerless minorities while absolving powerful institutions for their role in perpetuating the inequalities between the Black and white citizens of our nation?

It is an article of faith that education is a panacea for addressing the stubborn inequalities of race and class. However, this nostrum warrants critical reflection. Think about it. Were the missionaries in colonized countries who provided religion and education to the heathen acting out of noblesse oblige or were they unwitting accomplices of colonial rule? And what about the philanthropists who throw vast sums of money into educating Black children, whether in Tuskegee or Harlem? Is this "the conscience of capitalism," as Lorraine Hansberry exclaimed in her play *Les Blancs*?[44] Or is this an artifice whereby modern-day missionaries (read: neoliberals) demonstrate that the blessings of capitalism can reach even the most downtrodden subjects of an otherwise beneficent system?

A 2017 piece in *AlterNet*, a radical online publication, calls into question the illusion that education is a panacea for the deep divisions of race and class. *AlterNet* published an interview by Jennifer Berkshire, its education editor, with Harvey Kantor, a professor emeritus in the Department of Education, Culture, and Society at the University of Utah. Their dialogue has a conceptual umbrella for a title: "Education Can't Solve Poverty—So Why Do We Keep Insisting That It Can?"[45]

Berkshire posed a provocative question: "I read in the *New York Times* recently that education is the most powerful force for 'reducing poverty and lifting middle-class living standards.'" To which Kantor replied:

> One of the consequences of making education so central to social policy has been that we've ended up taking the pressure off of the state for the kinds of policies that would be more effective at addressing poverty and economic inequality. Instead we're asking education to do things it can't possibly do. The result has been increasing support for the kinds of market-oriented policies that make inequality worse.
>
> If we really want to address issues of inequality and economic insecurity, there are a lot of other policies that we have to pursue besides or at least in addition to education policies, and that part of the debate has been totally lost. Raising the minimum wage, or providing a guaranteed income, which the last time we talked seriously about that was in the late 1960s, increasing workers' bargaining power, making tax policies more progressive—things like that are going to be much more effective at addressing inequality and economic security than education policies. That argument is often taken to mean, "schools can't do anything unless we address poverty first." But that's not what we were trying to say.

Kantor poses the crucial question that is generally avoided in debates about schooling: Why do rich kids get better schools? This is the challenging question that shifts the debate to thorny questions about class, race, power, and inequality. Nor is it only a matter of social-class privilege. To quote Kantor again:

> Even while educational policy is focused on the schools that poor kids attend, we're not addressing the inequalities that have to do with the advantages richer parents have and work so hard to maintain. It works to create more inequality at the same time that it can't really do anything about the other things that are really driving income inequality: minimum wages, unions, tax policy, the concentration of income at the top. So we have this strange situation where we're trying to address educational inequality while economic inequality is expanding in ways that make educational inequality even worse. We don't address that kind of paradox at all.

If we were totally honest, we would confront the fact that schools, as they are currently constituted, are charged with an impossible mission: to compensate for societal inequities and injustices that the children bring to the classroom and that the teachers are charged with alleviating. Teachers and students are then told that they are failing, when the blame ultimately lies with the major institutions of our society and the vast and intolerable inequities that frustrate teaching and learning alike.

This dose of reality provides a basis for asking why financiers, philanthropists, and hedge fund managers, from Jacob Rosenwald to Stanley Druckenmiller—like the missionaries of yore—commit themselves to improving the schooling of poor Black children, otherwise consigned to live on the fringes of a capitalist system. With this in mind, let us examine the historical parallels between Tuskegee and the Harlem Children's Zone.

There are five parallels that shed light on why so many Blacks today find themselves, 150 years later, on a historical treadmill.

(1) Education in Political Context

Both Tuskegee and HCZ emerged during periods of revanchist backlash in the aftermath of revolutionary movements to secure elementary civil rights for African Americans.

Booker T. Washington rose to prominence and founded Tuskegee at the moment that Reconstruction had been dismantled, the Fourteenth Amendment had been effectively nullified, and the scaffolding for Jim Crow was being erected. Tuskegee represented a throwback to the status quo ante when "political questions" were put aside and even the proverbial "friends of the Negro" retreated from their commitment to the Black cause. In this context we can see the ideological function of Washington and Tuskegee: they provided a smokescreen for the retreat from race. Instead of political action and enforcement of the Reconstruction Amendments, Tuskegee substituted the gospel of education, on the supposition that racial uplift would come by acquiring education and skills that, in another leap of faith, would demonstrate that Blacks were worthy of citizenship.[46]

The civil rights movement of the 1950s and 1960s—its legislative victories and the subsequent implementation of affirmative action—was followed by a prolonged backlash that gradually chipped away those very gains. Like Tuskegee, the Harlem Children's Zone is a showcase promising opportunity and redemption, at least for the few who were lucky to be selected by lottery. Just as Tuskegee had its critics (including W. E. B. Du Bois), HCZ's critics regard HCZ as a neoliberal scheme to undercut public education.[47]

(2) The Role of Philanthropy

Both Tuskegee and the HCZ were projects of resourceful and energetic leaders who were lionized as saviors of the race. Geoffrey Canada, HCZ's president and CEO, was portrayed on the cover of the *New York Times Magazine* as a messianic figure: a tall Black man soaring above his flock of beleaguered children. Both Washington and Canada depended on the patronage of white philanthropy. What Peabody, Rockefeller, and Rosenwald were to Tuskegee, hedge fund managers, financiers, and corporate titans are to HCZ. Again, this raises an enigmatic question: What is the motive of plutocrats who donate huge subsidies to educate poor Black children in Harlem?

The answer has to do with neoliberalism. HCZ is a showcase project, motivated less by noblesse oblige than by ideology. Its whole purpose is to demonstrate that charter schools can succeed where the public schools have failed.

The problem is that despite the many advantages of HCZ, student scores on standardized tests have been disappointing. Canada acknowledges that "we live or die by the numbers," but despite long school hours, weekend classes, and test prep both in class and after school, HCZ student scores are not significantly higher than those of students in neighboring public schools. Nevertheless, this troubling fact does not diminish the hype, and HCZ was designated as the model for the Obama-Duncan education policy.

(3) The Making of an Icon

Booker T. Washington was catapulted to national prominence on the basis of his famed 1895 speech at the Atlanta Exposition in which he implored Blacks to put aside "political questions" and "artificial forcing." This was during the fraught moment when Reconstruction was being dismantled by the courts and legislatures (the *Plessy* decision came down just a year later). With his gospel of self-help and his disdain for politics, Washington advised Blacks to put down their buckets where they were—as subordinate laborers in the South's economy. With lavish patronage from wealthy philanthropists, he was catapulted to fame and influence.

But wasn't this also the effect of William Julius Wilson's 1979 publication *The Declining Significance of Race*, at a moment when racial backlash was on the rise, when liberals were in retreat and affirmative action was under attack, and the Democratic Party was eager to "put race on a back burner"? In 1895, "artificial forcing" entailed enforcing civil rights for Blacks. In 1979, "artificial forcing" meant dismantling affirmative action mandates in universities and the professions. Wilson's declaration that the problems of Blacks had more to do with "class" than with "race" sounded the death knell of Black militancy and the reliance on state power to attack the structures of racial inequality.

Though Wilson adopted a left veneer, arguing "class over race," on closer examination his conception of "class" amounted to little more than human capital, implying that Blacks needed to acquire the education and skills that would allow them to escape poverty—essentially the conservative bromide that was at the center of Washington's eschatology. Furthermore, like Washington, Wilson received lavish support from scores of foundations.[48] And like Washington, Wilson at times spoke out for other policy interventions—for example, his pie-in-the-sky advocacy of a new WPA program. When pressed, he also gave equivocal support for affirmative action. But what made both Washington and Wilson the pet of philanthropists and foundations was that they provided legitimacy for the retreat from a frontal assault on the structures of apartheid in schools, housing, and occupations.[49] No surprise, therefore, that Wilson emerged as a leading cheerleader for the Harlem Children's Zone and Obama's ineffectual educational policies.[50]

(4) Education as Exorcism

Both Tuskegee and the Harlem Children's Zone were predicated on the assumption that Blacks are saddled with an aberrant culture, and that this aberrant culture is an obstacle to progress. On this premise, the mission of education is to exorcize this dysfunctional culture and to inculcate the culture and work habits that will lead to academic achievement and put Blacks on the road to social and economic redemption.

Like Tuskegee and the Indian boarding schools, HCZ's goal is not merely to educate, but also to reconstruct these children psychologically and culturally. This begins with leaving all vestiges of hip-hop culture at the schoolhouse door. At the entrance of HCZ's Promise Academy, a sign prohibits hats, durags, hoodies, and body jewelry.[51] Students wear school uniforms: gray plaid skirts and white blouses for the girls, gray slacks and red vests for the boys. High school students are attired in preppy khakis and button-downs.[52] The unmistakable message is that the aberrant and dysfunctional culture of the home, neighborhood, and community must be extirpated and replaced with socially respectable—which is to say, "white"—alternatives. The problem is not that Black youth regard learning as "white," as is sometimes claimed, but rather that the schools themselves operate on the assumption of white cultural hegemony.

Beyond subjecting these students to a sartorial makeover, HCZ offers a rigorous academic program, including longer school days, a longer school year, much smaller classes, in-class and after-school tutoring, and Saturday classes for students who need remediation, with cash incentives for attending visits to elite colleges. According to one estimate, "Promise

Academy students who are behind grade level are in school for twice as many hours as a traditional public school student in New York City. Students who are at or above grade level still attend the equivalent of about fifty percent more school in a calendar year."[53]

Despite this demanding regimen, HCZ has produced mixed results at best. This was the conclusion of a special issue of *City Limits*, with the provocative title "Hope or Hype in Harlem."[54] This was also the reluctant conclusion of a detailed study by Will Dobbie and Roland G. Fryer, two Harvard economists, titled "Are High-Quality Schools Enough to Increase Achievement among the Poor? Evidence from the Harlem Children's Zone." Note that their study was funded by the Eli and Edythe Broad Foundation, whose stated mission was "Transforming K-12 urban public education through better governance, management, labor relations and competition."[55] Their neoliberal earmark is self-evident.

Note, too, that in the special issue of the *Annals of the American Academy of Political and Social Science*, William Julius Wilson gloated that "the preliminary results of this evaluation are spectacular."[56] Spectacular? The authors of the report were far less euphoric: "We conclude by presenting five pieces of evidence that suggest high-quality schools are enough to significantly increase academic achievement among the poor."[57] At best, this was a modest claim, based on a low threshold of success.

The contributors to the *City Limits* special issue on the HCZ offered an even less sanguine analysis of Dobbie and Fryer's findings. HCZ students had slightly higher scores than students in other public schools in Harlem and African American students citywide, but large gaps persisted when comparisons are made with white and Asian students citywide.[58] According to *City Limits*, "Both the Department of Education and New York State Regents Chancellor Meryl Tisch recognized that the Level 3 core—widely translated as 'at grade level' or 'proficient,' which is where most Harlem Children's Zone students scored—did not predict future academic success." Furthermore, Dobbie and Fryer's metrics were based on cohorts of approximately one hundred students enrolled in a particular class in a particular year, hardly a basis for shaping national policy on education. Undeterred, the Obama administration persisted in projecting HCZ as the model for their nationwide educational policies.

(5) Educationalizing Societal Problems

As David Labaree argues in "The Winning Ways of a Losing Strategy," all through American history, social reformers, with the complicity of the education establishment, have promoted education as a panacea for social problems. They have done so, according to Labaree, "even though schools have repeatedly proved that they are an ineffective mechanism for solving these problems."[59]

Like Tuskegee, Geoffrey Canada's Harlem Children's Zone is a laudable, even unassailable project to extend educational opportunity to disadvantaged children. However, problem arises when we consider the ideological and political *uses* of these projects. Why is it a "miracle," to use David Brook's designation, when HCZ students are brought up to citywide grade level?[60] And how does this experiment, bankrolled by tycoons, represent a model for national policy on schooling?

Labaree is right to challenge liberal orthodoxy with respect to education and to warn against the risks of educationalizing racism and poverty. The presumption that education is the key to mobility is a gross oversimplification. It not only evades the question of which children have access to good schools, but also the more vexing question of the relationship between social-class background and educational achievement.[61] The grand fallacy of education is that it treats the school as though it exists in a vacuum, and children as though they arrive at the schoolhouse door tabula rasa.

Geoffrey Canada was aware of this pitfall. The inspiration for his Promise Neighborhood is an array of pipeline schools and social services that aim to insulate children from the harsh realities of the neighborhood. These services include prenatal care, pregnancy prevention, a "baby college," preschool programs, a fitness center, legal services, and an employment and technology center. Canada's theory is that the combined impact of these services will transform the culture of the neighborhood, leading to a reverse "contamination effect" that will produce healthy and achieving schoolchildren.

However, it will take more than a patchwork of reforms to remedy the multiple and pernicious effects of poverty. In *Whatever It Takes*, Paul Tough probes the gritty reality of the lives of poor children outside of school. His journalistic eye focuses on the principal of a middle school who had to deal with behavioral issues in classrooms, the hallways, and the cafeteria:

> The more she learned about the home life of her students, the more their outbursts and breakdowns made sense to her. "Somewhat between 60 and 80 percent of our students have serious emotional needs or behavioral challenges," she told me. She could rattle off a list of the issues they dealt with at home: "substance abuse, domestic violence, foster care, involvement with ACS"—the city's child-welfare agency—"as well as mental illness or emotional disturbances within their family." Her students needed help, and lots of it, and she didn't always know how to give it to them.[62]

What is too often forgotten is that "poverty" is not one thing but a web of factors, circumstances, and institutions that pervade all aspects of life, defeating aspiration and eating away at the human spirit. The problem is far greater than can be addressed with Geoffrey Canada's ambitious patchwork of reforms to uplift the poor. The only answer is to eliminate racism and poverty "root and branch." Sadly, the *Brown* decision failed to end school segregation, and the lesson of Tuskegee and of the Harlem Children's Zone alike is that we must forego the shibboleth that education is a panacea for the deep divisions of race and class, which, on closer examination, are the failure of American democracy.

JOHN OGBU'S EPIPHANY

John Ogbu was born in 1939 and raised in a small village in Nigeria, where he was educated in missionary schools. As he came of age and taught in a missionary high school, he planned to enter the ministry and was sent to the Princeton Theological Seminary. Soon after, however, he enrolled in anthropology at the University of California, Berkeley. His book (which began as his dissertation) *The Next Generation: An Ethnography of Education in an Urban Neighborhood* was based on a case study of a school in Stockton, California, with the purported goal of learning why minority children did poorly in school.[63]

This was the abiding issue that defined Ogbu's intellectual project. His next book was a study not of a troubled urban school but of a high

school in the affluent Cleveland suburb of Shaker Heights, again exploring why middle-class African Americans lagged behind whites.[64] Trained
as an anthropologist, Ogbu's perspective and his empirical research centered on the role that "culture" plays in the transaction between schools
and academic achievement.

Upon graduating from Berkeley in 1971, Ogbu spent two years at
the Carnegie Council on Children in New Haven, Connecticut. As luck
would have it, the Institute of International Studies of UC, Berkeley, had
funded an exploratory study of minority education in six nations: the
United States, Great Britain, New Zealand, India, Israel, and Japan. Apparently, this cross-cultural framework spoke to Ogbu, and thanks to a
summer faculty fellowship in 1972, he devoted himself to exploring "the
historical and structural forces affecting Black education in the United
States." He then used his two-year stint at the Carnegie Council on Children to write a book, *Minority Education and Caste: The American System in Cross-Cultural Perspective*, that placed race and schooling in the
United States within a global framework.

This is what Ogbu found:

First and foremost, in all six nations under examination, there was a
pronounced performance gap between "caste-like minorities" and others. In three of these nations, the "minority" was not defined by race. For
example, in Israel, the fault line was between Ashkenazim and Oriental
Jews. In Japan, the Buraku were outcasts even though they were not identifiable in terms of physiognomy. In India, stratification was rooted in an
elaborate system of caste, ranging from Brahmins at the top to untouch-
ables at the bottom. In the other three nations—Britain, New Zealand,
and the United States—the dominant and minority groups were identified
by race. Thus, race as we know it in the U.S. was not the only driving
force behind the performance gap in academic outcomes. Other systems
of inequality also engendered sharp and enduring differences.

Second, all six societies developed bold initiatives to reduce the performance gap. Some focused on inadequacies of children. Others addressed the inadequacies of schools. Still others implemented affirmative
action (in some nations called "reverse discrimination"). Despite genuine
and assiduous effort, however, all three approaches generally failed to
make large and enduring differences in closing the performance gap.

One might conclude from this analysis that "nothing works." This was not Ogbu's conclusion. His "epiphany" is that patchwork reform has little effect, given the deep historical and structural conditions that limit the life chances of caste-like minorities. Rather, the only hope is through a large-scale and comprehensive assault on caste itself. Ogbu culminated with the following manifesto:

I have stressed . . . the need to develop a comprehensive national policy aimed at eliminating caste barriers. Within this planned policy, there
should be programs dealing simultaneously and in coordinated ways with
the three sources of the retardation: caste barriers, school discriminatory
policies and practices, and the "dysfunctional" influences of the home
and community environment on Black school children. Neither programs
aimed at changing or rehabilitating the individual nor those aimed at
reforming the schools can by themselves, or even combined, significantly
and permanently eliminate Black academic retardation.[65]

Ogbu ends on this lofty note:

What is required to achieve this is a comprehensive policy with the clearly
defined goal of incorporating Blacks into the mainstream of American
society, and this amounts to nothing less than a total elimination of caste
barriers.[66]

ROOT AND BRANCH

It goes without saying that it is one thing to call for "nothing less than a total elimination of caste barriers" and another thing to bring such a utopian vision to fruition. In the meantime, we must beware of the false promise that education is or ever can be a panacea for the deep and reprehensible racial divisions that are baked into American history, social structure, and culture.

To be sure, there is a bright side to schooling in America that emanates from the irrepressible spirit and energy of children. Public education is one of the great pillars of American democracy. Schools do much to propagate the democratic ethos, to cultivate norms of tolerance, to fertilize young minds, to provide steppingstones of mobility. However, schools as currently constituted can do only so much to counter the plethora of forces, both unseen and painfully familiar, that defeat the aspirations of students and teachers alike.

There is also an underside that is too often brushed over, especially by liberals who buy into the illusion that education is a magic bullet for the deep and persistent inequalities in American society. According to the Children's Defense Fund, in 2021, there were nearly 10 million children in poverty, 5 million of whom were in extreme poverty. Nearly three in four poor children were children of color.[67] These statistics are only the tip of an iceberg of the vast inequalities that are built into schooling in capitalist America.

Take No Child Left Behind as an example of false promises. This was a vacuous misnomer that promised deliverance, but gave us a soulless testing regime that deflated students and teachers alike. Where is the honesty and will to address the unconscionable disparities in the life chances of yet another generation of children? When and how do we confront the deep and enduring inequalities that are the ignominy of American democracy?

CHAPTER SEVEN

THEORIES OF ETHNIC SUCCESS

Three Narratives

If our children don't go to school, no harm results. But if the sheep don't eat, they will die. The school can wait but not our sheep.

Italian peasant quoted in Leonard Covello's 1944 study, *The Social Background of the Italo-American School Child*[1]

All I ever heard was "It's either education or the pick and shovel."

A student of Italian descent in my class at Queens College, ca. 1985[2]

The epigraphs epitomize the shifting currents in "culture" as Italians leapfrogged first from an agricultural to an industrial economy and then to a postindustrial economy. For an earlier generation of Italian peasants living in southern Italy, the exigencies of life required them to forego education: "The school can wait but not our sheep." However, for my student's generation, the "pick and shovel" was an iconic representation of a bygone area, and education had become a cultural imperative. This nugget of folk wisdom embodies an elemental truth: "culture," despite appearances to the contrary, is never fixed in time. On the contrary, culture adapts to the changing circumstances and exigencies of people's lives. Indeed, this is the guiding theoretical principle for making sense of whatever empirical relationships exist between ethnicity and social-class attainment.

The *fact* of ethnic success—the empirical correlation between ethnicity and social class—is widely observed and easily documented. But there is also a *theory* of ethnic success that traces the empirical outcomes to ethnic factors. Inasmuch as we conceive of ethnicity as a cultural phenomenon consisting of distinctive values and codes of behavior, it is readily assumed that culture is the fulcrum of "ethnic success"—whether groups advance in their class mobility or whether they lag behind. The danger here is of reifying culture—of failing to take into account its foundation in material and social-class factors. To assert "class" is not to deny "culture." Rather it is to explore its backward linkages to the constellation of historical and material factors that engendered and sustained those cultural factors in the first place.

This theoretical tenet provides a bridge for grasping the differential mobility patterns of three ethnic groups: Jews, Asians, and Blacks. My first example is the Jewish Horatio Alger story, which provides theoretical and historical explanation for why and how Jewish immigrants escaped poverty more rapidly than other groups, including Italian immigrants who arrived at about the same time but had a considerably slower trajectory of mobility.

Asians had a different immigrant "story" altogether. Though Chinese and Japanese have roots in the United States that go back to the mid-nineteenth century, most Asian Americans arrived after passage of the 1965 Immigration Act. This was a case of unintended consequences. The legislation was championed by Jewish and Italian advocacy groups who harbored resentment at the "national origins quotas" passed in 1924 that restricted immigrants from eastern and southern Europe. The 1965 act put all immigrants on an equal footing, though in practice, immigrants came disproportionately from Asia, Latin America, and the Caribbean.

THE JEWISH HORATIO ALGER STORY

Horatio Alger was a late-eighteenth-century novelist who wrote young-adult novels about boys from humble backgrounds who rose from rags to riches, exemplifying the virtues of hard work and determination. In his 1981 book, *Ethnic America*, the economist Thomas Sowell tagged Jews as "the classic American success story—from rags to riches against all opposition."[3] Against this background it behooves us to identify the historical circumstances that account for the Jewish success story.

In *The Ethnic Myth*, also published in 1981, I argued that Jewish immigrants escaped poverty sooner than other immigrants because they arrived with previous industrial experience and a higher rate of literacy than other immigrants who arrived at approximately the same time and settled in many of the same cities as Italians and other European immigrants. In making this argument, I relied heavily on the 1897 Russian census that was brought to light by an economist, Israel Rubinow, in a 1907 report for the U.S. Bureau of Labor.[4] The census showed that in the Pale, the area of Russia where most Jews lived, 32 percent were engaged in commerce, most often as traders in agricultural products such as grain, cattle, hides, and furs. Another 38 percent were employed in manufacturing or as artisans. Jews were dominant in clothing manufacture and the clothing trades, skills that they transferred to New York's burgeoning garment industry, providing immigrants with work and the Jewish community with a crucial economic anchor.

Studies by the 1911 U.S. Immigration Commission showed that Jews were first in a wide range of crafts, including hat and cap makers, furriers, tailors, bookbinders, watchmakers, cigar packers, and tinsmiths. Many others were jewelers, painters, dressmakers, photographers, locksmiths, bakers, butchers, metal workers, and workers in the building trades.[5] Not only were these skills in demand in cities where Jewish immigrants settled, but these trades also formed the basis for small businesses, which in turn served as a springboard of mobility for future generations. Historian Selma Berrol had it right in her 1976 article in the *American Jewish Historical Quarterly*:

> Most New York Jews did not make the leap from poverty into the middle class by going to college. Rather, widespread utilization of secondary and higher education *followed* in improvements in economic status and was as much a result as a cause of upward mobility.[6]

In other words, mobility was not a rags-to-riches story but rather an intergenerational phenomenon whereby immigrants first secured an occupational and economic foothold. Only then were their children and grandchildren positioned to use schooling as a springboard of mobility.

In their 1984 study *The Transformation of the Jews*, Calvin Gold-scheider and Alan Zuckerman show that literacy among Jews was not uniform but rather varied widely by region, reflecting economic conditions. They write: "Patterns of education among the Jews of Paris, Berlin, Vienna, and Budapest differed dramatically from those of Warsaw, Lodz, Vilna, and the medium-sized cities and towns that housed most of the Jews of Poland, Rumania, and half those of Hungary." They go on to argue:

> The intensity of modernization combined with the size, structure, and or-ganizational strength of the Jewish community to determine educational patterns among the Jews. There is no evidence that differential Jewish val-ues on education among these communities account for these differences.[7]

A problem of most mobility studies is that they are based on com-parisons between independent generational cohorts. The data may well indicate a pattern whereby the children of immigrants leaped over their parents, but the raw data obscures the process whereby "rags" morphed into "riches." With this in mind, I dispatched an older student who spoke Yiddish to interview elderly Jewish men in nursing homes in New York City and South Florida. Her marching orders were simple: interrogate these subjects about their occupational experiences before and after im-migrating to the United States, as well as the occupations of their adult sons and grandsons. These "occupational genealogies," extending across three generations, point up the pivotal role played by the occupational skills that immigrant Jews carried with them from Eastern Europe.[8]

For example, in Russia, one subject collected cowhides from farmers, tanned them, and in a classic middleman role, sold them to shoemakers and shoe manufacturers in urban centers. In New York, he started up a business tanning hides for bag manufacturers. After his three sons came into the business, they began manufacturing leather bags, wallets, and luggage. Together, they had seven sons: four doctors and three lawyers.

Another subject was a small grocer in Bessarabia, Romania. After the Cossacks destroyed his store, he emigrated with his five young sons and a daughter. With the help of a loan from a *landsmanshaftn* (a mutual aid society), he opened a grocery store, which prospered. Together with his five sons, he opened a larger store, and eventually they built a chain of thirty-two stores. The next generation of males all became professionals: seven doctors, three lawyers, and a psychologist.

I plead guilty here of highlighting two cases that illustrate my argument. However, a consistent pattern emerged from the interviews: Jewish immigrants parlayed skills they brought from Europe into small entrepreneurial business. In most cases, their sons did not go to college but entered the family business, often expanding it into a more lucrative enterprise. Typically, it was the grandchildren of these immigrant entrepreneurs who made the leap to college and, with astonishing regularity, entered the professions, usually as doctors or lawyers. As I like to add, tongue in cheek, the misfit became a professor.

To state that the Jewish success story was largely a matter of historical timing should not detract from the ingenuity and dogged enterprise of immigrants who developed successful businesses that improved the living standards of their families, including access to good schools. Pluck mattered but so did luck. Not only did Jews arrive with the right skills at the right time, but just at the point when they consolidated their class position, there was a vast expansion of higher education that opened up opportunities for their children. Today a far less favorable set of institutional forces are in place, which may well augur the demise of the Jewish success story.

THE MODEL MINORITY MYTH: ASIANS AS PROXY JEWS

As Toni Morrison has famously written, immigrants become American by joining the chorus singing praise to the American Dream.[9] They do so in their literature and drama and in their knowledge production as well. As part of their baptism as Americans, each ascendant ethnic group delegates one of its best and brightest to earn a PhD and, beginning with the dissertation, to tell their collective story of triumph over adversity. In addition to hard work, fortitude, and perseverance—all individual traits—these fledgling scholars give the success story a social-scientific twist, citing ethnic values and solidarities as the driving force of ethnic mobility.

Nathan Glazer cast the ideological mold for this genre. His first book, *American Judaism*, offered a narrative of crisis and redemption.[10] In his later work, Glazer spun the Jewish success myth: Jews succeeded, he argued, because of a reverence for learning, an entrepreneurial spirit, industry, fortitude, sobriety, and other such cultural virtues.[11] However, Glazer's fatal error was that he gave short shrift to premigration factors—in this case, previous industrial experience and higher rates of literacy—that gave Jewish immigrants a decisive head start and put them on a trajectory of intergenerational mobility. By lumping Jews together with the other "huddled masses," the props were in place for Sowell's "classic American success story—from rags to riches against all opposition."[12]

What Glazer did for Jews in propagating a success myth, Richard Gambino did for Italians, Andrew Greeley for Irish, Richard Novak for Slavs, and Betty Lee Sung for Chinese.[13] This genre of success stories continues among the progeny of the post-1965 immigrants who enter sociology and are eager to tell the story of their group's triumph over adversity. This might be called "the sociology of self-congratulation." Of course, a modicum of collective braggadocio can be forgiven, given the struggles these groups endured. The problem, however, is that self-congratulation has an insidious flip side when applied to the racial "other." In celebrating "our" cultural virtues and advancing a theory of how "we" made it, the implication is that "they" lacked "our" cultural virtues with respect to family, work, and education. The "model minority" is cast as the antithesis to the "problem minority."

A precursor of this discourse appeared in a 1957 article in the *New York Times* by William McIntyre under the title "Chinatown Offers Us a Lesson."[14] McIntyre marveled that in New York's Chinatown, there was virtually no juvenile delinquency. The reason? According to McIntyre, "growing up in such an insulated and emotionally snug family life, the child develops characteristics that seem peculiarly 'Chinese'—reservoirs of patience, unflagging capacity for work and dislike for physical violence." Again, McIntyre discerns that "as universal as brown eyes among the Chinese is the desire for education." His veneration for the Chinese extends even to his claim that "Chinese families are early to bed (10 P.M.) and early to rise (7:30 A.M.)"[15] Alas, what we see here is the invention of a model minority, one that combines Confucianism and Calvinism into an invincible amalgam.

It was not until January 1966 that the model minority myth entered scholarly discourse. This came with an article by sociologist William Petersen entitled "Success Story: Japanese-American Style," published in no less a public venue than the *New York Times Magazine*. The timing was perfect in terms of its racial subtext. The civil rights movement had attained its legislative objectives with the passage of the 1964 and 1965 Civil Rights Acts, and the movement was making a strategic shift from "liberty" to "equality" as Black leaders called for "compensatory programs" to open up channels of opportunity for Blacks in jobs and education. What better time to invoke the "success story, Japanese-American style."[16]

Indeed, the rhetorical frame for Petersen's article consisted of an invidious comparison between Japanese and Blacks. According to Petersen, centuries of racial oppression have permanently impaired the Black psyche—so much so that "when new opportunities, even equal opportunities, are opened up, the minority's reaction to them is likely to be negative—either self-defeating apathy or a hatred so all-consuming as to be self-destructive. For all the well-meaning programs and countless scholarly studies now focused on the Negro, we barely know how to repair the damage that the slave traders started."[17]

According to Petersen, what was unique about the Japanese is that they overcame oppression without governmental intervention or preferential treatment:

> Barely more than 20 years after the end of the wartime camps, this is a minority that has risen above even prejudiced criticism. By any criterion of good citizenship that we choose, the Japanese-Americans are better than any other group in our society, including native-born whites. They have established this remarkable record, moreover, by their own almost totally unaided effort. Every attempt to hamper their progress resulted only in enhancing the determination to succeed. Even in a country whose patron saint is the Horatio Alger hero, there is no parallel to this success story.[18]

Here Petersen has crafted the ideal formula: one who "revolts against re-volt" and resurrects himself or herself through sheer determination, but-tressed by those quintessential solidarities of family and ethnic group—along with education, which Petersen dubs as "the key to success."

With some rhetorical dressing, Petersen had refurbished Glazer's the-ory of Jewish success. As early as 1964, Norman Podhoretz, editor of *Commentary*, was on record as opposed to compensatory programs that would give "special treatment" to Blacks as a remedy for past oppres-sion.[19] After publication of his piece in the *New York Times*, Petersen would go on to become *Commentary*'s point man on affirmative action. On the one hand, he lampooned Robert O'Neil's 1975 book *Discrimi-nating Against Discrimination*, which defended preferential admissions in the 1974 *DeFunis* case.[20] On the other hand, Petersen showered praise on Glazer's 1976 book *Affirmative Discrimination*, which was the first book-length polemic against affirmative action in which Glazer com-pared affirmative action to the Nuremberg Laws.[21]

In 1981, Petersen was again on the pages of *Commentary*, heaping praise on Sowell's *Ethnic America*.[22] With a rhetorical sleight of hand, Sowell used the success of Asian Americans to argue that Blacks cannot blame "race" for their problems. If Blacks lag behind other races, it is because of cultural aberrations rooted in slavery itself. Alas, the hidden political agenda behind the model minority myth was never meant to exalt Asian Americans but rather to weave a success story that would undercut Black demands for compensatory programs and affirmative ac-tion in particular. Jewish opponents of affirmative action could invoke the myth of "success through education" without seeming to argue out of raw self-interest.

After the 1966 article in the *New York Times Magazine*, another ap-peared in *U.S. News & World Report* that shifted the focus from Japanese to Chinese: "Success Story of One Minority Group in U.S." In addition to "a tight network of family and clan loyalties," Chinese were exalted for their "strict discipline," leading children "to attend school faithfully, work hard at their studies—and stay out of trouble." This was followed by an invidious comparison to Blacks: "What you find, in the back of this remarkable group of Americans, is a story of adversity and prejudice that would shock those now complaining about the hardships of today's Negroes." Finally, the perverse subtext bubbles to the surface: "At a time when it is being proposed that hundreds of billions be spent to uplift Negroes and other minorities, the nation's 300,000 Chinese Americans are moving ahead on their own with no help from anyone else."[23]

Five years passed before the model minority appeared in another major publication. In June 1971, *Newsweek* published an article under the furtive title "Success Story: Outwhiting the Whites."[24] However, it was not until the 1980s, in the context of a fierce national debate over affirmative action, that the Asian American success story appeared in a spate of prominent mass circulation magazines.[25] To wit:

- *Newsweek*, "Asian Americans: 'A Model Minority,'" December 6, 1982.
- *Newsweek on campus*, "The Drive to Excel," cover story, April 1984.
- *Newsweek*, "A Formula for Success," April 23, 1984.
- *U.S. News & World Report*, "Asian-Americans: Are They Making the Grade?" April 2, 1984.
- *New Republic*, "The Triumph of Asian Americans: America's Greatest Success Story," July 15 and 22, 1985.
- *Psychology Today*, "The Oriental Express," July 1986.
- *Fortune*, "America's Super Minority," November 24, 1986.
- *Newsweek*, "A 'Superminority' Tops Out," May 11, 1987.
- *Time*, "The New Whiz Kids," August 31, 1987.

The article in *The New Republic* is especially noteworthy. With academic circumspection, David Bell concedes that some of Jewish and Asian American success is due to selective migration of highly educated immigrants. However, he joins the chorus by making invidious comparisons to Blacks:

Rather than searching for a solution to their problems through the political process, Jewish, Chinese, and Japanese immigrants developed self-sufficiency by relying on community organizations. The combination of their skills, their desire for education, and the gradual disappearance of discrimination led inexorably to economic success.[26]

In effect, Bell is rebuking Blacks for relying on "the political process" to break down discriminatory barriers, while extolling Asians for their self-reliance.

Leading Asian American scholars spoke out against the political agenda that lurked behind the exaltation of Asian Americans and objected to specious comparisons between Asian Americans and Blacks. In a 1971 review of Petersen's book *Japanese Americans: Oppression and Success*, Kiyoshi Ikeda rejected Petersen's contention that Japanese suffered worse oppression than African Americans. He could not have been more resolved in his argument: "The histories of oppression are not parallel or similar in level and type. From the inception of immigration, the Japanese in America always had the support of firm, cross-national agreements and legal protections to insure that they could develop and maintain ethnic institutions in a hostile environment." Ikeda concluded flat out: "The Japanese-Americans are not a self-made people."[27]

Sociologists Arthur Sakamoto and Keng-Loong Yap launched a critique of the model minority myth (MMM), which by the 1980s emerged "as a key theme in studies of Asian Americans. It is mentioned in virtually every academic book ever written for an Asian Studies audience."[28] A common objection in the discourse was that this upbeat narrative of success eclipsed the fact that many Asian Americans were poor and confronted barriers of racism. However, Sakamoto and Yap went a step further and objected to the politics behind MMM, especially the invocation of the Asian model minority to undercut support for affirmative action and other programs targeted for African Americans. They could not be more emphatic and impassioned on this point:

> According to the MMM, the "model minority" image has been used essentially as propaganda by politically conservative commentators to emphasize the openness of American society and to argue against government programs such as affirmative action and welfare that disproportionately help racial and ethnic minorities.[29]

In yet another exposé of the surreptitious politics of MMM, Theodore Hsien Wang and Frank H. Wu wrote:

One of the increasingly prominent fallacies in the attacks on affirmative action is that Asian-Americans are somehow the example that defeats the rationale for race-conscious remedial programs. House Speaker Newt Gingrich and California governor Pete Wilson are two of the many political leaders who point to Asian-Americans and their supposed success in American society to assert that affirmative action is not needed.[30]

In a section titled "Asian-Americans as Pawns in the Debate," Wang and Wu condemn the deployment of the MMM "for Machiavellian political purposes," adding that these divisive politics only feed racial backlash, deflecting attention away from the struggles of Asian Americans against discrimination.

Strangely, the model minority myth was not woven by ethnic insiders. Rather, as Thomas Nakayama has asserted, it is "a discursive practice by non-Asian Americans."[31] This is a puzzling circumstance. How or why did this discourse evolve, heaping encomiums on Asian Americans as "a model minority"? Nor are the encomiums aimed only at recent immigrants who have successfully made a leap "from pariah to paragon." Rather there is a sinister subtext, cited by Asian scholars quoted above, who see through the hype: Asian immigrants are celebrated for getting ahead without "government programs" or "affirmative action," unlike African Americans who demand "preference," "special treatment," and "reparations." The covert message is race is not an insurmountable barrier to mobility, but Blacks lack the pluck and determination displayed by Asians.

The Asian scholars cited above not only categorically reject the invidious comparisons between Asian immigrants and African Americans, but also are unsparing in their indignation that they are being coopted for somebody else's Machiavellian purposes.

Furthermore, we do not have to look far for the "ethnic outsiders" who crafted a popular discourse in leading journals and publications that surreptitiously use Asians to blame Blacks for their own detriments and failures. Their unworthy mission was to use Asians to impugn Blacks and, in doing so, to undercut the logic and purpose of affirmative action policy. To be blunt, Asians were being used as proxy Jews.

As late as 1990, *Commentary* published yet another article on America's "model minority." Louis Winnick, a new contributor, acknowledged that Asian American scholars had spoken out against the "hyperbolic ex-cesses" of the model minority construct, principally by calling attention to the struggles of poor and working-class Asian Americans who are far from a success story.[32] But Winnick dismisses these objections with the disclaimer that "all mass migrations are accompanied by hardship and privation" and returns to the familiar refrain that "the achievements of both Jews and Asians are largely the consequence of a common ensemble of cultural values." This statement leads to a recital of their shared devo-tion to family, the sacrifices they endure for education, the low rates of crime and welfare dependency, and their shared propensity for thrift and self-denial. Instead of examining the significance of two and half centu-ries of slavery and a generation of Jim Crow—and the myriad ways in which systemic racism still pervades all major institutions in American society—instead of "all that," we are left with the startling revelation that Blacks are neither Jewish nor Asian.

THE MYTH OF "ACTING WHITE"

"Acting white" entered the discourse with a 1986 paper by John Ogbu and Signithia Fordham under the title "Black Students' School Success: Coping with the Burden of 'Acting White.'" Invoking resistance theory, they argued that Black students sabotaged their own education by spurn-ing the behavior associated with academic success: speaking standard English, spending long hours doing homework, striving for high grades, enrolling in advance placement courses, and aspiring to college. Accord-ing to Ogbu and Fordham, instead of striving to do well academically, black youth do the opposite: they defiantly refuse to learn. Still worse, they ridicule and badger high-achieving Black students. In short, they reject "the code of the schools" for "the code of the streets."[33]

What is astounding—and itself begs for analysis—is the alacrity with which the "acting white" theorem was thrust to the center of both schol-arly and popular discourses.[34] In 2004 President Obama invoked the ter-minology in his keynote address to the Democratic National Convention:

> Go into any inner city neighborhood, and folks will tell you that govern-ment alone can't teach kids to learn. They know that parents have to par-ent, that children can't achieve unless we raise their expectations and turn

off the television sets and eradicate the slander that says a Black youth with a book is acting white. No, people don't expect government to solve all their problems.[35]

Poof! If only Black youth would turn off their televisions sets and cease regarding schooling as an act of racial betrayal, we could reduce the racial gap in academic outcomes. The political implications are clearly stated: government alone can't teach kids to learn, and people don't expect government to solve all their problems. What better example of the political use of the acting-white discourse! With a rhetorical sleight of hand, responsibility is shifted away from the powerful institutions of government that could make a difference and is placed on the shoulders of ordinary people who are virtually powerless against these forces.

Critics have challenged the factual accuracy of the acting-white thesis, as well as its implications for social policy. The most extensive empirical study was published in the *American Sociological Review* in 2005: "It's Not 'a Black Thing': Understanding the Burden of Acting White and Other Dilemmas of High Achievement." This was a rigorous study of eight public secondary schools in North Carolina based on intensive interviews with eighty-five students, forty of whom were Black.[36] They found that most students, Black and white alike, expressed a desire to do well academically. Relatively few Black students enrolled in AP courses, but this was not because they felt they could not hack the courses academically. The Black students (mostly female) who did enroll in AP courses came from affluent families. Thus, to the extent that "acting white" existed at all, it was rooted in notions of class and gender rather than in race per se.[37]

Corroborating evidence for this position is found in Paul Willis's classic study of white youth in a working-class town in England, *Learning to Labor*. Willis observed that these "lads" (remember, they are all white) regarded education as "a waste of time" and "for sissies," not "real men." Instead, they valorized physicality, chauvinism, and machismo. The striking parallels with Fordham's findings in her study of Capital High suggest that "acting white" has little or nothing to do with race per se, but is fundamentally a matter of poverty and joblessness.

In an afterword written for the second edition of *Learning to Labor*, Willis wrote the following with the United States in mind:

Far from being "ignorant," "anachronistic," "pathological," and in need
of eradication, such cultural responses may in certain important respects,
be *in advance* of the liberal agencies. "The lads'" culture, for instance
is involved in making its own realistic bets about its best chances in a
class society and how best to approach an impoverished future in manual
work. Meanwhile, their advisors are tying themselves up in humanistic,
developmental knots which bear very little relation to the actual labor-
ing future of their pupils. This suggests just how far liberal, humanistic,
generally "left" illusions can be from the reality of the oppressed and the
real possibilities facing them.[38]

Willis throws down the gauntlet to the liberal project on education and
its failure to link education to larger systems of domination and inequality. Indeed, we have to ask whether the liberal faith in education as "a
great equalizer" is a camouflage for the liberals' own failure to confront
the societal forces that stunt the lives of the children who inhabit our
classrooms. Instead, liberals raise false hopes that schools can remedy the
deep divisions of race and class that rend American society.

Like Willis, Ogbu captures the predicament of lower-class students
desperately trying to navigate the frustrations and perils of schooling. According to Ogbu, their efforts were destined for failure for two reasons:

First, Blacks still perceive and respond to their schooling, both consciously and unconsciously, in terms of how they see their chances in the
future to use and benefit from education like their white peers; second,
the cognitive and other school- and job-related attributes Blacks develop
continue to be those adaptive to their social and occupational roles rather
than those demanded by the positions occupied by the dominant whites
and stressed by their education.[39]

This is not an argument against school reform but rather against the
chimera of invoking the mantra of "education" as a magical solution for
the deep and persistent inequalities of race and class. It is either a leap
of faith or willful delusion to think we can live in a society where half
of Black children are born into poverty, pluck them out of ghettos that
are the repository for our nation's racial pariahs, funnel these students

into schools with droves of others like themselves, and expect teachers to redress conditions that ultimately reflect the patent failures of American democracy.

Nor is the problem simply that we don rose-tinted glasses and see education as a panacea. It is worse than that. The false promise of education is a subterfuge, deployed to camouflage the fact that the United States does not have the political will to link education reform to a larger project of class transformation and reparations for centuries of racial oppression. Until these inequalities are eradicated, Black children will continue to bear the onus of white racism.

CHAPTER EIGHT

"MAKING IT"

Fact versus Fiction

The problem with the thesis is that in setting out their claim, the authors ignore the more obvious explanation for differences in group success: history. To be specific, in their quest to make it all about culture, the authors either ignore or strongly discount the particular circumstances of a group's first arrival, and the advantages enjoyed by that first wave.

Daria Roithmayr, "The Flaw at the Heart of *The Triple Package*"[1]

In their 2014 best-seller, *The Triple Package: How Three Unlikely Traits Explain the Rise and Fall of Cultural Groups in America*, Amy Chua and Jed Rubenfeld, law professors at Yale University, tackle the question of why certain groups are overrepresented in the pantheon of success. They postulate that these groups are endowed with "the triple package": a superiority complex, a sense of insecurity, and impulse control. The skeptic asks, "How do we know that?" To which they respond, "They're successful, aren't they?"

Chua and Rubenfeld proffer no facts to show that their exemplars of ethnic success—Jewish Nobel Prize winners, Mormon business magnates, Cuban exiles, Indian and Chinese superachievers—actually possess this triple package. Or that possessing these traits is what explains their disproportionate success. For that matter, they do not demonstrate that possessing the triple package is connected, through the mystical cord of history, to Jewish sages, Confucian precepts, or Mormon dogma. As critics of Max Weber's classic study *The Protestant Ethic and the Spirit of Capitalism* (1905) contended, success came first and only later was wrapped in the cloth of religion. In other words, like elites throughout history, Chua and Rubenfeld's exemplars enshroud their success in prevailing cultural tropes, whether in the Talmud, Confucianism, Mormonism, or the idolatry of white supremacy. The common thread that runs through these success myths is that they provide legitimacy for social-class hierarchy.

Chua and Rubenfeld give us old wine in new bottles. They invoke the idea used the world over to justify entrenched systems of social stratification: success comes to the culturally deserving. For Chua and Rubenfeld, "the two million Eastern European Jews who immigrated to America in the early 1990s brought with them habits of heightened discipline, religious prohibition, and hard work that they cultivated and passed down to their children." There is a sinister flip side to this proposition. Like Chua and Rubenfeld, Thomas Sowell, in 1981, contrasted Jewish success in overcoming persecution and poverty with a deeply ingrained "defeatism" among Blacks who bear the scars of centuries of slavery and denigration:

> Groups today plagued by absenteeism, tardiness, and a need for constant supervision at work or in school are typically descendants of people with the same habits a century or more ago. *The cultural inheritance can be more important than biological inheritance, although the latter stirs more controversy.*[2]

There you have it: the problem of inequality resides not in the genes but in the cultural DNA, which according to Sowell, is even "more important than biological inheritance."

Anthropologists and sociologists have developed a canon of studies that debunk theories that reduce inequality to culture. This critical perspective was on display during Chua and Rubenfeld's book tour when they were challenged with querulous inquiries about the racist subtext of their book. Is their point that African Americans are culturally deficient?

Are they using "culture" to blame the victim and to deflect attention away from persistent racist barriers that limit opportunity? What about the 99 percent of people in "successful groups" who do not reach the top 1 percent? Are they less Jewish, Asian, Cuban, and Mormon than the Jews, Asians, Cubans, and Mormons who have "made it"? On closer examination, Chua and Rubenfeld simplistically invoke an idea that justifies entrenched systems of social stratification the world over: success comes to the culturally deserving.

If not culture, what does explain Jewish "success against all opposition"? As I argued in *The Ethnic Myth* (1981), Jewish success is chiefly the result of factors that date back to the condition of Jews in their countries of origin. The shtetls romanticized in *Fiddler on the Roof* were small towns, proximate to cities, where Jews carved out niches between rural and urban economies. Many were traders who purchased agricultural products, animal hides, and raw materials from peasants and sold them to importers in cities, eking out a small profit. By the end of the nineteenth century, there were large concentrations of Jews in cities, and they played a key role in the critical early phases of modernization.

As I showed in chapter 7, based on the 1897 survey of Jews in the Russian economy, Jews were on the forefront of commerce and industrialization. These skills were in demand in the burgeoning economies of the cities where immigrant Jews settled. In a nutshell, Jews were the right people in the right place and the right time, and this is why they were able to escape the poverty of the immigrant generation more rapidly than other immigrants.

None of this is to say that culture does not matter. The point is that culture does not exist in a vacuum. Rather, culture is one factor within a large matrix of social and material factors. As I argued in *The Ethnic Myth*:

> If Jews set high goals, it is because they had a realistic chance of achieving them. If they worked hard, it is because they could see the fruits of their labor. If they were willing to forgo the pleasures of the moment, it is because they could realistically plan for the future, for their children if not for themselves. In short there was much in the everyday experience of

Jewish immigrants to activate and sustain their highest aspirations. Without this reinforcement, their values would have been scaled down accord-
ingly, and more successful outsiders would today be speculating about
how much further Jews might have gone if only they had aimed higher.[3]

The fatal flaw of *The Triple Package* is that its authors treat their
magical trifecta as disembodied values, supposedly rooted in ancient
cultures. But they provide no evidence that their exemplars are actually
immersed in these cultural systems. Rather, there are more mundane de-
terminants of success connected with their social class and circumstances.
Chua's parents were not just struggling immigrants; they were educated
professionals with the social and material resources that allowed them
to sustain their aspirations for their children. Rubenfeld was raised in
upper-middle-class affluence, which put him on a fast track to success.
Their circumstances positioned these tiger parents to raise two achieving
daughters, one bound for the Harvard (their parents' alma mater), the
other for Yale (their parents' workplace). In other words, mobility is not
an individual achievement so much as it is a family project, one that occurs incrementally across generations.

The demystification of the Jewish success story has implications for
rendering a more truthful account of the success stories at the center of
Chua and Rubenfeld's book. In each case, pre-migration factors and selective migration go a long way to explaining group success:

- Nigerian immigrants at Harvard Business School are no success
  story whatsoever. Actually, they come from Nigeria's educated and
  affluent elite. If anything, this is a case of a transfer of human capital from one nation to another. Or, to put it bluntly, a brain drain.
  The same is true of many Middle Eastern nations, including Iran
  and Lebanon.

- A socialist revolution in 1959 made refugees of Cuba's political
  oligarchs and economic elites and sent them in flight to Miami.
  Recovery was not easy, but neither were they the "huddled masses"
  of yore. Cuban refugees received loans from the Small Business
  Administration whose purpose was to showcase the superiority of

American capitalism over Cuban socialism. In contrast the Cubans who arrived in the 1980 "Mariel boatlift" came from the poorest segments of the Cuban population. In this case, there were no articles in *Fortune* entitled "Those Amazing Cuban Émigrés."

- The first wave of Asian immigrants after passage of the 1965 Immigration Act consisted mostly of professionals who sought more lucrative employment in the United States. Later, these immigrants were able to send for their poorer relatives under the family reunification provision in immigration law. Like Jews, many Asians found a niche in the enclave economy and used their success as entrepreneurs as a springboard of mobility for their children.

- Chua and Rubenfeld have a field day with the statistic that Asians comprise nearly three-quarters of the students at Stuyvesant, New York City's elite high school. They exult in the fact that many of these students come from parents who are restaurant or factory workers, but they have no evidence of the actual class background of students who make the cut for Stuyvesant. Their source is a single local news story about a school in Sunset Park, Brooklyn, where children, at great expense to their working-class parents, are enrolled for years in a test-prep program called Horizons.[4] Nor is there any mention of the cottage industry of test-prep programs in Chinatown, which are now cashing in by enrolling non-Asians as well.[5]

The droves of foreign students in the nation's colleges and universities who overstay their visas are another source of immigrant achievers. These students come mostly from middle-class or affluent families, who can afford to enroll their children in American universities. This is not a success story so much as a case of selective migration.

- As for the Caribbean students who succeed, whether in college admissions or in business, they rarely come from affluent families, though they have other class advantages that place them a rung higher on the ladder than African Americans, and they encounter less racism as a result. Obviously, Jamaican seasonal farm workers who harvest apples in upstate New York are no success story.

- Why Mormons, regarded fifty years ago as a fringe group, have
made recent strides in the business world is something of a mystery,
but one thing is certain: Mormon religion did not change. As was
true of immigrant Jews, Mormons who were catapulted to success
had to break away from the strictures and doctrines of pre-modern
religions in order to achieve the success they sought in secular pursuits. Like Mitt Romney and like the protagonist in Abraham Ca-
han's 1917 novel, *The Rise of David Levinsky*, they may look back
nostalgically on their religious allegiances, but the discontinuities
are far more striking than the continuities.

When Chua and Rubenfeld appeared on Fareed Zakaria's weekly
show on CNN, Zakaria observed that the nations that supposedly embody the magic trifecta have, until recently, been "basket cases." Without
a moment's hesitation, Rubenfeld averred that in their home countries,
they had only two of the three requisite traits—an ingrained sense of
superiority and impulse control. Only when they arrived on American
shores did they develop the sense of vulnerability that completed the trifecta. Such are the absurd lengths that Rubenfeld must go to in order to
save his pet theory from its glaring overstatements and omissions.

It is worth asking how such a flawed book became a best seller. Its
launch was built on the notoriety of Chua's previous best-seller, *Battle
Hymn of the Tiger Mother*, published two years earlier. In addition, the
press gave the book extraordinary attention. The "tiger couple" published an opinion piece in the Sunday Review of the *New York Times*,
on January 26, nine days before *The Triple Package* was published.[6] A
week later the *New York Times Magazine* ran a feature article by Jennifer
Szalai, "Confessions of a Tiger Couple."[7] We learn that Chua was born in
Illinois, the daughter of Chinese parents from the Philippines. Not much
there to connect her with the Ming dynasty, much less contemporary Chinese culture. Nor was she of humble origins. Her father was a doctoral
student in electrical engineering and her mother was trained as a chemist
but gave up her career to raise her four daughters. True, Chua's parents
had high expectations for their daughters, but what is special about that?

They also had the education and the capital to sustain and finance their aspirations for their children.

Rubenfeld's family roots were entirely different. His father, a successful psychotherapist, and his mother, an art critic, revolted against the Jewish orthodoxy of their youth. Jed was not raised in Talmudic scholasticism but in the permissive dogma of Dr. Spock, free to find his own path in life. Yet for all their childhood differences, Chua and Rubenfeld converged on the same path of success as law students at Harvard. They met at a volleyball game and, long story short, they married and wound up tenured law professors at Yale.

"Confessions of a Tiger Couple" also reveals that the professional accomplishments of these two Yale law professors are meager. Both veered away from law into what Szalai calls "Gladwellian sociology." Rubenfeld penned two Freudian thrillers, one of which was a best-seller in England. Chua struck oil with her paean to boot-camp child-rearing. One wonders whether the book would have been relegated to the self-help section of book stores if not for her artful invocation of the "tiger mother," a trope that is pregnant with racist and sexist fantasies.

Then, for the third time in two weeks, manna from the *New York Times* fell on *The Triple Package*, this time a front-page review in the Sunday Book Review.[8] Sandra Tsing Loh, author of *Mother on Fire: A True Motherf%#$@ Story about Parenting* (2008), wrote a sardonic review, concluding that *The Triple Package* is "a dull but probably lucrative book." Indeed, two weeks later it made its debut in ninth place on the *New York Times* best-seller list, abetted by a grueling two-week book tour that included a flurry of interviews on major radio and television shows. However, no sooner did the media blitz end than *The Triple Package* disappeared from the best-seller list, leaving us to wonder whether this was a success story or a marketing feat playing on the tiger mother's notoriety and the ploys of the couple's three agents.

In their whirlwind interviews, Chua and Rubenfeld were often asked whether their theory had a racist flip side, and their prompt riposte was that Blacks, too, could achieve success if only they cultivated the magic trifecta. Never mind that most of the groups that Chua and Rubenfeld tout as exemplars of success would not be on American soil but for the 1965 Immigration Act that was passed on the heels of the civil rights movement. Not only that, but thanks to the Black protest movement, immigrants from Asia, Africa, and Latin America entered a nation with a far more favorable climate of tolerance than had existed in times past. Finally, it is safe to assume that some of Chua and Rubenfeld's exemplars reaped the advantage of affirmative action programs, which were developed in the cauldron of Black protest and gutted by the Supreme Court.

There is troublesome irony when the success stories in Chua and Rubenfeld's book are used to make invidious comparisons to Blacks who, throughout American history, have been pushed further back from avenues of opportunity by successive waves of immigrants. As Toni Morrison wrote twenty years ago,[9] their success came "on the back of Blacks," whose struggles are eclipsed in Chua and Rubenfeld's facile and fallacious book.

CHAPTER NINE

THE GOOSE-GANDER MYTH

Implications for the Black Lives Matter Movement

> I think there is blame on both sides. . . . You had a group on one side
> that was bad. You had a group on the other side that was also very
> violent. Nobody wants to say that. I'll say it right now.
>
> Donald Trump, Charlottesville, August 15, 2017[1]

> The best way to be fair is not to be falsely evenhanded, giving
> equal sides. It's to push for the truth, and tell it both accurately and
> powerfully.
>
> Margaret Sullivan, *Washington Post*, August 16, 2017[2]

"What's sauce for the goose is sauce for the gander." This English proverb dates back to the seventeenth century. Its American variant dispenses
with the sauce and professes: "What's good for the goose is good for the
gander."[3]

One has to marvel at the democratic spirit embedded in this nugget
of folk wisdom. At least at first glance, it stipulates that what holds for
one person should be applied equally to another. This is precisely the
logic embedded in the equal protection clause of the Fourteenth Amendment, stipulating that "no state shall make or enforce any law which shall
abridge the privileges or immunities of citizens . . . nor deny to any person

within its jurisdiction the equal protection of the laws." Thus enshrined in law, the goose-gander rule serves noble ends.

Yet we have to remember that the Fourteenth Amendment was prompted by one of the most glaring and treacherous systems of inequality in world history: over two centuries of slavery in a nation founded on the precept that "all men are created equal." Passed in the wake of the Civil War, the Fourteenth Amendment sought to secure full civil rights for Blacks. But only twenty-eight years later, the Supreme Court effectively nullified the Fourteenth Amendment when it ruled that Homer Plessy (who was seven-eighths white) could be consigned to a separate railroad car and that doing so did not constitute an abridgement of his civil rights. Thus we see that when it comes to race, the United States has never lived up to the democratic promise of the goose-gander rule: what was good for the white goose has rarely been good for the Black gander!

There is also a gender factor to consider in the construction of this proverb. The female goose is given primacy over the male gander, so the proverb asserts what is good for the female goose is good for the male gander. Perhaps we can read something into the fact that this four-hundred-year-old proverb is careful not to reverse the terms and to hold that what is good for the gander is good for the goose. Either which way, it is reassuring that this four-hundred-year-old proverb is gender neutral. This is precisely the logic behind the Equal Rights Amendment, which has yet to pass muster in the United States Congress, as is true for the concept of equal pay for equal work as well. Indeed, what was Marxism about, if not an assault on the ganders who extracted surplus profit from oppressed geese? I may be stretching a point, but the Communist Manifesto was a clarion call to the geese of the world to unite: you have nothing to lose but, well, your plumage!

My point is that the goose-gander rule is unassailable as logic or morality only when it is applied to individuals or groups that are roughly equal in power, wealth, and status. When disparities exist along these lines—especially when they are deeply rooted in history and social structure—the goose-gander rule not only falls apart, but actually operates against its democratic pretense: to reinforce or exacerbate existing inequalities.

Let us examine three cases where the goose-gander rule has perverse consequences that are inconsistent—even antithetical—to principles of social justice.

THE BLACK LIVES MATTER MOVEMENT

The Black Lives Matter (BLM) movement began on social media in 2013 after the acquittal of George Zimmerman in the shooting death of Trayvon Martin, an African American teen who was visiting family in a gated community in Sanford, Florida. The movement went national a year later after the deaths of Michael Brown in Ferguson, Missouri, and Eric Garner in New York City, both at the hands of police. By that time the BLM movement consisted of a national network of over thirty local chapters. It has been heralded by pundits as signifying a next stage in the struggle for full rights of citizenship.

The moniker Black Lives Matter was coined by three Black women and spread like wildfire on social media with the hashtag #BlackLivesMatter.[4] It also became the focal point of controversy and debate in popular discourses. By 2015 the moniker All Lives Matter sprang up as a retort and rebuke to the Black Lives Matter movement. Its self-explaining contention was that white lives were as important as Black lives. Before long, another refrain flooded the media: "Blue Lives Matter," alluding to police who lose their lives in deadly confrontations with Blacks. Finally, white supremacists got into the act by proclaiming that "White Lives Matter." Donald Trump weighed into the lexical battle, opining that Black Lives Matter is "a divisive term" and "inherently racist."[5]

This imbroglio raises the issue of "false equivalency." Defenders of Black Lives Matter contended that their moniker was a response to the horrific spate of police killings of Black men, most of whom were unarmed and in most cases constituted no threat whatsoever. It is difficult to escape the conclusion that these men would not have been slain if they had been white, thus validating the claim that Black lives do not matter as much as the lives of others.[6]

This position was passionately debated by commentators on *Real Time with Bill Maher*. Maher averred that the trouble with All Lives

Matter is that it "implies that all lives are equally at risk, and they're not."[7] Elsewhere, President Obama weighed in with the following rumination:

> I think that the reason that the organizers used the phrase Black Lives Matter was not because they were suggesting that no one else's lives matter. . . . . Rather what they were suggesting was there is a specific problem that is happening in the African American community that's not happening in other communities.[8]

Finally, Alicia Garza, one of the founders of Black Lives Matter averred that "changing Black Lives Matter to All Lives Matter is a demonstration of how we don't actually understand structural racism in this country." Carla Shedd, a sociologist at Columbia University went so far as to say that "All Lives Matter can actually be interpreted as racist."[9]

Thanks to a Rasmussen Reports poll conducted in August 2015, we can determine the outcome of this lexical tug-of-war among the American people. Pollsters asked respondents which statement was closer to their own point of view: Black Lives Matter or All Lives Matter. Seventy-eight percent chose All Lives Matter, and only 11 percent chose Black Lives Matter.[10] This suggests either that most Americans fall into the trap of making a false equivalency by assuming that it is virtuous to declare opposition to any destruction of human life. Or that they do not see or will not acknowledge that in matters of life and death, Blacks are at a fatal disadvantage.

TRUMP'S FALSE EQUIVALENCY OF "BOTH SIDES"

"The False Equivalency of Trump Blaming 'Many Sides' in Charlottesville."[11] So read the title of Vox's report on the violent clash in Charlottesville, Virginia, a progressive college town. On the one side were "white nationalists, white supremacists, the Ku Klux Klan, neo-Nazis, and other hate groups," as described in a joint congressional resolution that condemned the violence in Charlottesville. On the other side were counter-demonstrators, mostly students of color and white students from the nearby campus of the University of Virginia.

The catalyst for the conflict was the city council's 3–2 vote to remove the twenty-eight-foot bronze statue of Robert E. Lee, mounted on his legendary horse Traveler. In June 2017 Lee Park had been renamed Emancipation Park.[12] This was the third time in a few months that white nationalists gathered to protest the imminent removal of the statue. However, this time, according to *BBC News*, "some were dressed in full tactical gear and openly carrying rifles. Others wore black shirts, helmets, and boots."[13] The event was billed as a Unite the Right rally, and its battle cry was White Lives Matter. The torchlight procession on Saturday night was meant to invoke memory of Hitler Youth and other ultraright nationalist organizations, as marchers chanted the Nazi slogan "Blood and soil," along with "Jews will not replace us."

According to the BBC article, while white supremacists were marching with torches, "more than 500 people packed into St. Paul's Church for a multi-faith service. There were readings from the Bible and the Koran, spirituals sung by a choir, and a speech by activist and Harvard professor Dr. Cornel West that drew everyone in the house to their feet."[14]

On Saturday morning members of the Black Lives Matter movement staged a counterprotest. According to the report in the *Washington Post*, "Members of anti-fascist groups yelled at the rallygoers. Many also carried sticks and shields, and were joined by local residents, members of church groups, civil rights leaders and onlookers."[15] The situation was clearly inflammatory. For unknown but suspicious reasons, police were kept in the periphery until after a brawl broke out. According to the *Post*, "Both sides thought the police should have intervened earlier to keep the peace. But both sides were claiming victory."[16] The person who drove his car into the protesters was far from the rally itself, but one woman was killed and nineteen others injured.

Enter Donald Trump, who blamed "both sides" for the violence the previous day. As he declaimed:

> I'm not putting anybody on a moral plane. You had a group on one side
> and group on the other and they came at each other with clubs. There is
> another side, you can call them the left, that came violently attacking the
> other group. You had people that were very fine people on both sides.

Not all those people were neo-Nazis. Not all those people were white supremacists. Many of those people were there to protest the taking down of the statue of Robert E. Lee. So this week, it is Robert E. Lee. I noticed that Stonewall Jackson is coming down. I wonder, it is George Washington next week and is it Thomas Jefferson the week after? You know, you really do have to ask yourself, where does it all stop?[17]

Trump's message of moral equivalency elicited a storm of protest. Was it possible that our president could not discern the difference between the KKK and white supremacists armed for battle and chanting Nazi slogans, whereas the Black Lives Matter protestors and anti-fascists (dubbed "antifa") were defending democratic norms?

Trump's leading cheerleader was David Duke, who has been described as "an American white supremacist and white nationalist politician, anti-Semitic conspiracy theorist, Holocaust denier, convicted felon, and former Grand Wizard of the Ku Klux Klan."[18] Asked by a reporter what the events at Charlottesville represented, Duke replied: "It is a turning point for the people of this country. We are determined to take our country back. . . . That's why we voted for Donald Trump, because he said we would take back our country."[19]

Trump's false equivalence evoked much commentary from the press. Writing in the *Washington Post*, Margret Sullivan declared that Donald Trump is "the false-equivalency president." She added: "Elected with the help of false equivalency, Trump is now creating some of his own . . . by treating white supremacists and those who protest them as roughly equal." Sullivan went on to quote Winston Churchill as saying, "I decline utterly to be impartial as between the fire brigade and the fire."[20]

In 2016 Eric Alterman chimed in with a column in *The Nation* titled "How False Equivalence Is Distorting the 2016 Election Coverage." He berated the media for its need "to cover 'both sides' of every story . . . when one side has little regard for the truth."[21] Yet Alterman's formulation of "truth" is problematic. What if the two sides hold irreconcilable claims to "truth"? After all, the bloody Civil War was fought to the bitter end precisely because the two sides held different truths and were willing to die for them. In other words, "false equivalency" ultimately depends on the positionality of rival truth tellers, each holding that their truths are self-evident, while contending that their version of truth is disparaged by the other.[22]

It is difficult to avoid the conclusion that the brouhaha over the Lee statue is plain evidence that, as a nation, we are still fighting the Civil War.

AFFIRMATIVE ACTION: THE MOTHER
OF ALL FALSE EQUIVALENCIES

A favorite argument advanced by critics of affirmative action is that its proponents are guilty of contradicting the cardinal principle of the civil rights movement: the right to be judged by the content of one's character rather than the color of one's skin. Proponents of affirmative action are assailed for hypocritically doing the very thing they say they are against: introducing a racial classification. Applying the goose-gander rule, if it is wrong to use a racial classification to discriminate against Blacks, it cannot be right to use a racial classification to give Blacks preference, thus putting whites at a disadvantage. Or to use Justice Scalia's clever formulation: "You cannot use the disease as the cure."

Along with Scalia, some critics go as far as accusing proponents of affirmative action of advancing "a new racism," different from the old racism only in reversing which side wins and which loses. However, this position is preposterous. Although there are whites who are bumped from positions they might otherwise have had, the irrefutable point is that whites are not spurned or rejected *because* they are white.

For example, when Allan Bakke was denied admission to the medical school at UC, Davis, the class was predominantly white. His exclusion was not part of a systemic pattern to exclude or inflict harm on white people. Nor, unlike the case of Homer Plessy, was there a badge of inferiority placed on Bakke. Nor was Allan Bakke denied access to other equivalent medical schools. In short, Bakke's exclusion was motivated not by racism but, on the contrary, by an attempt, belated and meager at that, to counteract the effects of racism. Far from contravening democracy, affirmative action enhances democracy.

Yet leading scholars have advanced the facile and misguided argument I alluded to above: turning a blind eye to the differences between

Jim Crow—a system of oppression that trampled on the rights of an entire people—and affirmative action, a remedial social policy that provided relief to the victims of systemic racism. To quote Winston Churchill again, it is a failure to distinguish between a fire brigade and a fire.[23]

As we saw in chapter 3, as early as 1964, when affirmative action was still in its embryonic stage, Nathan Glazer—then the preeminent sociologist of race and ethnicity—spoke out against compensatory programs for Blacks, on the specious assumption that rights in American society are bestowed on individuals, not groups. So much for the goose and the gander. Both logic and racial justice would be better served if we adhered to another nugget of folk wisdom: the admonition against confusing apples and oranges!

Obviously, these learned jurists are capable of discerning between apples and oranges. And between Nazi genocide and German reparations. Clearly, the discourse over affirmative action is replete with sophistry, one of the weapons that intellectuals invoke when they wish to disguise their politics and self-interests behind a smokescreen of erudition. Whatever their motives in opposing affirmative action, whatever they told themselves when they placed themselves in the schoolhouse door, they must bear moral responsibility for the role they played in the subversion of affirmative action policy. And their role was considerable: not only did they foment the anti-affirmative-action crusade, but they also gave it indispensable legitimacy. They pretended to others, and perhaps even to themselves, that they were defending freedom and democracy. But now that the anti-affirmative-action crusade has achieved its nefarious purpose—the tantamount abolition of affirmative action policy—one thing is clear: the United States is not the more democratic nation that they imagined, but rather a nation ever more riven by racial divisions that are a blot on American democracy.

As we have seen in the foregoing pages, the trouble with the goose-gander rule is that, however convincing it may seem as an abstraction, it has adverse and paradoxical consequences when applied to the murky world of hierarchy and inequality: Where the playing field is not even. Where treating everyone "the same" ends up reproducing inequality. Where failing to take affirmative action to counter those structured inequalities only perpetuates and exacerbates the existing racial order.

Or worse! Let us take a lesson from history. In 1875 Congress passed a civil rights act that made it a criminal offense to deny accommodations at an inn, on a public conveyance, or in a theatre or other place of public amusement on the basis of race or color. Only eight years later, the Supreme Court held that the law was unconstitutional. In his majority opinion, Justice Bradley reasoned as follows:

> When a man has emerged from slavery, and by the aid of beneficent legislation has shaken off the inseparable concomitants of that state, there must be some stage in the progress of his elevation when he takes the rank of a mere citizen, and ceases *to be a special favorite of the laws*, and when his rights as a citizen, or a man, are to be protected in the ordinary modes by which other men's rights are protected.[24]

Think about it. Here were Blacks just emerging from over two centuries of slavery, and there sat erudite jurists declaring that it was time that Blacks cease "to be a special favorite of the laws." The repercussions were catastrophic: the dismantling of Reconstruction and the installation of a Jim Crow system, under the specious guise of "separate but equal," thereby subjecting Blacks and the nation to yet another century of hideous oppression.

Today, the same illogic undergirds the collapse of the Second Reconstruction, as the Supreme Court eviscerates affirmative action policy on the grounds that extending preferential treatment to Blacks violates the judicial principle of colorblindness. The predicable result, already evident in declining enrollments in college and the scaling back of affirmative action in employment, will be a steady erosion of the hard-won gains of the post–civil rights era.

The current Supreme Court is stacked by conservative jurists who are willing to turn a blind eye to the persistence of white supremacy. Tragically, the court is poised to pound the final nail into the coffin of affirmative action.

CHAPTER TEN

THE POLITICAL USES OF "CONCENTRATED POVERTY"

> There is no family structure. They sleep around and all that kind of
> thing. There is no family structure. That's the problem for the decade,
> as I see it. We have to break up that concentration, get those people out
> into society somehow. I'm about at the point where I think they ought
> to be all stuck in boxcars and sent out around, one family to each town.
>
> John Ehrlichman, assistant to President
>
> Nixon for domestic affairs, 1972[1]

All of us have stories that shape our worldview and lurk behind our scholarship. In 1996 I went to Chicago with my son, who was applying for admission to the University of Chicago. We stayed in the Marriott Courtyard on the edge of the Loop and took a taxi to campus. The driver told us that Lakeshore Drive was congested with traffic, and he made a detour through city streets. Within minutes, the window of the cab framed Cabrini-Green, identifiable by a massive rectangular sign in the middle of an open plaza. There it was—Cabrini-Green—the "project" that had achieved notoriety through sensational press reports of anarchy and violence. The realization that Cabrini-Green was situated on the edge of Chicago's legendary Gold Coast provided an epiphanic moment: I knew in a flash why Cabrini-Green was slated for demolition: it occupied immensely valuable real estate that was in the way of the growth machine. As two geographers put it, Cabrini was "an island of decay in seas of renewal."[2]

Let me say up front that I am no housing expert or policy wonk. However, Cabrini-Green remained on my personal radar, and in 2009 I attended a section at the annual conference of the American Sociological Association where a certified policy wonk presented a paper on her study on the deconcentration of poverty in Atlanta. The larger context is that this researcher was associated with a cadre of housing experts who conducted studies under the banner of Moving to Opportunity (MTO). Their mission was to rescue Black families from the perils of "the 'hood," and to relocate them in suburban areas with better housing and schools for their children. The presenter did a PowerPoint that mapped where these MTO recipients were situated before and after their "move to opportunity."

During the Q and A, I raised my hand and expressed my skepticism of her study. I averred that if we knew nothing about the laudable purposes of her research, the scattergram might be construed as portraying the relocation of Jews in Nazi Germany. A palpable hush went over the room, and the moderator—an erstwhile friend and a leading housing expert—disclosed how he and I have differed over the years, and that unlike him, I was willing to consign Black children to live in rundown and roach-infested high-rise projects and dangerous neighborhoods. He confided that we had quarreled for years and could never agree, and he proceeded to spare the audience from any more of my heresies. I suspect that the assembled policy wonks scoffed at the false equivalency between judenrein and MTO as they marched off to a scheduled lunch for members of the Community and Urban Sociology Section.

I plead guilty to false equivalency! Yet again, my mischief was a reminder that the demolition of Cabrini-Green, like scores of public housing projects across the nation, was conducted in the name of deconcentrating poverty, invariably over the rage and tears of the residents. As for the small number of volunteers who agreed to participate in MTO experiments, they were not exercising free will so much as responding to the lack of alternatives. Even then, as studies have found, they worried about their reception in the suburbs, as well as leaving behind friends and community in the 'hood. Indeed, two of the MTO doyens, James Rosenbaum and Stephanie DeLuca, reported that subjects gravitated back to the 'hood, and they therefore argued for relocating them further away from their former neighborhoods so that they would not be tempted or able to return.[3]

After my serendipitous encounter with the MTO crowd, my mind drifted to Alex Haley's account of Malcolm X's exhilaration when he moved to a Black neighborhood in Roxbury, Massachusetts, where he discovered the diversity, energy, and vitality of the city, including its streets, its hangouts, its ballrooms, and the pulse and drama of urban life generally. Incidentally, Malcolm X's home on 72 Dale Street, built in 1874, has been spared from the wrecking ball, at least so far. It was also the home of his sister, Ella Little Collins, a civil rights activist. Today it is a designated city landmark by the Boston Landmarks Commission.[4]

Let us return to the champions of MTO and deconcentration, who fit George Bernard Shaw's caricature of Major Barbara, the iconic white savior with good intentions who is an unwitting pawn for other less noble agendas. The same can be said of Matthew Hughey's white saviors who constitute a trope in recent films where whites rescue non-whites from unfortunate circumstances.[5]

In the case of the MTO advocates, the protagonists are advocates who rescue Black families from the degradation of the projects and the perils of the ghetto. However, the MTO advocates have an even more sinister theory, drawn from Oscar Lewis's research on the culture of poverty. The supposition is that after years in the projects, concentrated poverty "metastasizes" and takes on a life of its own.

Consider for a moment the semiotics of a metaphor that conflates poor neighborhoods with a metastasizing cancer, implying that it needs to be excised from the body politic. As I argue below, this optic provides specious legitimation for the demolition of the poor housing communities and the "relocation" of their residents, usually to other neighborhoods that are poor and segregated. What should be self-evident, however, is that deconcentration policy is applied selectively with other interests in mind: when developers and politicians conspire to clear the way for lucrative development, especially in neoliberal cities that were previously "distressed" and are now ripe for gentrification.

This position has been forcefully argued by Edward Goetz, a professor of urban planning at the Humphrey School of Public Affairs and the director of the Center for Urban and Regional Affairs at the University of Minnesota. Goetz thoroughly discredits the claim that Moving to Opportunity and other schemes to deconcentrate poverty are a gift or advantage to the groups being "relocated." In the concluding paragraph of his 2003 book *Clearing the Way: Deconcentrating the Poor in Urban America*, he writes:

> A responsible antipoverty policy should not lead with the demolition of low-cost housing and the forced relocation of the poor. This nation's history with the urban renewal program suggests that without complementary actions to reduce exclusionary barriers and incentives that foster and facilitate growing socioeconomic disparities—and the geographic expression of those disparities—the scattering of poor people, in itself, accomplishes little.[6]

THE RAVAGES OF HOPE VI

The Fair Housing Act of 1968 was passed to prohibit racial discrimination in sales and rentals of housing. However, no public housing was built under the Nixon administration. Under President Clinton, HUD Secretary Henry Cisneros created HOPE VI, whose policy objective was to replace "severely distressed" public housing with low-rise apartment complexes that would be mixed income and mixed race. A new generation of architects and urban planners at the University of Chicago conceived of a "new urbanism" whose architectural features would blend residents of public housing into the surrounding neighborhood. Against the specter of crime-ridden high-rise towers that "warehoused" the poor, we were given the promise of decorous row houses that would foster integration in terms of race, ethnicity, and class. A compelling imaginary, to be sure.

However, local newspapers told a different story—one that depicted grassroots organizations opposing the Cabrini-Green demolition as a flagrant land grab that served the interests of developers and politicians, that trampled over the interests and rights of the residents, and that would leave most of the displaced families worse off as they gravitated to other densely poor neighborhoods, further away from the jobs, transportation, and services they had relied on.[7]

To these aggrieved families, fearful of losing their homes and communities, it was clear that HOPE VI was a ruse for "Negro removal," a term coined by James Baldwin in the early 1960s and embraced by Malcolm X to convey their opposition to the "urban renewal" projects that displaced poor Blacks from their homes and communities. Nor can "Negro removal" be dismissed a hyperbole. In the case of Cabrini-Green alone, 14,000 African Americans were evicted, and this was only one of a score of Chicago's "projects" that were demolished.[8] By the time that HOPE VI was ended in 2010, 255,000 units had been demolished, impacting half a million people at a cost of $6.2 billion.[9] Critics were vehement that the promise of building mixed-race and mixed-income housing was only a smokescreen to conceal what amounted to the cleansing of the Black underclass.

So let us address the uncomfortable question of whether HOPE VI amounted to Negro removal by another name, one that would cleanse the urban landscape of the Black nemesis and clear the way for developers? This raises another question: Were scholars and policy wonks complicit in providing indispensable legitimacy for ethnic cleansing under the ruse of "deconcentrating poverty"?

As James Baldwin presumably knew when he deployed the term "Negro removal," it conjured up memory of another ignominious policy, the Indian Removal Act that was signed into law in 1830, authorizing Andrew Jackson to remove Native American tribes to federal territory west of the Mississippi River. The parallels to Negro removal are not far-fetched. In the case of Cabrini-Green, the rule for one-to-one replacement of low-income housing was abrogated by Cisneros, the allotment of low-income housing was severely scaled back, and stringent tenant screening criteria, including strict work requirements, assured that only a handful of displaced residents would be allowed to return to the small allotment of public housing units in the new mixed-income development.[10]

Thus, Cabrini-Green was demolished and the new development was refurbished with a new name: Parkside of Old Town. By September 2007, a local real estate blog offered this rhapsodic account of the neighborhood's transformation from slum to Gold Coast:

PARKSIDE OF OLD TOWN BRINGS DEVELOPMENT TO CABRINI

Cabrini was once one of the most notorious neighborhoods in Chicago. When public housing was built in the neighborhood, many of the old homes were destroyed and families left in the neighborhood.

During the 1980s and 1990s, crime and drugs levied a heavy cost on the neighborhood, making it one of the most dangerous in the city.

Today, Cabrini is the scene of one of the largest real estate redevelopment projects in all of Chicago. Most of the housing projects are gone now, replaced by cranes and new developments that offer a mix of luxury condominiums and affordable housing for former residents of public housing in the neighborhood.

One of the largest developments underway in Cabrini is Parkside of Old Town. Buyers can choose from condos and townhomes that start at $300,000. The townhomes sell for as much as $700,000.

This 18-acre development will offer park space with basketball courts and a playground. There are also several other new condo developments around the neighborhood that are attracting new families and bringing back the neighborhood feel that characterized Cabrini before the construction of public housing.

Many new residents choose Cabrini for the excellent location just minutes from downtown. Prices in the neighborhood are competitive when compared to other areas of north Chicago such as the Gold Coast and Streeterville.[11]

Determined efforts of community activists and years of litigation had come to naught, and according to one estimate, 97 percent of dislocated families moved into areas that did not meet either the "low poverty or racial integration requirements set out in the relocation rights contract."[12] Broken promises: another parallel with the nation's treatment of Native Americans.

CONCENTRATED POVERTY RECONSIDERED

Where is the evidence that "concentrated poverty" has explanatory significance above and beyond the effects of poverty itself? Do we know that
concentration magnifies or exacerbates poverty? Studies that advance
this theory devote tomes proving that poverty has become more concentrated, but they utterly fail to prove that concentration has an additive
effect to poverty per se.[13] To demonstrate this, they would have to show
that poor people who do not live in high-poverty census tracts—and who
are not warehoused in "soulless high-rise apartment buildings"—are less
prone to aberrant behavior than poor people who live in concentrated
poverty. We also know from studies of rural poverty, whether in Appala-
chia or upstate New York or the farm belt, that all these "urban" pathologies run rampant there as well.

Urbanists have fallen into the trap that Manuel Castells cautioned
against long ago: positing the reified "city" or aspects of urban ecology as
the cause of "urban ills," rather than a political economy that engenders
deep and persistent inequalities.[14] Before we dynamite housing projects,
obliterating 200,000 units, shouldn't there be ironclad evidence that deconcentration will have the beneficial effects that are presumed?[15]

Not only do mobility programs fail to magically transform the lives of
the small number of people who are delivered from "the 'hood," but studies find that relocatees are often worse off than before. With or without
a Section 8 voucher, most relocatees gravitate to other poor neighborhoods where rents are low, thus moving the poor from one neighborhood
of concentrated poverty to another, ironically validating the fears of the
NIMBYs.[16] Nor do the suburbs provide the magical solution. Xavier de
Souza Briggs, a leading advocate of mobility programs, concedes that
"many minority families that moved to the suburbs in the 1990s, even if
they became homeowners, did not escape the pattern that contains poverty, school failure, and job isolation in particular geographic areas."[17]

In a study of a HOPE VI relocation program in Tampa, Florida, Susan
Greenbaum and her collaborators found that even when relocatees acknowledged that their housing was improved, "many . . . expressed feelings of loss and nostalgia for the neighborly relations they had in the public housing complexes where they used to live. In addition to enjoyment,

patterns of mutual assistance and exchange among the residents had made survival easier on their very low incomes and offered a sense of community"[18]

There is an ironic addendum to the personal narrative at the outset of this essay. When my son was enrolled at the University of Chicago and rented a house on Kimbark Avenue, his back porch provided a telescopic view of a strip of low-rise, subsidized housing that had been built on 55th Street. Architecturally, the houses were a New Urbanist nightmare: fortified bunkers, walled off to the street, with a small, internal courtyard. My son observed that on Sunday mornings, women dressed in their Sunday best would stand on the corner, waiting for a bus that would transport them back to "the 'hood" where their church was located.

HOPE VI and mobility programs were predicated on demonized images of the poor within "severely distressed" housing projects. Implicitly and often explicitly, theorists and planners have pictures in their mind of aberrant individuals who are the source of violence and disorder. To be sure, it is easy to conjure up such images and compile statistics that present a bleak picture of gangs, drugs, and violence. But another picture emerges from ethnographic research: of ordinary people, desperately poor and struggling to survive; of networks of resourceful women, men, and extended families engaged in mutual support; of neighborhoods and churches that provide people with a sense of belonging and access to services and resources; and of activists and advocacy groups who valiantly represent the poor against the powerful institutions that seek their expulsion.[19]

Why is it, one might ask, that social scientists valorize the solidarities of white ethnics as "Gemeinschaft," whereas in the case of racial minorities, these same solidarities are disparaged as "hypersegregation" whose prescribed remedy is "deconcentration by demolition?"[20] These scholars forget that when white ethnics were poor—like the Italians who were the first occupants of Cabrini-Green or the Jewish immigrants on the Lower East Side—they manifested the same "pathologies" associated with today's minorities. If their "pathologies" were not as prevalent or as enduring, this is because white ethnics had the advantage of white privilege, were not encircled by discriminatory barriers, and consequently were not mired in poverty for generations.[21] As a result, they were able to fulfill the American Dream by eventually moving to suburbia, though they typically also cling to memories of their struggles in the tenements.[22]

In short, a policy predicated on the claim that the demolition of their homes will advance the interests of the very people whose homes are being destroyed is a preposterous sham. Here we confront the cold reality: HOPE VI was never an anti-poverty program but a bureaucratic experiment that stomped over the rights and interests of the poor and sacrificed them on the altar of political and economic power. This is how an agency whose putative mission was to provide housing of last resort for the poorest Americans devolved into a wrecking ball for public housing.[23] As with Indian removal, this policy had to be implemented in a way that does not foment violent resistance or "political problems." This is where the theory of deconcentrated poverty comes into play, which is trotted out in Congressional hearings and in Congressional Research Service reports, to paste over the patent injustices and to make a virtue of the unconscionable.[24]

It is not my contention that minus the theory of deconcentrated poverty, HOPE VI might have lived up to its promise. Powerbrokers heed the sage advice of housing experts only when it is in their interest to do so. We have to be honest about the *political uses* of the theory of concentrated poverty, which is invoked wherever the poor occupy valuable real estate that is coveted by developers and which is part of the neoliberal project of reclaiming urban space that previously was relinquished to the nation's racial and class pariahs. Neil Smith aptly called this "the revanchist city."[25]

In recent years, Atlanta also demolished most public housing, including housing occupied by stable families with regular employment.[26] In New Orleans, after Hurricane Katrina, housing projects that escaped the ravages of Katrina were nevertheless bulldozed despite the anguished protests of its residents.[27] Indeed, while bodies were still being plucked from Katrina's floodwaters, William Julius Wilson and Bruce Katz appeared on the *PBS NewsHour*, declaring that Katrina presented an opportunity to break up pockets of concentrated poverty.[28] And when Xavier de Souza Briggs posted a petition on an urban sociology listserv under the evocative title "Moving to Opportunity in the Wake of Hurricane Katrina," nearly two hundred urban experts rushed to affix their signatures, oblivious to the political uses of their dogma.[29]

A final point. Let us concede for the sake of argument that deconcentration and mobility programs provided better housing and schools for some poor people, and advanced the cause of racial integration. Even so, we have to ask whether such policies merely divert attention away from the vastly greater problem: the millions of poor people who still inhabit ghettos and barrios—or who are homeless altogether—whose plight has been exacerbated by the dismantling of the welfare state and who are now threatened with the gentrification of the neoliberal city.

As Greenbaum argues with blunt eloquence, "A poverty alleviation policy that excludes the majority cannot be judged a success."[30] Not only do mobility programs provide relief only for a select few, but they provide an ideological façade for the neoliberal war against the poor and for disinvestment in the inner city. As Goetz puts it: "When accepted as a political strategy, deconcentration justifies the redirection of community development efforts away from the declining housing stock of poor neighborhoods and/or away from poor residents."[31] This argument is extended in his most recent book, *The One-Way Street of Integration: Fair Housing and the Pursuit of Racial Justice in American Cities.*[32]

Goetz's argument is incontrovertible. Instead of comprehensive policies that would revitalize these communities, provide jobs—the sine qua non of anti-poverty policy—and include grassroots organizations in the reconstruction of their communities, we have demonstration projects that, at best, help a select few and throw others to the winds, with or without a Section 8. Furthermore, the dispersal of the minority poor makes it all the more difficult to mobilize politically and to put pressure on political and economic elites to live up to their responsibility to address the problems in their own backyard. Instead, in the name of deconcentrating poverty, they use dynamite as a remedy and transfer the problem to somebody else's backyard—with the sanction of urban experts who labor under the illusion that they are advancing racial and economic justice.

PART III

From Backlash
to Frontlash

This play on words conveys the seismic transformation in public understanding and attitudes following the police murder of George Floyd in 2020. Pundits and protesters alike have speculated on whether or not the eruption of protest marks the beginning of a national reckoning on racial inequalities and injustices.

The core argument advanced in this book is that the passage of landmark civil rights laws in 1964 and 1965 marked the high point of the civil rights revolution, but over the past half century, we have witnessed the evisceration and rollback of hard-won gains. It began with the whittling away of school desegregation, then the erosion of safeguards against job discrimination, and today it is extending, even more dangerously, to voting rights. Remember, as Reconstruction came to an end in the aftermath of the Civil War, W. E. B. Du Bois wrote with prophetic wisdom: "The slave went free. Stood a brief moment in the sun. Then moved back again toward slavery." We must fear that we are on the cusp of a similar reversal in the Second Reconstruction.

On the other hand, for an optimistic moment there was an unexpected shift in the mood of the nation and the prospect of "a current reckoning on race." How can we reconcile these opposing developments? To state the obvious, the nation stands again at the crossroads:

between advancing civil rights and racial equality or seeing these rights whittled away.

The chapters in part III assess the politics and possibilities for racial transformation. The overarching question is whether the nation has the ability and the will to live up to its democratic promise.

CHAPTER ELEVEN

DECOLONIZING RACE KNOWLEDGE

Exorcizing the Ghost of Herbert Spencer

During the years 1870 to 1890, Spencer was probably more widely read and discussed in the United States than any other philosopher. His works were known and debated throughout the literate population, and he enjoyed a vogue that has not been known by any philosopher before or since. He became the emblem of what was referred to as the "scientific spirt," an unbounded confidence in the power of systematic observation to advance any and all utilitarian goals, and to replace other forms of knowledge from other sources.

Daniel Breslau, "The American Spencerians"[1]

What choice did he [Du Bois] have but to invent a counter-sociology, perhaps even an anti-sociology, in an intellectual context in which the Anglo-American founding fathers indulged in broad theoretical speculation on race relations, championing a theoretical model—Social Darwinism—that "instinctively placed Blacks at the primitive end of the evolutionary scale."

Pierre Saint-Arnaud, *African American Pioneers of Sociology*[2]

In his 1937 opus *The Structure of Social Action*, Talcott Parsons, notorious for turgid prose, began with a startling first sentence of four words:

"Who now reads Spencer?" Actually, Parsons was quoting Crane Brinton, a British intellectual historian, who declared that Spencer's theory of evolution was obsolete, predicated on a spurious teleology that human society was bent on an inexorable path of progress from "primitive man" to "civilized man." Parsons delivered the coup de grace: "We must agree with the verdict. Spencer is dead."[3]

As others commented, rumors of Spencer's demise were premature. In a paper titled "The American Spencerians," Daniel Breslau writes: "It is beyond dispute that Herbert Spencer was the most influential source of 19th century sociology in the United States."[4] Nowhere was this more pronounced than in the sociology of race knowledge. Let me quote again from Herman Schwendinger and Julia Schwendinger's *The Sociologists of the Chair*, sadly neglected, presumably because of its unabashed politics, which are inscribed in the book's subtitle *Radical Analysis of the Formative Years of North American Sociology, 1883–1922*:

> The degree to which Spencer's theory was permeated with racist ideas cannot be overemphasized. He claimed that "savage" and "semicivilized" people represented a lower stage of biological evolution. These people were regarded as mental and moral inferiors and their sense of justice, according to Spencer, was less evolved than that of the "civilized" races.[5]

These beliefs are commonly dismissed as social Darwinist tripe, but there is more to it than that. To echo Oliver Cox, social Darwinism was merely "the attitudinal expression of imperialism."[6] As Schwendinger and Schwendinger write, "The founders of American sociology adopted the tenets of Social Darwinian ideas in order to buttress their own racist and imperialistic doctrines."[7]

Nor can the sins of sociology's founders be exculpated with the caveat that they were merely "men of their time." As the Schwendingers demonstrate, there was all along an alternative paradigm that the men of the Chicago school chose to disparage or occlude altogether. Marxism preceded the rise of American sociology by half a century, and approached issues of race and racism with penetrating insight.[8]

To quote Marx again, fifteen years before the Civil War, he wrote: "Without slavery there would be no cotton, without cotton there would be no modern industry."[9] In one epigrammatic sentence, Marx summed up the relationship of slavery to the emerging industrial economies of both the United States and England. Cotton provided the raw material that was exported to manufacturers in New York and Birmingham for use in their burgeoning textile industries, which in turn made the products sold in the consumer market. Indeed, one can trace the entire history of race and racism as providing the labor that spawned the early phases of capitalism, including the concentrated wealth that subsidized still other capitalist ventures. It can be said without hyperbole that American capitalism was built on the backs of the enslaved.

However, the august founders of sociology recoiled from the specter of Marxism. At the very time that Albion Small sought to secure the consent of the university's trustees to establish the nation's first department of sociology, the city of Chicago was a cauldron of political unrest. Progressive activists assailed the oligarchs, the trusts, and the captains of industry, some of whom were trustees at the University of Chicago. In *Advocacy and Objectivity*, Mary Furner devoted a chapter to the "perils of radicalism." She writes, "Sympathy with the labor movement was tantamount to subversion; support of public ownership of gasworks or streetcar lines attacked the interests of the private capitalists who owned them and the politicians who dispensed the franchises."[10]

Indeed, several faculty of the University of Chicago were purged because they were regarded as too closely aligned with radical ideas.[11] Albion Small and others in the fledgling Sociology Department had to avoid any taint of radicalism.

Robert Park is legendary for telling his students that they should regard the world with the same detachment and objectivity with which the zoologist dissects the potato bug.[12] This was the pretense for rationalizing away both overseas colonialism and its domestic equivalent: two and a half centuries of slavery and a century of Jim Crow. Indeed, at the very time University of Chicago was established in 1892, the scaffolding of Jim Crow was being erected, with the indispensable sanction of the Supreme Court, the very institution that had previously provided the warrant to slavery.

According to Howard Winant, "in the early years of sociology, race was not viewed as a political issue except by opponents of the disciplinary consensus. In the United States it was seen as 'natural' that the Black South and Native peoples would be subdued by the 'more advanced' white races."[13] Note Winant's caveat: "except by opponents of the disciplinary consensus." As Schwendinger and Schwendinger remind us: "The founders of American sociology should not be considered 'waxen tablets' who merely reflected the racism of their times. Their writings were based on the *active selection* of compatible ideological ideas."[14] And this included keeping a safe distance from the specter of socialism.

Simply put, the pioneers of sociology had a choice between Marx and Spencer, and they chose Spencer. Indeed, it can be said with only slight exaggeration that the whole purpose of Chicago sociology in its formative years was to provide a politically respectable alternative to Marxism.

Other forces were at work. As R. W. Connell has shown, sociology was born in the crucible of imperialism, and its founders were obsessed with the "difference between the civilization of the metropole and an Other whose defining attribute was its primitiveness."[15] Indeed, the whole logic and shibboleth of colonialism—that it brought the blessings of civilization to backward peoples—is so baked into the models of Chicago sociology and so mired in obfuscation that the complicity of the fabled pioneers of Chicago sociology is rarely subjected to critical scrutiny.

For example, take Robert Park's famed "race relations cycle." Doctoral students to this day recite its four stages like a catechism: contact, competition, accommodation, and assimilation. On closer examination, this model is suffused with the language of colonialism, and its four stages mirror Spencer's stages in the evolution from "primitive man" to "civilized man." Put another way, although regarded as one of the primogenitors of Chicago sociology, Park spouted the language and logic of Spencerism.

As Stanford Lyman has pointed out, "It is noteworthy that in restating the character and terminal phase of the race relations cycle, Park made no prediction about the future status of Blacks or any other of the nonwhite peoples in the American variant of that cycle."[16] In a diary discovered near the end of his life, Park quoted William James as saying: "Progress is a terrible thing. It is so destructive and wasteful."[17] As though the ravages of colonialism can be dismissed with an imperial shrug!

From its inception, race knowledge in the social sciences has been what Charles Mills has called "an epistemology of ignorance." With this intentional oxymoron, Mills calls into question the assumption that the mission of social science is to pursue knowledge. Rather, against its professed intentions, mainstream social scientists have masked or obfuscated the incriminating truths about genocide, slavery, and colonialism and their legacies of domination that extend to the present.[18] And while Chicago sociology still bathes in self-congratulation for having repudiated scientific racism, it basically substituted "culture" for "genes." In effect, Chicago sociology gave us Spencerism without biology.

THE TWO FACES OF CHICAGO SOCIOLOGY

There is an unexpected coda to this narrative concerning race and Chicago sociology. As far as I know, until now nobody has critically addressed the question of what prompted Robert Park and his colleagues to breach the color line and to accept Black doctoral students into the citadel of the University of Chicago. This is generally accepted at face value, as an unassailable expression of anti-racism. However, Roger Salerno, a sociology professor at Pace University, provides other troubling insights. According to Salerno: "Taken as a whole, the work of these particular African-American sociologists provides us with some central features that resonate with the Chicago School sociology touted by Park and Burgess, but much of their work challenged some of its underlying assumptions— particularly the more conservative assumptions of Park such as temperament and innate racial antipathies."[19] Never mind Salerno's revelation that Park frequented the university's Quadrangle Club that prohibited the admission of women, Blacks, and Jews.[20] Besides, the inclusion of some Black students at the hallowed University of Chicago was consistent with the claim that the gospel of imperialism was "to uplift and to civilize."

Salerno also discloses that there was monetary incentive behind noblesse oblige: "Rockefeller Foundation monies funneled through the

Laura Spellman Fund and the Social Science Research Council provided financial assistance to African Americans seeking graduate education. The University of Chicago received much of this funding by inviting students of colour to the institution."[21] Insofar as race relations was Chicago's signature area of specialization, "it was natural for it to open its doors to these students—most of whom were mature men with track records in research returning to school for advanced degrees."[22]

The inclusion of Black students into the august doctoral program served as a showcase for demonstrating that the backward races could be elevated to the level of the advanced races. A correlate of this proposition was that "the race problem" could be ameliorated through education. It is telling, however, that none of the original cohort of talented Black students admitted into the University of Chicago's Sociology Department received teaching appointments at white universities. Rather they were funneled into historically Black colleges; "they were expected to take the word back to the masses of the 'lesser educated' in colleges in the South."[23]

Nevertheless, something quite remarkable happened. In a collective spirit of resistance, the quietly insurgent Black sociologists admitted into the citadel of higher learning surreptitiously revolted against the orthodoxies of Chicago sociology. To be sure, they knew that they were "walking a fine line," as Oliver Cox once said of E. Franklin Frazier. Some of these enterprising students had been educated at Howard, which at the time was a hotbed of radical thought.[24] Howard's administration was almost exclusively white, as were most of the faculty, but students flocked to hear occasional lectures by W. E. B. Du Bois and were also exposed to the heresies of Marxism. This is the intellectual alchemy of race and class that eventually coalesced in a unique brand of "Black sociology."[25]

This intersectionality of race and class—centered on Du Bois and Marx—not only challenged many of the assumptions and theoretical underpinnings of the prevailing "white sociology" but also invented a unique method of scholarship and analysis that came to be known as "ethnography." Arguably, ethnography was born out of a determination shared by these pioneering Black scholars to tell their own story and to write their own history.

The fruit of this scholarly breakthrough became evident in works that received little recognition at the time but decades later were celebrated as classics. Consider the following works and scholars:

- Du Bois's *Philadelphia Negro* (1899) is now considered a pioneering study and the genesis of sociological inquiry that was appropriated as "Chicago sociology." Although an instant success, Du Bois was denied a teaching position at the University of Pennsylvania and accepted a position at Atlanta University, the oldest Black university in the country, founded in 1865. Along with other Black faculty, Du Bois organized the Atlanta University Conferences, which convened annually to assess the state of Black America.

  As Pierre Saint-Arnaud wrote in *African American Pioneers of Sociology*, Du Bois "unquestionably deserves to be known as the founding father of a distinct sociological tradition. He remained the dominant intellectual of his generation until after the First World War, when others came on the scene: Charles S. Johnson (late 1910s), E. Franklin Frazier (early 1920s), Oliver C. Cox and Horace R. Cayton (early 1930s), and J. G. St. Clair Drake (late 1930s)."[26]

- Charles Sturgeon Johnson, the first Black protégé admitted by Robert Park, conducted a groundbreaking study of the 1919 Chicago race riot. This has an illuminating subtext. After the outbreak of the race riot, the VIPs at the Urban League went to Robert Park, the venerated "father of race relations," to conduct a study of the riot. However, Park demurred and instead recommended his bright graduate student Charles Johnson to take his place. Three years later, Johnson published a comprehensive study of over eight hundred pages that not only provided a critical analysis of the riot, but also documented, in graphic detail, the influx of Southern Blacks into Chicago's South Side and their rapid absorption into the burgeoning industrial sector, including interracial unions.[27]

- E. Franklin Frazier's *The Negro Family in the United States* (1939) emanated from his Chicago dissertation. Although some elements were later appropriated by Daniel Patrick Moynihan to validate his screed concerning the weakness of Black families, Frazier's contention was that the struggles of Black families were a product of white racism, particularly their exclusion from jobs that entailed more than servile labor.

Let me digress with an irresistible anecdote about Frazier, who earned the moniker "Forceful Frazier" for his resolute demeanor.[28] In 1927, Frazier published an article that had been rejected by various publications but finally accepted by *Forum*, a popular periodical on social policy. Its title was "The Pathology of Race Prejudice." Tongue in cheek, Frazier asserted that whites in the South were driven mad by a "Negro-complex," evident by the fact that "otherwise kind and law-abiding" citizens would "indulge in the most revolting forms of cruelty towards Black people." After Frazier's article was published, he received death threats and fled Atlanta with a .45 tucked in his belt. The *Atlanta Constitution* carried an editorial condemning the "psychopathologician" as "more insane by reason of his anti-white complex than any southerner obsessed by his anti-Negro repulsions." Furthermore, the Morehouse College's Board of Trustees decided not to renew Frazier's contract because his "ideas on race equality went too far."[29]

- G. St. Clair Drake and Horace R. Cayton's *Black Metropolis* (1945) was a landmark study of Black Chicago in the 1940s, one that straddled history, sociology, and ethnography. The book ran eight hundred pages and probed various facets of social life. The opening narrative traced the "flight to freedom," the "land of promise," and "the Great Migration," capped off with a chapter centered on the racial tensions leading to the 1919 race riot. Another chapter explored life "along the color line," followed by a chapter titled "Crossing the Color-Line," which centered on intermarriage. Another key chapter, "The Job Ceiling," foregrounded the exclusion of Blacks from coveted jobs in Chicago's expanding economy. Other chapters, including "Breaking the Job Ceiling" and "The New Unions," provided a hopeful perspective on the acceptance of Blacks as allies, "adding *fraternity* to *liberty* and *equality*."[30]

The chapter "Bronzeville" is named for the "continuous eddy of faces—black, brown, olive, yellow, and white."[31] This was a lively and diverse neighborhood of "drugstores, grocery stores, theaters, poolrooms, taverns, and churches."[32] Segregation was endemic, yet a far cry from the oppression and violence that drove African Americans to migrate to the North. One can see from this brief synopsis why *Black Metropolis* is still regarded as a classic in the sociological canon.

- Oliver Cromwell Cox started out in economics but shifted to sociology, which he regarded as more theoretical. His masterpiece, *Caste, Class, and Race* (1948), had a pronounced Marxist orientation and is now regarded as the forerunner of world systems analysis. Cox revolted against the reductive tendencies of most sociological research. In his words: "Race prejudice is the social-attitudinal concomitant of the racial exploitative practice of a ruling class in a capitalist society.[33]

  Cox earned a reputation as outspoken and irascible. In *Caste, Class, and Race*, he took issue with Robert Park, his erstwhile professor, with this devastating critique: "His teleological approach has diverted him from an examination of the specific causal events in the development of modern race antagonism; it has led him inevitably into a hopeless position about 'man's inhumanity to man,' a state of mind that must eventually drive the student into the open arms of the mystic."[34]

Salerno is correct in identifying the foundations and evolution of a distinct Black Chicago school, beginning with Du Bois and the research and pedagogy promulgated by the Atlanta school and centered on the Black experience. However, during the 1920s there emerged a second "Chicago school" of predominantly white scholars who pioneered the empirical study of urban life, including such memorable works as *The Hobo* by Nels Anderson (1923), *The Gang* by Frederick M. Thrasher (1927), *The Strike* by E. T. Hiller (1928), *The Gold Coast and the Slum* by Harvey W. Zorbaugh (1929), and *The Taxi-Dance Hall* by Paul G. Cressey (1932). Other Chicago sociologists dealt with the ecology of city life, including family disorganization, ethnic communities, occupational social types, and the analysis of social trends. According to Schwendinger and Schwendinger, "these studies produced mainly by third-generation sociologists, pioneered in the empirical study of urban life."[35]

Thus, there were two distinct streams of epistemology and research in the development of American sociology: one unequivocally Black, the other predominantly white.[36] Robert Park straddled these two streams, though he was the person most responsible for admitting Black students to the University of Chicago. However, as Ralph Turner, a professor at UCLA, wrote in 1968, "For all of his concern with race relations, it is striking that the achievement of social and economic equality never emerges as a dominant goal in Park's thought."[37] Cox described Park as a Spencerian, preoccupied with lofty issues of natural history and social evolution. This put him strangely at odds with the Black students he admitted into the Chicago doctoral program, whose research was empirical, pragmatic, and driven by a commitment to advance racial justice.

The 1930s witnessed another influx of philanthropic support for Black students admitted into the Chicago school, thanks to the largess of the Julius Rosenwald Fund. Rosenwald was the child of German immigrants who started out as a peddler and eventually emerged as one of the founders of Sears, Roebuck, and Company. Though not in the league of Rockefeller or Carnegie, Rosenwald invested millions of dollars to build thousands of Black schools in the South. He also contributed substantial sums to Booker T. Washington at Tuskegee. Between 1928 and 1948 Rosenwald funded scholarships for artists, writers, and cultural figures, including Black students admitted into the Sociology Department at the University of Chicago. These were the Depression years and therefore his philanthropy was all the more influential.

However, there is a disturbing coda to this record of philanthropy. At the same time that Rosenwald poured extravagant sums to advance Black education in the South and, later, to doctoral students at the University of Chicago, Sears had a color line that excluded Blacks from its workforce. After Rosenwald's death in 1948, Edwin Embree, the president of the Rosenwald Fund, wrote a biographical essay that ruefully acknowledged that "Mr. Rosenwald was saddened by his inability to change the discriminatory practices in his own firm and the Chicago office building that he owned."[38]

This hypocrisy did not go unnoticed in the Black community. A 1938 editorial in the *Pittsburgh Courier*, a Black newspaper, triggered a storm of protest from Jews who cited the extravagance of the Rosenwald Fund in helping Blacks. In a subsequent editorial, the *Courier* asserted that "we are not ungrateful," but went on to cite the fact that Sears refused to hire Black workers. The *Courier*'s editorial ended with this zinger: "Thus the graduates of Rosenwald schools can go without bread so far as the Rosenwald business is concerned. We are grateful but we are hungry."[39] Presumably, this refrain reflected the ambivalence among aspiring Black students to philanthropic largesse.

MERELY NEGROES STUDYING NEGROES: THE MARGINALIZATION AND REDEMPTION OF W. E. B. DU BOIS

There is an illuminating contrast between the life course of W. E. B. Du Bois and that of his intellectual biographer Aldon Morris. As Du Bois acknowledged in his autobiography, he grew up "in amoebic innocence" as the only Black child in a small town in Massachusetts. By his own account, he mixed freely with schoolmates, was welcomed in the homes of friends, and was barely conscious of the color line, despite its hideous ramifications. Nevertheless, his internal radar led him to enroll as an undergraduate at Fisk University. There he found that "the problem of race was faced openly and essential racial equality asserted and inferiority strenuously denied."[40]

Du Bois's first encounter with the color line occurred when, to the consternation of his teachers and fellow students, he volunteered to teach at a Black school in rural Tennessee for two summers, where he experienced raw, vicious racism for the first time. His next jolt was when he enrolled as a junior at Harvard in 1881. There he learned that Blacks were the laggards of evolution and that the cephalic index was a measure of their intellectual inferiority.

In his preface to *The Scholar Denied*, Morris reveals that he grew up in rural Mississippi in the 1950s, at the height of Jim Crow. "In blistering hot weather," he recalls, "whites sat under shade trees while we worked the fields dripping sweat from sun up to sundown."[41] To evade the draft during the Vietnam War, Morris enrolled in Southeast City College on Chicago's South Side, where an elderly Black professor introduced him to *The Souls of Black Folk*, in which Du Bois challenges Booker T. Washington's politics of accommodation.

As a graduate student in sociology at SUNY, Stony Brook, Morris was taken aback to discover that Du Bois was conspicuously missing from courses on inequality, sociological theory, and social movements. Lewis

Coser, an illustrious sociologist, had his office festooned with photos of
Marx, Weber, Durkheim, and Mannheim. Morris had the audacity to ask
Coser why there was no photo of Du Bois. Coser's retort was that "mas-
ters of sociological thought are those rare scholars who build theoretical
systems, and Du Bois did not build such a system."[42] From that moment,
Morris resolved that he would "one day, set the record straight."

The Scholar Denied makes good on Morris's pledge to himself and his
vow to history. Indeed, there is poetic justice in the fact that this child of
"the Emmett Till generation," as Joyce Ladner called it, grasped the significance of the marginalization of Du Bois's prodigious scholarship. But
Morris's book is more than a vindication of Du Bois. Its larger purpose is
to challenge dominant discourses in sociology that, ever since the inception of sociology at the University of Chicago in 1892, have provided
epistemic justification for racial hierarchy.

Du Bois is renowned for providing readers with "the big picture,"
and doing so with penetrating logic and rhetorical eloquence. Less well
known is that as a graduate student at Harvard, he received a two-year
fellowship to study in Berlin, where he was trained in statistics and quantitative analysis. The credo of the German school of economics was that
scientific knowledge could be an instrument for social reform, which Du
Bois seized upon as a weapon against racism. Rejected from white universities, he accepted a professorship at Atlanta University, a historically
Black college, where he launched a series of studies of Black communities, which flourished for thirteen years.

Despite a paucity of funds, under Du Bois's tutelage the "Atlanta
Studies" probed a broad spectrum of topics: mortality, urbanization,
business, schooling, and crime, along with institutions within Black communities such as "the Negro church," "the Negro artisan," and "Negro
morals and manners." Annual conferences sought to publicize the findings and explore avenues for reform. This prolific research agenda is the
basis for Morris's claim that "the Du Bois–Atlanta school deserves recognition for founding scientific sociology in America."[43] Indeed, Morris
calls into question sociology's origin myth, since Du Bois's pioneering
community studies preceded the work of Robert Park and his colleagues
by two decades. Yet as Morris shows with undisguised pique, "this

distinctive contribution has nevertheless been attributed to the Chicago school."[44]

A year prior to assuming his position at Atlanta University, Du Bois was commissioned by the University of Pennsylvania to conduct a study of the Philadelphia's Black population. Though resentful that he was not offered a professorial appointment, Du Bois launched his investigation with energy and conviction. He interviewed every family in the Seventh Ward, conducted surveys, collected archival data, and engaged in participant observation—a prime example of what is today acclaimed as "a mixed-method approach."

Nor did Du Bois gloss over shortcomings and flaws within the Black community. For example, he acknowledged that crime was a problem, but he rejected any suggestion that crime was rooted in degeneracy. Rather he traced crime to an all-encompassing system of oppression that "trapped Blacks in a vicious cycle of subordination."[45]

The Philadelphia Negro, published in 1899, is now recognized as a classic, though it was "largely ignored by mainstream white social scientists for decades."[46] Morris takes another jab at Lewis Coser, his erstwhile professor, for writing that W. I. Thomas's 1918 study *The Polish Peasant in Europe and America* was "a monumental achievement, the earliest major landmark of American sociological research."[47]

Morris also challenges contemporary critics, mostly from the Left, who portray Du Bois as "an elitist who had contempt for the Black masses."[48] Du Bois did not attempt to sugarcoat the dark side of Black life in Philadelphia, though as Morris concedes, he often deployed language that described poor Blacks as "backward," "low social grade," "undeveloped people," "ignorant," and in a state of "race-childhood" that rendered them "in need of guidance." Morris counters with two arguments: (1) Du Bois deployed the vernacular of the time, and cannot be blamed for "not using social constructionist language that had not been invented."[49] And (2) these critics "privilege a selective assortment of phrases and concepts extracted from Du Bois's writings and present them as pillars of Du Bois's thought."[50]

Beyond these quibbles, Morris's main point is that Du Bois never subscribed to the essentialism that was the hallmark of racist discourses.

Thus, while contemporary critics may regard his concept of "a talented tenth" as elitist, Morris argues that Du Bois was not disparaging the Black masses but only recognizing the necessity of a cadre of leaders to spearhead a movement for political transformation. Indeed, this prognosis came to fruition with the mobilization of the civil rights movement in the 1950s and 1960s, as Morris copiously documented in his 1986 study *The Origins of the Civil Rights Movement.*

Thus, it is not surprising that "Park and the Chicago School locked Du Bois out of the intellectual fraternity of sociology by systematically ignoring his scholarship."[51] The erasure of Du Bois from mainstream sociology continued throughout the twentieth century. As I have argued here, the whole purpose of the fabled Chicago school of race relations was to offer an alternative discourse to Marx and Du Bois, both of whom were excluded from mainstream sociology.[52]

Morris reaches a delicious high point in his chapter "Max Weber Meets Du Bois." He bridles at claims that Weber mentored Du Bois during the latter's student days in Germany and shows that it was the other way around: it was Du Bois who influenced Weber's transformation away from Spencerism and social Darwinism. As proof, Morris cites a 1910 symposium of the German Sociological Society in which Alfred Ploetz, founder of the *Society for Racial Hygiene*, averred that segregation in America existed because of intellectual and moral inferiority. Weber retorted: "Nothing of the kind is proven. I wish to state that the most important sociological scholar anywhere in the Southern states in America, with whom no white scholar can compare, is a Negro—Burckhardt [*sic*] Du Bois."[53] Indeed, when Weber visited the United States in the fall of 1904, Du Bois was the only sociologist he sought out, and Weber waged a campaign, unsuccessfully, to have *The Souls of Black Folk* translated into German.

Du Bois gradually came to the painful realization that the idea that the Negro problem could be remedied through scientific knowledge was an illusion. He wrote in 1944 that, despite the success of the annual Atlanta Conferences, "so far as the world of science and letters was concerned, we never 'belonged'; we remained unrecognized in learned societies and academic groups. *We rated merely as Negroes studying Negroes, and after all, what had Negroes to do with America or Science?*[54]

During his years at Atlanta, Du Bois was the major driving force behind the Niagara Movement, which culminated with the founding of the NAACP in 1910. That same year he resigned from Atlanta University and assumed the position of director of publicity and research for the NAACP. In this capacity he was the founder and editor of *The Crisis*, a position he held until 1934. Thus, Du Bois made the leap from sequestered scholar to political activist, and he used his position as editor of *The Crisis* to introduce a score of progressive voices into the public domain and advance the cause of racial justice. As Morris observes, Du Bois was "the discipline's first preeminent public scholar long before such a role was lucrative and celebrated."[55]

Aldon Morris has thrown down the gauntlet. It is time not only to give Du Bois the recognition so long denied, but also to rethink sociology's origin myth and its roots in the language and logic of colonialism. And while we are at it, it is also time to rescind the gamut of victim-blaming discourses that sociology spawned and continues to propagate, albeit under new rhetorical guises. As Morris observes in his concluding chapter, "an intellectual nonhegemonic school can emerge outside conventional routes if certain conditions are established"[56]

Of course, Du Bois was not alone in forging the Du Bois–Atlanta school of sociology. His team of researchers at Atlanta included Monroe Work, George Edmund Haynes, and Richard R. Wright, among others. Together they provided the foundation and inspiration for a second generation of Black sociologists who consciously built on Du Bois's groundbreaking work. They developed a canon that represented a critical alternative to the dominant paradigm that obscured racial oppression in a morass of theoretical abstraction and in a litany of victim-blaming discourses.

This second generation of black sociologists included Oliver Cromwell Cox, E. Franklin Frazier, Charles Sturgeon Johnson, St. Clair Drake, and Horace Cayton, among others. Together they formed "an epistemic community" that cultivated what Pierre Saint-Arnaud has termed "a peripheral sociology" that countered and subverted hegemonic discourses on race.[57] To be sure, these black doctoral students who were admitted to the University of Chicago had to tread carefully, lest they fall into disfavor with the professors on whom their careers depended. As it was, their work was generally disparaged as "Negroes merely studying Negroes," and they were relegated to teach at black colleges in an academy that was thoroughly segregated. Such was the stranglehold of marginalization.

However, there is a supreme irony that is worth pondering. As outsiders—not *despite* the stigma but *because* of it—these pioneers of a distinctive "peripheral sociology" had the perspicacity to see through the shibboleths and the pompous falsifications of "white sociology."[58]

CHAPTER TWELVE

THE MYTH OF BLACK PROGRESS

You don't stick a knife in a man's back nine inches and then pull it out six inches and say you are making progress.

Malcolm X, TV interview, March 1964[1]

The Black people will never gain full equality in this country . . . [and] even those Herculean efforts we hail as successful will produce no more than temporary 'peaks of progress,' short-lived victories that slide into irrelevance as racial patterns adapt in ways that maintain white dominance.

Derrick Bell, "Racial Realism," 1992[2]

Thanks to their extraordinary ingenuity, talent, and roots in musical traditions across generations, Black youth developed a transformative musical form with a hypnotic cadence: hip-hop music. It was a genuinely indigenous creation that emerged in New York City parks and gradually mushroomed into a domestic music phenomenon that was an instant cultural sensation. Its tentacles extended to art, style, and an array of inventive consumer products. Before long, hip-hop excited audiences in nations the world over, especially youth who grasped its immanent politics that transcended national boundaries.

Hip-hop was more than a temporary sensation and kept morphing into a wider panorama of musical and artistic expression, with its distinctive style and sartorial innovation. Its huge popularity and success also affected how the rest of the world regarded Black people in the United States. This dimension of the hip-hop phenomenon is the subject of an incisive analysis by Roopali Mukherjee, a professor of media studies at Queens College and author of an article entitled "'Ghetto Fabulous' in the Imperial United States." Its provocative subtitle speaks to the core issue of this book: "Black Consumption and the 'Death of Civil Rights.'"[3]

According to Mukherjee, hip-hop is both a music form and a commodity that has defined attitudes toward American Blacks and "the American way":

> With cheering audiences both in the United States and overseas, hip hop music and, in particular, the swagger and style of its "bling" aesthetic capitalize on the power of blackness to "sell everything." The influence of Black popular culture has cajoled audiences worldwide to find freedom in conspicuous consumption, security in commodities, and life's contentment through "the American way."[4]

Consider how this enviable spectacle of black celebrity and talent, not to speak of the music itself, is regarded through the optic of outsiders:

> The visible presence of hip-hop moguls and sports icons offered incontrovertible evidence of the distance that African Americans had traveled since the marches, sit-ins, and boycotts of the 1960s. . . . After all, how oppressed could a minority be if its most visible representatives were fixtures on the nation's television screens, sporting thousand-dollar suits and million-dollar diamonds? Could African Americans still claim discrimination in a culture that found them among its highest-ranking political, economic, and cultural elites? Were continued mandates for redistributive social justice—social welfare, affirmative action, and so on—justified given that the social revolutions of the civil rights era appeared to have effectively succeeded?[5]

Poof! Through dazzling music and the glamor of Black celebrities, America's perennial race problem is consigned to history. Not only that, but the image of the United States as an imperial power is whitewashed from the stain of racism. Never mind that the United States, to quote Martin Luther King in 1967, is "the greatest purveyor of violence in the world today." Never mind that the United States has been enmeshed in "permanent warfare" and imperialistic policies in the Middle East, Africa, and Latin America. What a feat when the irrepressible talent of hip-hop performers is appropriated to win the hearts and minds of oppressed nations the world over. Even as African Americans endure the legacy of slavery in multitudinous ways, including voter suppression that is a throwback to centuries of disenfranchisement. Are we allowing the magnetism of hip-hop to drown out Derrick Bell's premonition of "short-lived victories that slide into irrelevance as racial patterns adapt in ways that maintain white dominance"?

With that sobering viewpoint, let us consider the perennial question of whether the United States has made "racial progress" during the half century since the civil rights revolution. Ibram Kendi has shrewdly observed that both racists and antiracists have made progress: "Both forces—the racist force of inequality and the antiracist force of equality—have progressed in rhetoric, in tactics, in policies. Both forces have drawn inspiration from American's founding creed of liberty."[6]

Kendi implicitly takes issue with Obama's contention that "the arc of history bends toward justice," a nugget that he deployed in his second inaugural address and at least a dozen of his speeches.[7] For Kendi, this is a figment of naïve optimism: "But what if there have been *two* historical forces at work: a dual and dueling history of racial progress and the simultaneous progression of racism? What if President Trump does not represent a step back, but a step forward?"[8] Ouch! Kendi artfully goes a step further:

> Americans have been well schooled in racial progress. That progress has
> been real over the course of history, and to deny its forward march is to
> deny all successes of courageous activists who challenged slavery, and

who are challenging segregation and poverty and the 45th president today.

But to deny the forward march of racism is to deny the successes of American racists. We have paid less attention to the progression of racism that often follows racial progress: how the law, the lyncher and the creditor replaced the master, the whip and the slave patrol in locking black people into destitution to white exploiters.[9]

As Hannah Arendt put it, revolution is inexorably a prelude and catalyst to counterrevolution.[10]

Martin Luther King was acutely aware of this inexorable transition. So was Lyndon Johnson, despite his lofty rhetoric as he signed the Voting Rights Act before students at Howard University in June 1965: "Today is a triumph for freedom as huge as any victory that's ever been won on any battlefield. . . . Today we strike away the vast major shackle of . . . fierce and ancient bonds."[11]

Actually, there is still lively debate on whether Johnson was cognizant that he was signing away the votes of "the solid South" from the Democratic Party. One school dismisses the claim that Johnson told an aide (according to one account, Bill Moyers), "We have lost the South for a generation."[12] Whether or not Johnson make this pronouncement, a 2018 study by two economists raised the paramount question: "Why Did the Democrats Lose the South? Bringing New Data to an Old Debate." Their conclusion was as follows: "Using newly available data, we reexamine one of the largest partisan shifts in a modern democracy: Southern whites' exodus from the Democratic Party. We show that defection among racially conservative whites explains the entire decline from 1958 to 1980."[13]

A year after the passage of the 1964 and 1965 Civil Rights Acts, a white backlash surfaced, which King described as "a witches' brew of bigotry, prejudice, half-truths and whole lies."[14] King spoke the bald truth: "white America was ready to demand that the Negro should be spared the lash of brutality and coarse degradation, but it had never been truly committed to helping him out of poverty, exploitation or all forms of discrimination."[15] Furthermore, many of his white allies "had quietly disappeared."[16]

Alas, even before the ink was dry on the two landmark civil rights acts, it was evident that a tide of counterrevolution had emerged. The handwriting was on the wall that these laws would themselves die a slow death. It is testimony to King's acumen as a politician that he could see that "the inevitable counterrevolution that succeeds every period of progress is taking place."[17]

RACIAL PROGRESS: TALE OF TWO DATA POINTS

In 1984, Alphonso Pinkney, a sociologist at Hunter College, published a book under the title *The Myth of Black Progress*. His preface began as follows:

> Reports of the ongoing oppression of Afro-Americans are commonplace: In 1983 a five-year-old Black child was murdered in California by a white police officer who claimed that the child had a handgun; four Blacks were indiscriminately killed by New Orleans police offers following the murder of a white police officer; a Black transit worker was killed by a white mob in Brooklyn as he stopped with coworkers in a delicatessen for food; white voters refused to support well-qualified Black candidates; the Black candidate for mayor of Chicago, along with a Democratic candidate for president, was refused permission to speak by a crowd of white racists at a Roman Catholic church on Palm Sunday; spokespersons for the administration continued to take positions opposed to the aspirations of Blacks; twice as many Black adults were unemployed as whites and among teenagers it was three Blacks for every white; Little Rock resegregated its schools because of white boycotts.[18]

Pinkney conceded that racism was "less visible and vocal" than in times past, but it remained "an ever-present part of the American way of life."[19]

This was not the prevalent view at the time. As Pinkney observed: "We are bombarded with books and articles, by Blacks and whites, claiming that in this country race is no longer a salient variable in relations between Blacks and whites."[20] And if we leapfrog three decades to the election of Donald Trump on an unabashedly racist policy agenda, it behooves us to ask whether Blacks had been making progress or, on the contrary, falling behind. Or is it the case that, as Ibram Kendi asserts, *both* racists and anti-racists have made progress?

In his recent bestseller, *Enlightenment Now*, Steven Pinker, a psychology professor at Harvard University, reassures his readers that contrary to the prevailing mood, the world is not coming to an end.[21] He amasses data from a plethora of sources that prove that people are living longer, healthier, freer, and happier lives. I wondered whether Pinker would also present a rosy picture of inequality, the Achilles' heel of optimists. Alas, he does not disappoint. He reports that at the turn of the twentieth century, there was an average of three lynchings a week, but today "racially motivated killings of Blacks occur at a rate of zero to one per year." However, the recent scourge of racially motivated killings of Blacks obviously belie Pinker's rosy claims of racial progress.

Pinker then reached deeper into his potpourri of feel-good statistics. He found that whereas only 4 percent of Americans approved of marriages between Blacks and whites in 1958, the figure today soars to over 87 percent, one of the largest shifts of public opinion in Gallup history. By this twisted logic, racism is a thing of the past, and the congenital pessimists of the Black Lives Matter movement should take cheer in knowing that they can marry 87 out of 100 white partners! And readers should take heart that Bill Gates has blurbed that Pinker's frivolous book is his "new favorite book of all time."

This specious use of statistics should alert us to the pitfalls of relying on statistics to assess the extent of Black progress. For our purposes here, I will review the findings of the Economic Policy Institute, which issued a report in 2018 titled *50 Years after the Kerner Commission*.[22] The context for this commission was the 1968 assassination of Martin Luther King Jr., which unleashed a score of protests across the nation, including major conflagrations in Newark and Detroit. President Johnson appointed the commission ostensibly to investigate "the causes of the riots." According to his chief speechwriter, LBJ came up with his own report card: "I've moved the Negro from D+ to C−. He's still nowhere. He knows it. And that's why he's out in the streets. Hell, I'd be there, too."[23] This was an unmistakable message, from the bottom up, that passing laws did not go far enough in addressing the deep inequalities that beg for major policy initiatives.

It is an open secret that presidential commissions are commonly appointed to buy time, to cool tempers, to assuage grief, and "to appear to be doing something, while actually doing nothing."[24] However, the report issued by the Kerner Commission came as a surprise. Instead of blaming Blacks for violence and mayhem, the report was a radical departure from past commissions.

The Kerner Commission Report made history for two unexpected pronouncements:

> What white Americans have never fully understood—but what the Negro can never forget—is that white society is deeply implicated in the ghetto. . . . White institutions created it, white institutions maintain it, and white society condones it.
>
> Our nation is moving toward two societies, one Black, and one white—separate and unequal.

To his credit, Kerner did something that is uncommon for the head of a presidential commission. According to Jill Lepore, the author of a recent history of the Kerner Report, when the commission travelled and garnered media attention, "Kerner went out on the street to talk to people." Here is an example:

> He went for a walk in Newark and stopped to speak to a group around the corner from Prince Street. They told him they had three concerns: police brutality, unemployment, and the lack of a relocation program for displaced workers. One man told the Governor that he hadn't had a job in eight years.[25]

What a revolutionary turn of events. He listened rather than pontificated, and instead of casting blame, he engaged the perspective of the actors themselves: the "rioters" who elicit headlines in newspapers but whose life experiences and point of view are rarely considered. So here we are, fifty years after the original Kerner Commission, still scratching our heads regarding the "causes of the riots."

Enter the Economic Policy Institute, nominally a nonprofit, nonpartisan think tank, founded in 1986 by a group of prominent economists with progressive credentials. Its report *50 Years after the Kerner Commission* began with the good news: lower rates of infant mortality, longer life expectancy (at least if you are not a Black male), and significantly higher rates of high school and college graduation.

Now the bad news: "With respect to homeownership, unemployment, and incarceration, America has failed to deliver any progress for African Americans over the last five decades." Especially vexing is why the increases "in the absolute levels of formal education would not translate into large improvements in economic and related outcomes for African Americans." Let me answer this question with a couple of questions: To what extent does this anomaly reflect the fact that these graduates confront a wall of discrimination in labor markets everywhere? And to what extent does this reflect the impact of the effective gutting of affirmative action by a revanchist Supreme Court?

The most startling racial disparity is in terms of family wealth, a measure of family assets, including wealth derived from earnings and home ownership. In 1968, the typical Black family had almost no wealth: $2,467, to be exact. However, in 2018, "the figure is about six times larger ($17,409), but it is still not that far from zero" when considering mounting costs for children's college education and other routine expenses.

These paltry gains are also related to mass incarceration. The "war on drugs" during the 1960s and the passage of the crime bill in 1994, signed by Bill Clinton, with provisions like "three strikes and you're out," greatly increased incarceration, especially among Black and Latinx men. The number in prison or jail nearly tripled between 1968 and 2016 (from 604 per 100,000 to 1,730 per 100,000). This in turn had devastating consequences for families, increasing joblessness and poverty.

To return to the question I raised earlier, Was the civil rights revolution a revolution in name only? On the one hand, it was a monumental success insofar as it brought an end to the reign of terror in the South and the degrading segregation in schools and other public spaces. On the other hand, as Derrick Bell averred in the epigraph at the beginning of the chapter, other avenues were adapted to maintain white domination. What else is the wanton killing of Blacks by police than lynching in another name?

Furthermore, it was only a matter of time before segregation in schools, housing, and employment reverted to old ways. Indeed, the "crown jewel" of the civil rights movement—the right to vote—has been defiled by the Supreme Court, using artifices that existed under Jim Crow. The familiar adage that "we've come a long way, but we have a long way to go" might be stated in reverse: "We made a lot of progress, but much of it has been rolled back."

The bottom line is that Black wealth is still "not far from zero." Indeed, what else was the scandal of the 2008 foreclosure crisis, in which over 240,000 Blacks lost their homes, than a looting of the Black middle class? And it was exacerbated by the 2014 subprime scandal, which, according to Natalie Baptiste, led to another "staggering loss of Black wealth.[26]

In 2020, the Economic Policy Institute published another study under the banner headline "Black Workers Face Two of the Most Lethal Preexisting Conditions for Coronavirus—Racism and Economic Inequality." Its overall argument was that "persistent racial disparities in health status, access to health care, wealth, employment, wages, housing, income, and poverty all contribute to greater susceptibility to the virus— both economically and physically."[27] Aside from the loss of jobs, Blacks were disproportionately in the ranks of essential workers in front-line jobs, "forcing them to risk their own and their families' health to earn a living." Households headed by Black women were especially precarious since they were less likely to have multiple earners. In addition, Black workers were less likely to have life insurance and more likely to have preexisting health conditions. And they were less likely to have cash reserves to draw on, and more likely to live in densely populated housing.

Overall, Blacks make up 12 percent of the U.S. population but account for 22 percent of COVID-19 deaths. In short, the pandemic has brought to light "the ongoing legacy of racism that continues to produce unequal outcomes affecting nearly every aspect of life in the United States."[28]

To repeat, if this is "progress," it is the progress of a people on a historical treadmill.

CHAPTER THIRTEEN

SYSTEMIC RACISM

The Elephant in the Room

The Black revolution is much more than a struggle for the rights of Negroes. It is forcing America to face all its interrelated flaws—racism, poverty, militarism, and materialism. It is exposing evils that are rooted deeply in the whole structure of our society. It reveals systemic rather than superficial flaws and suggests that radical reconstruction of society is the real issue to be faced.

Martin Luther King Jr., "A Testament of Hope," 1969[1]

If we are to have a true reckoning with race, we must challenge white comfort in all its valence and cadence. . . . Most every entity whose name ends in the word "system" has been used to methodically exclude Black bodies and to prevent Black wellbeing—while providing comfort to the white masses.

Michael Eric Dyson, *Long Time Coming*, 2020[2]

In the aftermath of George Floyd's 2020 murder at the hands of the Minneapolis police and the ensuing avalanche of protest, a terminology previously deployed by professional sociologists reentered political discourse: *systemic racism*, or its facsimile, *structural racism*. These terms are the conceptual flip side of the race relations paradigm, a prevailing discourse that regarded racism as a system of distorted or hostile beliefs harbored by the dominant group, visited on disparaged minorities, and perpetuated from one generation to the next.

In the prosaic language of the race relations paradigm, the roots of prejudice begin in childhood. As Gordon Allport wrote in his 1954 study *The Nature of Prejudice*:

> As early as the age of five, a child is capable of understanding that he is a member of various groups. He is capable, for example, of a sense of ethnic identification. Until he is nine or ten he will not be able to understand just what his membership signifies—how for example, Jews differ from gentiles or Quakers from Methodists, but he does not wait for this understanding before he develops fierce in-group loyalties.[3]

Prejudice in turn leads to discrimination—that is, to deleterious acts that deprive minorities of access to employment, housing, and education. The remedy, or so it was held, was education, which would disabuse people of these distorted and malicious beliefs and cultivate racial harmony. The trouble with this simplistic model is that it turned a blind eye to the systemic and structural manifestations of prejudice and discrimination, which are rooted in systems of domination and exploitation.

In her 2015 book *From Power to Prejudice*, Leah Gordon shows how a discourse tagged as "racial individualism" evolved in the decades after World War II, in the shadow of the Holocaust:

> Bringing together psychological individualism, rights-based individualism, and belief in the socially transformative power of education, racial individualism presented prejudice and discrimination as the root cause of racial conflict, focused on individuals in the study of race relations, and suggested that racial justice could be attained by changing white minds and protecting African American rights. This social theory and agenda for change grew in influence between the publication of Gunnar Myrdal's *An American Dilemma* in 1944 and the passage of the Civil Rights Act in 1964.[4]

Ironically, long before the emergence of racial individualism in the 1940s, there were robust discourses that theorized racism from the perspective of political economy. Karl Marx, W. E. B. Du Bois, and Oliver Cox developed incisive theories that examined race and racism within the framework of capitalism and the role that Black labor played in the production and reproduction of racial hierarchy. Indeed, Cox dismissed racial individualism with one devastating salvo: "If beliefs per se could oppress a people, then the beliefs that Negroes have about whites should be as effective as the beliefs that whites hold about Negroes."[5]

In the decades after passage of the Civil Rights Acts of 1964 and 1965, theories of political economy reemerged with renewed force. In the 1970s, Martin Luther King's strategy of nonviolent protest was superseded by a more militant phase that included violent protest. The larger context was the struggles for national liberation in the Third World. No longer was racism sugarcoated as merely distorted ideas that could be remedied through education. No longer could race experts promulgate the notion that racism was a psychological aberration that could be remedied through education.

Indeed, during the 1960s, civil rights activists and movement leaders had gained a new respectability and had written books eagerly published by major publishing houses. Among the celebrated writers were James Baldwin, Ralph Ellison, Richard Wright, Lorraine Hansberry, Malcolm X, Eldridge Cleaver, Julius Lester, Stokely Carmichael (renamed Kwame Ture), and countless other movement leaders who found eager audiences for their books. In 1969 the *New York Times Book Review* declared that there was a "Black revolution in books."[6] Race, for so long a taboo subject, was at the center of literary and political discourse.

Given the fact that race relations was a designated field of inquiry in sociology, one might have thought that sociologists would be in the forefront of the seismic changes that were taking place in the society at large. This was far from the case. If anything, these men and women of science, precisely because they were wedded to an outdated paradigm, were slow to recognize, much less engage the shifting political terrain.

The single most important book that challenged the prevailing race relations paradigm was Bob Blauner's 1970 publication *Racial Oppression in America*. By foregrounding "racial oppression," the title itself marked a break from the prevailing orthodoxy. It is noteworthy that Bob was a doctoral student in sociology in the late '50s and received his PhD at Berkeley in 1962, just as the student movement was gaining steam. In retrospect, he was the right person, in the right place, at the right time, in that he challenged established orthodoxies on racism and broke new ground. I once asked him, naively, how he came to embrace the word *oppression*, and he responded, with characteristic diffidence: "I don't know. *Oppression* was a word that was bandied about a lot in radical circles." A glaring understatement!

In the opening pages of *Racial Oppression in America*, Blauner states that his book owed little or nothing to the race relations dogma:

> Virtually all the new insights about racism and the experience of the oppressed have been provided by writers whose lives and minds were uncluttered by sociological theory. Probably the best have come from outside the academic establishment entirely—for example, *The Autobiography of Malcolm X* and Harold Cruse's *The Crisis of the Negro Intellectual*. . . . The most valuable products of the sociological method have been case studies rather than theoretical understanding—for example, E. Franklin Frazier's *Black Bourgeoisie* and Elliot Liebow's *Tally's Corner*.[7]

According to Blauner, the emergence of the civil rights movement "took sociology by surprise" and "exposed the depth and pervasiveness of racism in a society that appeared, on the surface, to be moving toward equality."[8] He added sardonically, "There were still sociologists celebrating the impressive decline in racial prejudice at the very moment that Watts burst into flames."[9] One can see the parallels between the political embers in the 1970s and the awakening following the murder of George Floyd in 2020.

In another footnote, Blauner makes the case for "a systematic theory of social oppression":

> For a number of intellectual and political reasons, including the rejection of Marxist perspectives, sociologists were caught short without a

systematic theory of social oppression, one that could stipulate the conditions under which oppressed groups would challenge their long-standing subjugation.[10]

He follows with a key distinction that is still lost on sociologists who are fixated on the subjective dimensions of racial victimization: "The distinction between racism as an objective phenomenon, located in the actual existence of domination and hierarchy, and racism's subjective concomitants of prejudice and other motivations and feelings is a basic one." At the same time, Blauner warns against economic reductionism—namely, the tendency on the part of radical theorists and liberal policy makers to "reduce race to class."[11]

One can readily see from these passages how Blauner's groundbreaking book vitiated the "racial individualism" of previous generations, which had "assumed that this movement toward equality depended primarily on the reduction of prejudice in the white majority, rather than upon the collective actions of the oppressed groups themselves or upon basic transformations in the society."[12] This deeply flawed paradigm had left sociology and the society at large unprepared to grasp, much less address the escalating forces that were tearing the nation apart. Note, however, that Blauner was not forging a wholly new paradigm so much as reclaiming and reconceptualizing the pioneering scholarship advanced generations earlier by Marx, Du Bois, and Cox.

THE STRANGE CAREER OF SYSTEMIC RACISM

In the aftermath of the murder of George Floyd, the concept of systemic racism entered popular and political discourses with the Black Lives Matter movement. This new political formation originated in the summer of 2013 after the acquittal of George Zimmerman for the death of Trayvon Martin and was consolidated after the police murder of Michael Brown in 2014. However, it was not until the killing of George Floyd in 2020 that support for BLM galvanized with mass public protest. This is a prime example of how marginal political groups sometimes lay the groundwork for political mobilization that comes to fruition when the conditions are favorable.[13]

The leaders of the BLM movement seized the moment and were conscious of the fact "reform" was woefully inadequate to address the persistent and pervasive racial wrongs. A startling example is the stop-and-frisk practice, involving over five million incidents targeted at Black and Latinx men in New York City, notwithstanding its claim as a citadel of tolerance.[14] Another example is the phenomenon dubbed "driving while Black," the ironic tag for the disproportionate surveillance and ticketing of Black drivers.[15] Equally egregious are the institutionalized practices of "aggressive policing" that are both humiliating and a patent violation of civil rights.

The Michael Brown case in Ferguson, Missouri, exposed insidious police misconduct against Blacks in low-income neighborhoods who were targeted for minor traffic offenses, including suspended licenses. Under the guise of public safety, fees and fines were levied upon people who could afford them least. As the costs mounted, people were subject to arrest, which incurred still further penalties. Furthermore, these revenues were used to balance municipal budgets, including bloated police departments. Small wonder that the Black Lives Matter movement has spearheaded a demand to defund police departments.

According to an incisive study conducted by law professors at Saint Louis University Law School, "police and municipal courts were using a racially discriminatory and regressive local tax system that violates the tax limitations of the Missouri constitutions."[16] These examples are merely the tip of an iceberg. We need look no further than the burgeoning system of mass incarceration that consigns young Black men and women to upstate prisons located in remote areas that separate them from their families. The final straw is that these prisons then function as a boon to economically depressed rural communities.[17]

Generally speaking, the concept of systemic racism is a lexical attempt to make sense of the despicable abuses visited upon African Americans, which are reminiscent of the "Black codes" that were invented in the aftermath of the Civil War.

As I argue in the opening chapters of this book, the passage of civil rights legislation was the high point of the Black struggle for rights, and we have been going downhill ever since. Here we are, more than one hundred and fifty years after the Civil War and almost sixty years after the landmark civil rights legislation in the mid-1960s, still running in place. Without doubt, one can cite progress. However, to again paraphrase James Baldwin, we cannot use the crimes of the past to gloss over the crimes of the present. Nor can we claim progress when an entire people are traumatized with the fear that the local police department will unleash lethal violence on their children.

With that in mind, it behooves us to ask what the connective tissue is among police departments across the nation. In the aftermath of the public uprising over the killing of George Floyd, liberals were left scratching their heads in disbelief that these events continued unabated, in defiance of public condemnation.

One explanation is found in a 2017 report in *The Intercept*, an online news publication, whose banner headline reads: "The FBI Has Quietly Investigated White Supremacist Infiltration of Law Enforcement."[18] According to journalist Alice Speri, in 2006 a heavily redacted version of FBI intelligence found that white supremacist groups had been "infiltrating law enforcement communities or recruiting law enforcement personnel." Furthermore, "law enforcement had recently become aware of the term 'ghost skins,' used among white supremacists to describe 'those who avoid overt displays of their beliefs to blend into society and covertly advance white supremacist causes.'"[19]

More is involved here than "bad actors." Because of the qualified immunity that shields police from personal liability for actions within the scope of their jobs, the deck is stacked against any prosecution, no matter how egregious or violent the police behavior. Ironically, officers with supremacist proclivities are protected by First Amendment rights and therefore are hard to identity, much less prosecute.

According to reporting in *The Intercept*, after the election of Barack Obama in 2009, an intelligence study by the Department of Homeland Security in coordination with the FBI warned of a resurgence of right-wing extremism. White supremacists had infiltrated the ranks of police departments; the report "singled out the Oath Keepers and the Constitutional

Sheriffs and Peace Officers Association for their anti-government attitudes and efforts to recruit active as well as retired law enforcement officers."[20] The *Intercept* article concludes on the following note:

> For some reason, we have stepped away from the threat of domestic ter-
> rorism and right-wing extremism. The only way we can reconcile this
> kind of behavior is if we accept the possibility that the ideology that per-
> meates white nationalists and white supremacists is something that many
> in our federal and law enforcement communities understand and may be
> in sympathy with.[21]

Fortunately, the concept of systematic racism has been resuscitated by
leaders of the Black Lives Matter movement. Although this term has its
origins in academic discourses, as I show below, it has not received the
centrality that it deserves among "race experts" who too often are preoccupied with minutiae and avoid the big picture. All the more credit to
the leaders of the Black Lives Matter movement for bringing the discursive argument of systemic racism into current political discourses..

JOE FEAGIN'S THEORY OF SYSTEMIC RACISM

Given the recent reincarnation of the concept of systemic racism in public discourses, it behooves us to revisit a 2006 book by Joe Feagin titled
Systemic Racism: A Theory of Oppression. A few biographical details are
in order. Feagin grew up in Houston, Texas. After graduating from Baylor
University in 1960, he earned his PhD at Harvard and was the scholar-in-
residence at the U.S. Civil Rights Commission in 1974–1975. In 2000 he
was elected president of the American Sociological Association, and his
presidential address was titled "Social Justice and Sociology in the 21st
Century." Feagin is author of scores of books on race, many coauthored
with doctoral students whom he mentored at Texas A&M University,
where he is a distinguished professor. He is also the pioneer, along with
Jesse Daniels, of a blog, *The Racism Review*, which is a forum for students, scholars, journalists, and activists for debating racial issues.[22]

In the opening pages of *Systemic Racism*, Feagin offers this rebuke to
mainstream sociologists for their methodological reductionism and their

studious neglect of "the big picture" of racism in American history and society:

> Missing in both the mainstream and race-ethnic relations approach and much of the racial formation approaches is a full recognition of the big picture—the reality of this whole society being founded on, and firmly grounded in, oppression targeting African Americans (and other Americans of color) now for several centuries.[23]

The thrust of *Systemic Racism* is to undercut the methodological reductionism of mainstream sociology and to provide a broad history and analysis of systematic racism across the span of American history.

Nor does Feagin consign slavery and Jim Crow to the distant past:

> Evaluating the contemporary United States, we see that systemic racism has in some ways changed significantly from the racialized patterns of slavery and legal segregation, yet in certain fundamentals—such as the enduring racial hierarchy, persisting white-imposed discrimination, and white privilege and advantage in all major institutional areas—systemic racism today remains rather similar to the systemic racism of earlier eras.[24]

In Feagin's epistemology, racism is not an attribute of "sociological individualism" but rather is a highly structured and enduring system of domination that reduces the life chances of an entire people across the span of American history.

Let us examine the relevance of the concept of systemic racism to the exigencies of the current moment.

Feagin presents us with a startling paradox. Whites as a group have never been the staunchest defenders of liberty, equality, and social justice. Rather, it is African Americans who "have been at the forefront of those pressing strongly and organized aggressively *within this country* for these ideals to be put into practice."[25] Put another way, it is not the perpetrator but rather the victim who has been the champion of democratic ideals.

In this context, Feagin delivers a stinging rebuke to John Rawls, the illustrious American philosopher who exalted liberty and equality.[26] The trouble with such noble precepts is that they are pitifully contradicted by the omnipresence of systemic racism. As Feagin puts it: "Equal liberties do not exist where there is still widespread discrimination in employment, housing, public accommodations, and schooling, and where the substantial socioeconomic inequalities of this society are neither beneficial to disadvantaged Americans of color nor the result of an equality of opportunities."[27]

Finally, Feagin leaves the reader with this illuminating quote from W. E. B. Du Bois, reminding us of the extent to which African Americans have provided the inspiration and defense of American democracy:

> It was the rise and growth among the slaves of a determination to be free and an active part of American democracy that forced American democracy to look into the depths. . . . One cannot think of democracy in America or in the modern world without reference to the American Negro.[28]

CHAPTER FOURTEEN

BRING BACK AFFIRMATIVE ACTION

Why have the Republicans been so much more effective at dragging the
judicial branch rightward than Democrats have been in yanking it back?

Dahlia Lithwick, *Washington Monthly*, 2012[1]

Affirmative action is *about* history: the exclusion of whole groups from
entire job sectors for all of American history. This needs to be under-
scored because so much of affirmative action discourse lapses into facile
reductionism: Whether individuals should be penalized for crimes that
they did not commit. Whether it is fair to give preference to the son of a
Black doctor over the daughter of a white garbage collector. Whether affirmative action engenders feeling of inferiority among its recipients. And
whether, as Justice Scalia quipped, we are using the disease as the cure.

To repeat, when we take up the issue of affirmative action, we are
dealing with the exclusion of whole groups from entire job sectors for
all of American history. Nor is this a matter of random incidents of "discrimination." This tepid word fails to capture the scope and cumulative
harm wrought by these individual acts of racism. A more effective term
would be *occupational apartheid*—a term that also provides the warrant
for affirmative action, whose purpose is to eliminate the monopoly that
privileged groups have on coveted jobs and opportunities.

In *When Affirmative Action Was White*, Ira Katznelson shows how whites reaped the benefits of affirmative action as a matter of white privilege. Specifically, he documents how the federal government systematically excluded Blacks from social programs enacted during the Depression: Social Security, unemployment compensation, the minimum wage, the right of workers to join labor unions, and the GI Bill of Rights. To make matters worse, Southern Congressional leaders spearheaded legislation to administer these programs locally, thereby drastically curtailing benefits to African Americans. Imagine the impact of the GI Bill alone, which provided white veterans with college loans, job training, and other programs that helped them to purchase their first homes. Thanks to occupational apartheid, Blacks were written out of the American Dream from the outset of the welfare state.[2]

In its original incarnation, affirmative action programs were targeted to increase Black representation in education and job markets. This began with court decisions in the early 1970s affirming the constitutionality of the Philadelphia Plan and ended with a series of Supreme Court rulings in the late 1980s that essentially gutted affirmative action policy. By July 2003, the title of the cover story of *The Black Commentator* was a lament: "The Slow and Tortured Death of Affirmative Action." The subtitle was equally blunt: "Redress of Racial Wrongs No Longer Public Policy."[3]

THE FALLACIES OF ANTI-AFFIRMATIVE-ACTION DISCOURSE
One would have to go back to the discourses over slavery to find such an outpouring of misguided erudition, of philosophical treatises by learned scholars that elide elemental truths or obscure these truths behind a smokescreen of sophistry and obfuscation.

Given that the political Right has played such a prominent role in the crusade against affirmative action, it would be easy to blame them for the dismantling of affirmative action. In point of fact, much of the culpability rests with liberals and leftists—those proverbial "friends of the Negro." Not only have they equivocated or defaulted in the struggle to save affirmative action policy, but as I show below, most of the earliest and most vehement opposition came from the ranks of liberals. As was discussed in chapter 3, long before the phrase *affirmative action* entered the political lexicon, opposition came from an unexpected quarter: namely, Jewish liberals at *Commentary* magazine who forged an anti-affirmative-action discourse that later was appropriated by conservatives. Not only did conservatives stoke popular antagonism to the evolving affirmative action policy, but as Nancy MacLean has shown, they used this issue to resuscitate conservatism from a long period of senescence and decline, making it a potent rival for political hegemony.[4]

The extent of bad faith and spineless capitulation on the part of the liberal/left is not only deplorable, but it had dire political consequences. Here we can take a lesson from history. As Reconstruction unraveled at the end of the nineteenth century, Southern Redemptionists gloated that "all the fire has gone out of the Northern philanthropic fight for the rights of man."[5] Unfortunately, historians will look back on the end of the Second Reconstruction and conclude that liberals were again complicit in the restoration of the status quo ante.

Admittedly, affirmative action is difficult to justify in terms of abstract principle. It *does* classify individuals on the basis of race and gender. It *does* conflict with the cardinal principle of the civil rights movement itself: a colorblind society. It *does* institute a system of preferences that evoke distaste and *seems* to conflict with democratic principles. We might even echo the defenders of slavery by conceding that affirmative action is "a necessary evil," one made necessary by over three centuries of legal segregation that left Blacks at an unfair disadvantage. Simply put, affirmative action is one way of "leveling the playing field."

In *The Racial Contract*, Charles Mills argues that alongside the social contract at the center of Western political thought is an unacknowledged racial contract that provides the framework for the white supremacist state. Like donning a new pair of glasses, recognition of this racial contract casts American political institutions in a wholly different light. Mills writes:

> The "Racial Contract" throws open the doors of orthodox political philosophy's hermetically sealed, stuffy little universe and lets the world rush into its sterile white halls, a world populated not by abstract citizens but by white, black, brown, yellow, red beings, interacting with, pretending not to see, categorizing, judging, negotiating, allying, exploiting,

struggling with each other in large measure according to race—the world, in short, in which we all actually live.[6]

Thus, to talk about affirmative action, we need to talk about the world in which we actually live: a society riven by race and a system of occupational apartheid drawn along racial and gender lines. To repeat, we must confront the brute reality of whole groups excluded from entire job sectors for all of American history. How else can we salvage American democracy from its hypocrisy and contradictions?

AFFIRMATIVE ACTION AS DRAMATURGY

The historical trajectory of affirmative action resembles the dramatic arc of a play: rising action, climax leading to crisis, and the tragic denouement.

1. Prologue: "Compensatory Programs," 1963-1965

It is too often forgotten that the nation's vaunted democratic institutions utterly failed to rectify the monumental injustices of the Jim Crow era until the rise of a grassroots insurgency in the South, and even then, not until the entire society was thrown into crisis. Moreover, as important as the 1964 and 1965 Civil Rights Acts were, they only restored rights that had supposedly been guaranteed by the Reconstruction Amendments a century earlier but had been effectively nullified in the 1890s. The question we must confront is whether the nation is repeating history with the gutting of affirmative action—that is, wiping out in the 1980s and the ensuing decades rights that were won in the 1960s and 1970s.

As is often pointed out, the civil rights revolution was about "liberty," not "equality." It nominally conferred the rights of citizenship on Blacks, but it did nothing to address the deep inequalities that were the legacy of two centuries of slavery and a century of Jim Crow. Martin Luther King reminded readers that "the practical cost of change for the nation up to this point has been cheap. The limited reforms have been obtained at bargain rates."[7] The rallying cry for the 1965 March on Washington was "For Jobs and Freedom," with the implication that without jobs, freedom is an empty promise. As King wrote in 1968, "What good is it to be able to eat in a restaurant if you can't afford a hamburger?"[8]

The upshot of this conceptual shift from liberty to equality was a demand for "compensatory treatment" in jobs and education. In 1963—a year before passage of the 1964 Civil Rights Act and a decade before affirmative action evolved as policy—this idea was debated in the *New York Times Magazine* under the title "Should There Be 'Compensation' for Negroes?"[9] Whitney Young was arguing that the enormous gap in incomes and living standards required some kind of "special effort" to open up job opportunities for Blacks.[10] Already on the defensive, he grumbled that this reasonable demand was obfuscated with scare phrases like "preferential treatment" that "go against the grain of our native sense of fair play." The "no" side was argued by Kyle Haselden, an editor at *Christian Century*, who struck the chord that later would emerge as the keynote of anti-affirmative-action discourse: "Compensation for Negroes is a subtle but pernicious form of racism."[11]

By 1963 the words *compensation, reparations,* and *preference* had already crept into the nation's political discourse. Indeed, this issue rapidly fractured liberals into opposing camps. Some liberals pledged their support. A notable example was Charles Silberman, an editor at *Fortune* magazine, whose book, *Crisis in Black and White* appeared on the *New York Times* best-seller list for ten weeks in 1964. Silberman wrote:

> If those who make the decisions in this country are really sincere about closing the gaps, they must go further than fine impartiality. We must have, in fact, special consideration if we are to compensate for the scars left by 300 years of deprivation.[12]

However, other white liberals were troubled by this turn of events. "Wherever this issue of compensatory or preferential treatment of the Negro is raised, some of our friends recoil in horror," King observed in *Why We Can't Wait*. "The Negro should be granted equality, they agree, but he should ask for nothing more."[13] King's statement, penned in 1963, was tragically prescient. The underlying message of the crusade against affirmative action, waged over the past half century, is that the nation has gone as far as it is willing to go by passing landmark civil rights legislation that restored elementary civil rights.

2. The Plot Thickens: The Philadelphia Plan, 1969

Affirmative action was never formulated as a coherent policy, but evolved through a series of presidential executive orders, administrative policies, and court rulings, all reflecting shifting political currents.[14] It began with executive orders issued by Presidents Kennedy and Johnson, directing government contractors to take "affirmative action" to end discrimination in hiring. But these orders lacked enforcement power and were generally ineffective. By far the most important initiative was the Philadelphia Plan, initially drawn up by faceless bureaucrats in Lyndon Johnson's Department of Labor, shelved after Humphrey's defeat in 1968, only to be resurrected soon after Richard Nixon took office in 1969.

The unsung heroes of affirmative action are Arthur Fletcher, the Black assistant secretary of labor, who has laid claim to the title of "father of affirmative action"; his boss, George Shultz, who provided indispensable support; Attorney General John Mitchell, who successfully defended the Revised Philadelphia Plan before the appellate court in 1969; and Nixon himself, who not only backed the plan but also risked a great deal of political capital in rallying Congressional Republicans to defeat a move by Democrats to kill the plan before it could be implemented. Strangely, throughout this period, particularly during the crucial Congressional debate, the Philadelphia Plan received only equivocal support from civil rights leaders, and it faced fierce opposition from labor and liberals.

There has been much speculation about why Nixon backed the Philadelphia Plan, and rightly so. After all, he was elected on the basis of a Southern strategy that appealed to the white backlash, and he promptly nominated two white supremacists to the Supreme Court, both of whom were rejected by the predominantly Democratic Senate. Some contemporaneous opponents to the Philadelphia Plan, including Bayard Rustin, regarded Nixon's action as a cunning ploy to break up the liberal coalition by driving a wedge between the civil rights movement and organized labor and Jews, both of whom regarded affirmative action as antithetical to their respective interests.[15]

This reasoning was later given academic respectability by historian Hugh Davis Graham, author of the influential *The Civil Rights Era*. According to Graham, as Nixon pondered Shultz's proposal to resurrect the

Philadelphia Plan, he was swayed by "the delicious prospect of setting organized labor and the civil rights establishment at each other's Democratic throats."[16] Elsewhere Graham has written: "Nixon wanted to drive a wedge between Blacks and organized labor—between the Democrats' social activists of the 1960s and the party's traditional economic liberals—that would fragment the New Deal coalition."[17]

This, I submit, is a fallacious version of history. It has been repeated so often that it has assumed the dimensions of a myth, invoked by liberals to camouflage their default on affirmative action. Let me suggest another explanation for Nixon's dogged support for the Philadelphia Plan.

During the summer of 1969 there was an eruption of highly publicized demonstrations by Blacks protesting discrimination in the construction trades. For documentary proof, we need go no further than Graham's *The Civil Rights Era*:

> In Chicago, job protests launched by a coalition of Black neighborhood organizations shut down twenty-three South Side construction projects involving $85 million in contracts. . . . The demonstrations in Pittsburgh were more violent than in Chicago, but were similarly organized and focused on job discrimination in construction. One clash in Pittsburgh in late August left 50 Black protestors and 12 policemen injured. . . . Racial violence over jobs occurred in Seattle, and Black coalitions announced job protest drives for New York, Cleveland, Detroit, Milwaukee, and Boston.[18]

Whatever political calculations led Nixon to back Fletcher's proposal to resurrect the Philadelphia Plan, one thing is clear: without pressure from below, the plan would have remained in the Labor Department's files, where it had been deposited by the outgoing Democratic administration.

As Graham claims, Nixon had little to lose by "sticking it to the Democratic unions." Furthermore, against the background of the war in Vietnam, Nixon had political reason to defuse Black protest, lest he find himself confronted with a second front at home. Consider, too the larger historical context. Nixon came to power at a juncture when liberalism was in decline and conservatism was ascendant, and he oscillated

between these two poles throughout his administration.[19] For example, in
the wake of the civil rights revolution and the spiral of "riots" following
King's 1968 assassination, highlighted by the Kerner Commission Report
with its far-reaching recommendations for national action, Nixon sought
to mollify the violent protests emanating from the Black community.

Despite appearances to the contrary, Fletcher's advocacy for a revised
Philadelphia Plan was consonant with core tenets of Republican ideology. Consider Fletcher's own account:

> I decided to go ahead with the Philadelphia Plan of putting specifications
> of minority employment goals in all contracts. I did this because my study
> and experience had convinced me that such targets were essential if we
> are to measure results in terms of minority employment. Without such
> targets, the paper compliance, and the indeterminable ineffectiveness of
> the government programs would go on. I had not come to Washington
> to preside over the continuation of the ineffective programs of the past.[20]

The Philadelphia Plan was ideologically congenial to Republicans in that
it envisioned no new government programs, no make-work schemes, and
no major public expenditures. Instead it looked to the private economy
to lead the nation out of its racial morass. Thus, the claim that Nixon
revived the Philadelphia Plan as a Machiavellian ploy to fragment the
liberal coalition is patent nonsense. Nixon backed Arthur Fletcher's proposal because it allowed him to preempt the liberal agenda on civil rights
with a policy predicated on contract compliance.

However—and this is where Graham's theory has some credence—
once the Philadelphia Plan was enacted, it triggered fierce opposition
from labor and many liberals, as well as from "Nixon Democrats" and
hardhats who had been instrumental in his election. The Philadelphia
Plan had become a political liability. What did Nixon do? He did an
about-face and attached the very "quotas" that he previously endorsed.

This was also the context in which Daniel Patrick Moynihan, in his
capacity as adviser to the president, issued his infamous call for "benign
neglect." In 1970 Nixon reached out to the building-trades unions to
mend fences. "Professing agreement with them on the need for 'voluntary' approaches," as historian MacLean writes, "the administration

backpedaled from the Philadelphia Plan and promised no 'undue zeal' in putting it into practice." The Philadelphia Plan was doomed, at least as far as the Nixon Administration was concerned. According to MacLean, "within one year of its proclamation word spread that it [the Philadelphia Plan] was to die a quiet death."[21]

3. Climax: The Golden Years of Affirmative Action, 1972-1988

Notwithstanding the mounting popular backlash, affirmative action was destined to live and even flourish before succumbing to a slow and tortured death. The die was cast when John Mitchell's Department of Justice successfully defended the Philadelphia Plan in the federal courts. By 1972 affirmative action mandates were extended to over three hundred thousand firms doing business with the government, thus covering approximately half the non-farm private sector workforce.[22] This was the inception of affirmative action as we know it.

No more efficient mechanism has ever existed for influencing employment practices and outcomes on such a large scale. However, one by-product of the extension of affirmative action mandates to all government contractors was that colleges and universities were included under the umbrella of affirmative action, and therefore subject to contract compliance reviews by the Office of Federal Contract Compliance. One of the ironies of affirmative action is that it elicited far more heated opposition in the university than in the business world. According to John Skrentny, "businesses, if left alone, do not seem to mind hiring by the numbers, or at least giving the appearance of compliance."[23] Of course, in the business world, where hiring is on a larger scale, it is easier to implement goals and timetables. In contrast, hiring decisions in the university are decentralized among a score of academic departments. Besides, despite its liberal pretensions, the university is notorious as a site of class privilege and snobbery. Just as northern liberals supported integration so long as it meant integrating schools and public accommodations in the South, liberal elites supported affirmative action until it encroached on their institutional turf and threatened their entrenched prerogatives.

Thus, affirmative action mandates triggered fierce opposition to a vocal segment of the professoriate, including *Commentary* intellectuals who regarded the university as a sacrosanct refuge for Jews. For them, any semblance of "quotas" was reminiscent of the numerus clausus, the quota system in Eastern Europe that restricted Jewish enrollment in higher education. As Jacob Heilbrunn wrote in *They Knew They Were Right*:

> The demands of Black radicals for race-based affirmative action came as a particular shock. The Jews had experienced a Jewish quota; were the Blacks now, perversely, to insist on a special quota for themselves? Was merit to be supplanted by skin color?[24]

The idea that students would be admitted to elite universities based on racial "quotas" was anathema, as was the practice of collecting data on the racial and ethnic identity of faculty and students.

In *Running* Commentary: *The Contentious Magazine That Transformed the Jewish Left into the Neoconservative Right*, Benjamin Balint documents *Commentary*'s outpouring of scathing articles against affirmative action during the 1990s.[25] To be sure, there were countless other organizations vehemently opposed to affirmative action. What was unique about *Commentary* is that it gave the anti-affirmative-action crusade an articulation and legitimacy that it had previously lacked.[26] This also marked an ideological shift in the affirmative action debate. Now affirmative action was portrayed as a tug of war between merit and preference, and controversy centered almost exclusively on elite colleges and professional schools.

"When we debate using racial preferences to admit more Blacks and Hispanic students to the nation's best colleges," Alan Wolfe has observed, "we are considering the fate of a shockingly small number of people."[27] Furthermore, as the affirmative action debate shifted from employment to education, it obscured the historic impact of affirmative action as an instrument of racial integration in the world of work—not only in the professions and corporate management but also in major blue-collar industries and in the vast public sector, where nearly a third of Black workers were found.

The implementation of affirmative action mandates over several decades amounted to a social engineering of the first large Black middle class that was anchored outside the ghetto economy. Not only did this respectable middle class signify racial progress, but it had a transformative effect on the semiotics of Blackness for Blacks and whites alike. "No longer is whiteness the unquestioned cultural norm," Ellen Willis observed in 1999.[28]

Yet we should not lose sight of the fact that the progress of the Black middle classes did not signify a deracialization of labor markets as much as it reflected the steady implementation of affirmative action mandates over three decades.[29] Eventually, the increasing appointment of conservatives to the Supreme Court set the stage for an ultimate clash.

4. Denouement: The Unraveling of Affirmative Action Policy, 1988-2012
Advocates of affirmative action were elated when Justice Powell saved the 1977 *Bakke* case from defeat by ruling with the majority that "diversity" was a legitimate goal for a university and therefore could be taken into account in college admissions. In retrospect, the "Powell compromise" only prolonged the death throes of affirmative action. No longer was it predicated on the logic of reparations and the moral imperative of remedying for past wrongs. Now "diversity" emerged as a reigning principle for increasing minority representation in employment and education.

Though Justice Powell contended that diversity was a long-standing practice in college admissions, Harvard's Board of Overseers had discovered the virtues of geographical diversity only in the 1920s, when Jewish enrollment at Harvard reached an "alarming" level of 20 percent.[30]

The deeper problem with the Powell compromise is that it wiped away the logical underpinning of affirmative action as a remedy for past injustices. As David Hollinger wrote, "affirmative action lost an element of clarity it once had when it became entangled with multiculturalism."[31] As "preference" was extended to recent immigrants from Asia and Latin America, affirmative action drifted far from its original purposes as a remedy for the victims of slavery and genocide. According to Peter Schrag, by 1995 three-fourths of all legal immigrants qualified for group preferences.[32]

By the 1980s, what had begun as a squabble within the liberal coalition emerged as a full-blown anti–affirmative action crusade centered on the political Right. What explains this political metamorphosis?

As early as the 1970s, conservative pundits had realized they could reap political hay from white resentment over "quotas." Now it was conservative scholars who put their talents as wordsmiths to work, and once again, *Commentary* provided a venue for the attack against affirmative action. In April 1973, *Commentary* published an article that railed against "the equalitarian orthodoxy."[33] It was penned by Richard Herrnstein who two decades later would collaborate with Charles Murray to write *The Bell Curve*, which resurrected the idea that racial differences in IQ were rooted in biology.[34] Never mind that *Commentary*'s erstwhile liberals had acquired strange bedfellows.

According to MacLean, William Buckley found common cause with the neocons. Irving Kristol, for example, argued that conservatives were defending liberal institutions from liberals' own mounting complaints."[35] Indeed, affirmative action provided conservatives with an issue that went beyond fighting Communism and championing free enterprise. At the same time, it dispelled suspicions that conservatives were driven by bigotry and harbored a latent anti-Semitism.

With this ideological facelift, conservatives could now present themselves not as the enemy of equality but as the champions of colorblindness. Instead of antagonism toward Blacks and civil rights, they rallied to the defense of white males against "the new equality," which Robert Nisbet decried as "the gravest single threat to liberty and social initiative."[36]

With the help of the neocons, old-line conservatives used the escalating dissension over affirmative action to turn the tables on liberals and to develop an ideological blueprint for the restoration of conservatives to power. Who better to orchestrate this political escapade than the nascent neocons at *Commentary* who, according to Heilbrunn, saw it as "their self-anointed role to serve as the court theologians of the Right."[37]

Fierce opposition was marshalled by right-wing pundits and publications, not to mention right-wing foundations and think tanks.[38] As in the case of the revolution that the partisans of counterrevolution sought to negate, the shifting political currents reached into the university and the ranks of social science. Charles Murray's 1984 book *Losing Ground* argued that the welfare state created the conditions that it purported to remedy: welfare dependency, non-work, family breakdown, rising crime, moral dissolution. Thomas Sowell, Glenn Loury, and a cadre of Black conservatives, lavishly funneled by foundations and ensconced in leading universities, put a Black face on "white sociology," parrying those who claimed that sociology had sunk into the abyss of racism. Publication of *The Bell Curve* in 1994 marked the apogee of the intellectual backlash, with the reinstatement of the scientific racism that supposedly had been relinquished to the trash heap almost a century earlier.

This was the historical moment when racism receded into code words and circumlocutions that tapped broader ideological currents. The electoral success of Republicans during the post–Civil War period was not the result only of a conspicuous racial backlash. It also reflected the inroads that the burnished conservative philosophy had on voters with conservative proclivities who wavered in their loyalty to the Democratic Party.

The anti-affirmative-action backlash also provided the context and warrant for a series of reversals of previous Supreme Court decisions that sanctioned affirmative action policy. Nor for that matter was there much support from President Clinton, notwithstanding his nebulous "mend it, don't end it" slogan. As Joe Klein shrewdly observed in a column in *Newsweek*, Clinton's doublespeak provided a rhetorical façade for the quiet dismantling of affirmative action policy, which always depended on vigorous enforcement by the Office of Federal Contract Compliance and the Department of Justice.[39]

In effect, affirmative action had been allowed to die the quiet death that Nixon operatives had pronounced as early as 1970.

By 1995, the obituary for affirmative action was emblazoned on the cover of *Newsweek*, proclaiming "The End to Affirmative Action."[40] A year later, another nail in the coffin of affirmative action was delivered by an appellate court in *Hopwood v. Texas*, which stipulated that a college could implement affirmative action only as a remedy for past discrimination at that very institution, thus rejecting the goal of educational diversity as a general principle. In response, the Texas State Legislature passed a "10 percent plan," permitting major state universities to admit all undergraduate applicants who graduated in the top 10 percent of their high school class. Nevertheless, a year later the percentage of Blacks entering the University of Texas Law School dropped precipitously: from

5.8 percent (29 students) in 1996 to 0.9 percent (6 students) in 1997.
Latinx students also declined, though not as sharply: from 9.2 percent
(46 students) in 1996 to 6.7 percent (31 students) in 1997.[41]

The conclusion is inescapable: affirmative action today is all but dead,
eviscerated by a relentless crusade waged over four decades. To be sure,
there were desperate attempts to resuscitate the patient. However, adverse rulings by the increasingly conservative Supreme Court made it illegal to target affirmative action to particular minorities, on the grounds
that this amounted to a system of "reverse discrimination" in violation
of the Fourteenth Amendment. However, it was still held that promoting "diversity" was a legitimate goal, whether in employment or college
admissions. This was the saving remnant that allowed advocates of affirmative action to breathe a sigh of relief, on the assumption that African
Americans and other protected minorities might fit under the expanded
umbrella of "diversity."

As affirmative action morphed into diversity, however, it lost its original logic and intent. Instead of advancing the cause of racial justice, corporations came to recognize the uses of "diversity" in both the domestic
consumer economy and the global market. This was documented in an
incisive paper by Sharon Collins under the title "Diversity in the Post Affirmative Action Labor Market: A Proxy for Racial Progress?" The question mark conveyed Collins's skepticism. She cited a 1995 survey of the
fifty largest U.S. industrial firms, 78 percent of which either had a formal
diversity management program or were developing one. Another survey
in 1998 found that 75 percent of *Fortune* 500 companies had instituted
programs to promote diversity.[42]

A similar trend has emerged in higher education as affirmative action
morphed from "minority" to "diversity." In 2005, Peter Schmidt, a senior
editor at the *Chronicle of Higher Education*, published a book entitled
*Color and Money: How "Rich White Kids Are Winning the War over
College Affirmative Action*. In 2006, he wrote:

> Over the last three years, mainly in response to two landmark U.S. Su-
> preme Court rulings in June 2003 that defined the limits of affirmative
> action, colleges across the country have been concluding that they are in

legal jeopardy if they continue to offer some services or benefits solely to minority students. As a result, the institutions abandoning the use of race-exclusive eligibility criteria in determining who can be awarded scholarships and fellowships or can participate in recruitment, orientation, and academic enrichment programs.[43]

Schmidt documented the abandonment of "minority" programs at colleges across the nation, over the protest of the NAACP Legal Defense and Education Fund. Its protestations fell on deaf ears as philanthropies and federal agencies withdrew their support for college programs with race-exclusive criteria.

From a historical perspective, the gutting of affirmative action signifies the end of the Second Reconstruction and a return to the status quo ante: the period before affirmative action when there were laws on the books that were ineffectual in combatting institutional racism in employment and education. As for the present, with Trump's appointment of three arch conservatives to the Supreme Court, the majority seems poised to deliver the coup de grace to the remaining vestiges of affirmative action.

IS RESURRECTION POSSIBLE?

For a passing moment, it appeared that the 2020 election might lay the groundwork for resurrecting affirmative action. The political landscape changed with the uprising following the police killing of George Floyd and raised hopes that we were on the cusp of "a national reckoning on race." There was hope that if Democrats prevailed, then the 5–4 majority was only one appointment away from a liberal majority with the power to "bring back affirmative action."

However, that hopeful scenario was dashed with the sudden death of Ruth Bader Ginsberg, whom the Republicans quickly replaced with Amy Coney Barrett. Alas, the current 5–3 majority on the court drives a fateful nail in the coffin of affirmative action for the foreseeable future.

Sadly, our only recourse is to give affirmative action a decent burial. During its brief life, affirmative action succeeded in its core policy objective. It drove a wedge into the system of apartheid that historically restricted Black access to employment and education. Thanks to affirmative action, Blacks developed the first substantial middle class outside the ghetto economy. Furthermore, significant numbers of Blacks gained access to higher education, including elite colleges and graduate schools. Despite the epithet of "affirmative action babies," this cadre of Black professionals—including Barack and Michelle Obama—not only broke through barriers of racial exclusivity but also transformed the semiotics of Blacks and Blackness in American society and culture.

One facet of affirmative action that is rarely acknowledged is that a minority presence has had a profound impact in developing critical epistemologies in various academic disciplines. Indeed, the civil rights "revolution in books," alluded to in chapter 13, transformed knowledge production, including the study of race itself.

William Julius Wilson and others have portrayed affirmative action as primarily helping middle-class Blacks. However, this statement does not withstand scrutiny. Remember that affirmative action mandates began with lily-white construction trades in cities like Philadelphia, Chicago, and New York and eventually were extended to such major industries as automobiles and steel. It is precisely because of affirmative action, that Blacks gained access to coveted jobs in major blue-collar industries, as well as the corporate world and the professions.

The pity of it all is that affirmative action has been systematically dismantled by judges nurtured by the Federalist Society. In a perverse mockery of constitutional law and common sense, these jurists chose to ignore the difference between behavior that was designed to *injure* Blacks and behavior designed as a *remedy* for those very injuries. The result was a relentless denigration of affirmative action programs that account for so much of the celebrated "racial progress" of the post–civil rights era.[44]

The one bright spot is that if or when pressures mount for change, insurgent groups will have the memory and precedent of a robust affirmative action policy that, in its short life, passed muster with the Supreme Court and succeeded in breaching the wall of occupational and educational apartheid that had its origin in slavery itself.

Indeed, the current national reckoning with white supremacy raises the question of whether, like the legendary phoenix, affirmative action might rise from the ashes. Let us take hope and inspiration from

Keeanga-Yamahtta Taylor, who ended her book *From #Blacklivesmatter to Black Liberation* with this prophetic message:

> No one knows what stage the current movement is in or where it is headed. We are very early in the most current rendering of the Black awakening. But we do know that there will be relentless efforts to subvert, redirect, and unravel the movement for Black lives, because when the Black movement goes into motion, it throws the entire mythology of the United States—freedom, democracy, and endless opportunity, into chaos.[45]

It is important to remember that in the early 1970s affirmative action was settled law, until jurists appointed by Richard Nixon and Ronald Reagan threw stare decisis out the window. The time is ripe, perhaps under the leadership of the Black Lives Matter Movement, to mobilize youth—Black, Latinx, Asian, and white—in a campaign to bring back affirmative action.

AFFIRMATIVE ACTION IS DEAD. LONG LIVE AFFIRMATIVE ACTION.

CHAPTER FIFTEEN

TRUMP, TRUMPISM, AND THE RESURGENCE OF WHITE SUPREMACY

Whatever the rhetoric, the message remains the same as it has been for a century and a half: The "other" is not to be trusted; the "other" threatens the white, Christian, heterosexual hegemony.

Barbara Perry, "'White Genocide': White Supremacists and the Politics of Reproduction"[1]

We cannot change this country without winning over some portion of the white working people, and I am not talking about gaining votes for the Democratic Party. I am talking about opening a path to freeing white people from the prison house of whiteness.

Robin D. G. Kelley, "After Trump"[2]

On November 4, 2008, Barack Obama was elected president of the United States. Just after midnight, he appeared on stage in Grant Park, Chicago, along with Michelle Obama and their daughters, Sasha and Malia. The stage was festooned with American flags. After exuberant applause, Obama intoned:

If there is anyone out there who still doubts that America is a place where all things are possible, who still wonders if the dream of our founders is alive in our time, who still questions the power of our democracy, tonight is your answer. . . . It's the answer spoken by young and old, rich and poor, Democrat and Republican, black, white, Hispanic, Asian, Native American, gay, straight, disabled and not disabled, Americans who sent a message to the world that we have never been just a collection of individuals or a collection of red states and blue states.

We are, and always will be, the United States of America.[3]

These words were greeted with euphoria by Obama's fervent followers, as well as historians and pundits who regarded his election as "a transformational event," one that signified the end of white supremacy and portended the arrival of a post-racial society. At long last, the nation had erased the stain of racism. Or so it seemed at this historic moment.

On the other side of the racial divide, Obama's soaring rhetoric was regarded with anathema among the legion of white supremacists. In his 2013 book, *Angry White Men*, Michael Kimmel captured the idiom and politics of the white supremacists whom he interviewed:

Electing a Black president was the symbolic final straw. . . . All over the country, the extreme Right was apoplectic—we'd elected a Black president. This was all the evidence they needed that we had turned a corner and that only a desperate and courageous group of true patriots could save America from itself. It would be bloody, but it was now necessary.[4]

"Bloody, but . . . necessary." In retrospect, this was a forewarning of the events that would materialize twelve years later, when white supremacists stormed the Capitol in Washington, DC. Ironically, Obama's election fit the playbook of David Duke, an erstwhile Ku Klux Klan leader, who realized that "apoplexy and rage" are a useful ploy for stoking the fires of racial hatred. A campaign headline on *NBC News* on August 8, 2008, had read: "Supremacists Hope for Boost from Obama Win." The article had reported:

They're not exactly rooting for Barack Obama, but prominent white supremacists anticipate a boost to their cause if he becomes the first black president. His election, they say, would trigger a backlash—whites rising up, a revolution of sorts—that they think is long overdue.[5]

Indeed, Duke gloated that Obama "will be a clear signal for millions of our people. Obama is a visual aid for White Americans who just don't get it yet that we have lost control of our country, and unless we get it back we are heading for complete annihilation as a people."[6]

According to the Southern Poverty Law Center (SPLC), in 2008 there were some two hundred thousand people nationwide active in white supremacist organizations and militias. SPLC also reported that nativist extremist groups increased nearly 80 percent since Obama took office. Antigovernment "patriot" groups more than tripled.[7] Here was a forewarning of the incendiary politics already seething beneath the surface during the Obama presidency. Twelve years later the chickens came home to roost with the storming of the Capitol in Washington, DC.

THE RISE OF THE RADICAL RIGHT

"The Radical Right" entered the sociological lexicon in a 1955 anthology with that title, edited by Daniel Bell, a political sociologist. Among the contributors were Seymour Martin Lipset, another political sociologist, who coined the term "the Radical Right," and Richard Hofstadter, a historian and public intellectual. They were struck by the fact that the Radical Right was a new and dangerous political constellation that, to their consternation, had emerged at a time of relative prosperity and full employment. As Bell put it:

> This is a turbulence born not of depression, but of prosperity. Contrary to the somewhat simple notion that prosperity dissolves all social problems, we see that prosperity brings in its wake new social groups, new social strains and new social anxieties. Conventional political analysis, drawn largely from eighteenth- and nineteenth-century American experience, cannot fathom these new social anxieties nor explain their political consequences.[8]

Lipset was also mystified that the Radical Right bore no resemblance to political movements that engaged in pressure-group practices, lobbying, and the ballot box. They were not like unions demanding higher wages. Nor were they swayed by ideologies that promoted equalitarian values or social democracy. On the contrary, the singular feature of Radical Right agitation is that it facilitated the growth of practices that threaten to undermine the social fabric of democratic politics.[9]

Lipset drew a crucial distinction between "class politics" and "status politics." Whereas class politics favor redistribution of income and gain strength during times of unemployment and depression, status politics favor the status quo, are irrational, and seek scapegoats among ethnic or religious groups who represent their status resentments.[10] Lipset provides an illuminating example:

> Historically, the most common scapegoats in the United States have been the minority ethnic or religious groups. Such groups have repeatedly been the victims of political aggression in periods of prosperity, for it is precisely in these times that status anxieties are most pressing.[11]

Consistent with their preoccupation with an idealized past, the Radical Right was doggedly opposed to immigration, which they regarded as a disruptive purveyor of alien values and purposes. Lipset cites anti-Catholic and anti-immigrant agitation before the Civil War and the Know-Nothings, who polled one fourth of the popular vote for president in 1856. Another example is the Ku Klux Klan in the 1920s, which was aimed against Jews, Catholics, and Blacks. The litany of resentment against scapegoats who are targets of declining status groups seems to have no end in American history and sheds light on the current conjuncture as well.

The singular possession of declining status groups is the badge of being "real Americans." Paradoxically, this moniker only stokes bitterness and resentment aimed at unworthy competitors, especially in the world of work. As Lipset observed with a note of irony: "If foreigners may become American, then Americans may become 'un-American.'"

Richard Hofstadter titled his essay "The Pseudo-Conservative Revolt," a term that he borrowed from Theodore Adorno, author of *The Authoritarian Personality*, published five years earlier. Like Bell and Lipset, Hofstadter sought to demystify this new phenomenon, and he was struck by its relentless demand for conformity:

Its exponents, although they believe themselves to be conservatives and usually employ the rhetoric of conservatism, show signs of a serious and restless dissatisfaction with American life, traditions, and institutions. . . . Their political reactions express rather a profound if largely unconscious hatred of our society and its ways—a hatred which one would hesitate to impute to them if one did not have suggestive clinical evidence.[12]

Here was a new, enigmatic, and dangerous brand of politics that was a threat to democracy and that prefigures the political gestalt that contributed to the storming of the nation's capital sixty-five years later. Indeed, its seeds were planted by the resentment and rage of these earlier generations.

The subtext to the critique of the birth of the Radical Right has to do with whiteness, as synecdoche for its underlying grievances. In his recent book *All-American Nativism*, Daniel Denvir points up the semiotics of whiteness:

As I tell it in this book, the proximate story of the Trump administration begins in the 1960s and 70s. But the *longue durée* of European settlement serves as historical backdrop and founding condition: government has tried time and again to ensure that the United States is a white country for white people—and sometimes to ensure that it belongs to a specific subset of whites at that.[13]

For good measure, Denvir adds: "That is not hyperbole." Indeed, whiteness and the trope of "the forgotten white American" is the hallmark of the white supremacist movement.

Before going further in this narrative, let us examine the interregnum between the rise of the right in the 1950s and the fulminations of those "real Americans" who stormed the nation's capital on January 6, 2021.

FROM HEARTLAND TO RUST BELT

With the onset of the industrial revolution in the late nineteenth century, the nation's heartland transitioned from agriculture to manufacturing, and the Midwest emerged as the epicenter for the production of steel, automobiles, and a host of allied industries. For nearly a century, the Great Lakes Megalopolis prospered beyond imagination. According to the Brookings Institution, if the economy of the Great Lakes region stood alone as a country, it would have been one of the largest economic units in the world, with a $4.5 trillion gross regional product.[14] By another estimate, about 200 million tons of cargo was shipped through the Great Lakes each year.[15] Nevertheless, in the decades after the Second World War, the industries that produced "the American economic miracle" began to succumb to competition and technological advances from abroad. By 1980 this extraordinary icon of industrialization was on the verge of a deadly spiral as American manufacturing came under mounting pressure from automation and foreign competitors.

For example, steel mills fell into obsolescence, with their open-hearth furnaces and sulfur-burning coal-fired plants. Bethlehem Steel and the U.S. Steel Company were reduced to industrial dinosaurs. The automobile industry had storied names that still resonate in American iconography— names like Buick and Ford, Oldsmobile and Studebaker—not to speak of Dearborn Engines and Trucks. However, they were losing market share with competitors in Japan, Germany, and Scandinavia. In their wake, they left abandoned plants and jobless workers.

The ravages of deindustrialization extended even to New York City, legendary for its garment trades, textiles, printing, and light manufacturing. From a base of 1 million manufacturing jobs in 1950, by the early 1960s New York's manufacturing sector had shrunk to 200,000 workers. By 2015 it was a mere 76,000. However, unlike factories in the Midwest, New York City was able to recover through growth in real estate, insurance, and finance. Mass media, publishing, and entertainment also emerged as new sources of spectacular growth. By the 1970s, New York City had not only recovered but was celebrated as one of the nation's first "postindustrial cities."[16]

In the 1992 presidential debate with Bill Clinton and George H. W. Bush, third-party candidate Ross Perot famously exclaimed that you could hear a giant sucking sound of jobs being pulled out of the United States. Though NAFTA is widely blamed for the collapse of American manufacturing, as you can see from the above account, these industries were already losing their advantage in global markets. No doubt, NAFTA hastened the outsourcing of American factories to low-wage nations, both in Latin America and Asia, but this outcome was inevitable. From an economic standpoint, NAFTA shifted production to Mexico and other low-wage nations in exchange for access to domestic markets in these nations.

Nevertheless, deindustrialization had gut-wrenching effects on the lives of workers who were displaced from jobs and thrown into personal crisis. The effects were equally devastating on the surrounding communities, evident in deteriorating land values, declining tax revenues, poor schools, and high rates of drugs and crime.

Kimmel interviewed young men buffeted by global political and economic forces beyond their control. Family farms were lost to foreclosure, and small shops were squeezed out by Walmarts and malls, leaving these families facing a spiral of downward mobility and economic uncertainty.

Kimmel found that a large proportion of the extreme Right were military veterans, like Timothy McVeigh, the domestic terrorist who bombed the Federal Building in Oklahoma in 1995, killing 168 people.[17] From the standpoint of young men in the rust belt, "the government has abandoned the very men who have fought and died to protect it, the corporations have abandoned the very guys who have worked tirelessly to create the wealth the owners and shareholders enjoy, and our doors have been flung open to allow all sorts of unworthy types to come and take our jobs, our homes, even our women. Feminism is just one more straw, the symbolic straw that signals a complete reversal."[18]

Nor were these "angry white men" immune to the rapidly shifting social and economic transformations of the larger society. In the 1960s, it was the student movement, the peace movement, and the gay and lesbian movement, along with increased immigration from Mexico and Latin America. In the 1970s, it was the Black revolt and the women's movement that stoked fears and resentment. In the 1980s and 1990s, the farm crisis and globalization "added fuel to the sense that the very people who had built America were the ones who were being pushed aside."[19]

Put another way, whiteness is a double-edged sword. On the one hand, it is a badge of privilege in a society that derogates the racial "other." On the other hand, its rewards are illusory and whip up false expectations, disappointment, and ultimately anger. As is evident from the epigraphs to this chapter, these "angry white men" may imagine themselves as belonging to the master race, but this illusion only stokes anger when they observe others, especially the racial other, as connected to the society and its system of rewards.

To quote Kimmel: "They harken back now to some mythic era, before feminism, before civil rights, before gay liberation." Kimmel observed that "emasculation is a dominant theme in white-wing websites, blogs, magazines, and newsletters."[20] In addition, they are contemptuous of multiculturalism, which includes everyone who is not a white man. They are literally drowning in the contradiction of whiteness:

> Theirs are the hands that built this country; theirs is the blood shed to defend it. And now, they feel, no one listens to them; they've been all but forgotten. . . . They're downwardly mobile, contemptuously pushed aside by the fast-talking, fast-driving fat cats and bureaucrats. And they're mad as hell.[21]

STRANGE BEDFELLOWS

The trajectory of the Radical Right derived inspiration and momentum from an unexpected source: the Black Power movement of the 1970s. This concept was inspired by Kwame Ture (aka Stokely Carmichael), who sought greater independence in the struggle for equal rights. "Black power" also expressed itself as a celebration of Black culture, and "ethnic fever," as it was called, spread like wildfire to other ethnic groups.

Eventually ethnic fever spread to whites, albeit in a reactionary form. In his article "Trumpism and the Collapse of the Liberal Racial Consensus in the United States," anthropologist Jeff Maskovsky depicts how whites in the rust belt jumped onto the ethnic bandwagon:

> Once vilified as ignorant, dangerous, and criminal in comparison to mainstream WASP culture, white ethnicity became politically legitimate and even fashionable as a white ethnic identity politics formed in direct

reaction to Black Power and other militant protest movements of the 1960s and 1970s. In the 1980s and 1990s, the culture wars were effective in further linking the politics of white ethnic pride to white racial resentments. The neoconservative condemnation of "illiberal" causes such as affirmative action, multiculturalism, political correctness, and liberal immigration policy also helped to shift white ethnic politics to the right.[22]

The Radical Right adopted the language and flamboyance of "White Power." If Blacks could trumpet "Black Power," then what was there to prevent whites from claiming and embracing White Power?

Actually, for David Duke and white supremacists, "white power" was the antithesis of Black Power. In their eyes, "White power means a permanent end to unemployment because with non-Whites gone, the labor market will no longer be overcrowded with unproductive niggers, spics, and other racial low-life. It means an end to inflation eating up a man's paycheck faster than he can raise it because our economy will not be run by a criminal pack of international Jewish bankers, bent on using the White worker's tax money in selfish and ever destructive schemes."[23] These exponents of white power are not the white version of the Black Power movement. On the contrary, they gravitate to such groups as the neo-Nazis and the Ku Klux Klan, as well as militias, Aryan survivalists, white supremacist youth groups, and violent religious cults.

ENTER DONALD TRUMP

Trump did not stumble onto the stage of history by masquerading as a faux business tycoon on reality TV. Nor was it his bombast or atmospherics, as he descended the escalator of Trump Tower, with a cranked-up soundtrack of Neil Young's "Rockin' in the Free World." Rather, according to David Neiwert, author of *Alt-America: The Rise of the Radical Right in the Age of Trump*, "these dark forces had been building for years, waiting for the right kind of figure—charismatic, rich, fearlessly bombastic—to come along and put them into play. . . . What really stood out was Trump's open, unapologetic expression of bigotry toward Latinos and other minorities."[24] No sooner did he step off the escalator than he unleashed a screed against Mexicans: "They're bringing drugs, they're bringing crime, they're rapists."

New York City's tabloids erupted with a mixture of scorn and satire, including a dose of condemnation from prominent Republicans. However, *Fox News* projected an altogether different image: "Trump has drawn support from Americans who say he is openly confronting the severity of the immigration problem that others won't publicly knowledge [*sic*]."[25]

From that iconic moment, white supremacists in the red states embraced Trump as their white savior, certain that this business tycoon who condemned immigration and globalism would provide salvation consistent with his political rhetoric.

"Once in office, Trump rendered in administrative and legislative prose a nativist presidential campaign suffused with the toxic poetry of race, nation, and religion," writes Daniel Denvir in *All-American Nativism*. "Trump had won by portraying a country under siege from a globalist elite that prioritized themselves and the interests of a foreign-born underclass over those of forgotten white Americans."[26]

Ah, those "forgotten white Americans." The same refrain that harkened back to the rise of the political Right sixty-five years earlier, presciently identified by Bell, Lipset, and Hofstadter, who grasped that this was a dangerous new political constellation, fundamentally different from other political formations. This was a political movement that sought to recover prerogatives and power they had enjoyed in the halcyon days of white supremacy. Trump rambled through speeches, but whenever the crowd grew restless, he snapped them back to attention with a phrase that summarized it all: "Build the wall." Nothing tied his multifarious warnings of criminal, economic, and even existential threat together as tightly as immigration.[27]

As Denvir points out, the excoriation of immigrants was not a new phenomenon: "For decades, hard-core xenophobia had seeped into conservative politics, transmitted across an ascendant network of right-wing television, radio and, ultimately, internet outlets."[28] Trump used this platform to reinvent himself as the nation's leading nativist. Never mind that he had no compunction when it came to hiring immigrant workers in his hotels and construction business.

Even before he entered presidential politics, Trump had a dress rehearsal with his ploy over Obama's birth certificate. The birther movement was a trial run for his assault on people of color and immigrants and, ultimately, to nonwhites collectively. It delivered a sinister message to the right wing: Obama was not a "real American," much less a legitimate president of the United States. Trump, in desperation, would attempt to use a similar ploy to disqualify millions of voters in the 2020 election.

Actually, this mindset has deep roots in American history and iconography. The Naturalization Act of 1790 limited naturalization to "free white persons of good character." As recently as 1957, William Buckley, a conservative pundit who was editor of the *National Review*, penned an editorial titled "Why the South Must Prevail." Buckley declared that the white race was "the more advanced" race and, as such, the most fit to govern.[29] It followed that "so long as Blacks remained backward in education and economic progress, Southern whites had a right to 'impose superior mores for whatever period of time it takes to effect a genuine cultural equality between the races.'"[30]

Buckley eventually backed away from his unvarnished racism, though his vitriol has found renewed support among the alt-right, who regard Blacks and immigrants as undeserving of the franchise. Trump then deployed this logic to allege voter fraud in cities with high concentrations of African Americans. Ditto for Latinx immigrants in such states as Texas, California, and New Jersey. As Trump would have it, if only votes of "real Americans" were counted, he would ipso facto be the legitimate president of the United States.

Trump's unabashed embrace of nativism earned him the instant adulation of the white supremacists. As did his denunciation of NAFTA and his promise that jobs would come streaming back to the rust belt. Trump staged grandiose photo ops with local industrialists to provide visual proof that he had superior powers. Never mind that jobs in manufacturing and coal were rapidly disappearing due to globalization and climate change.

In an illuminating monograph entitled *The Old Is Dying and the New Cannot Be Born*, political theorist Nancy Fraser shows how Trump resorted to the old bait and switch.[31]

> [He] failed to lift a finger to rein in Wall Street. Nor has he taken a single serious step to implement large-scale, job-creating infrastructure projects; his efforts to encourage manufacturing have instead been confined to symbolic displays of jawboning and regulatory relief for coal, whose gains have proved largely fictitious.[32]

Furthermore, instead of proposing an overhaul of the tax system that could have provided relief to working and middle-class families, Trump pushed for "tax reform" that funneled billions of dollars to the 1 percent.

Trump's whole purpose in stoking anger was to provide a smokescreen for selling out the very workers that he pretended to champion. Instead of jobs, says Maskovsky, these displaced workers were treated to enactments of "xenophobic, racist, and ethnonationalist forms of politics."[33]

According to Fraser, two political formations—progressives and neoliberals—dominated the political landscape in the rust belt, and neither made any serious effort to salvage these communities. She writes: "To the neoliberals, their economies were uncompetitive and should be subject to 'market correction.'" On the other hand, "to the progressives, their cultures were stuck in the past, tied to obsolete parochial values that would soon disappear in a new cosmopolitan dispensation."[34] With their backs against the wall, these displaced workers had no choice but to resort to "precarious, low-wage McJobs, the rise of predatory debt; and the consequent decline in living standards for the bottom two-thirds of Americans."[35]

Despite his blatant hypocrisy, Trump retained the loyalty and reverence of white supremacists who believed his flagrant lies, even as he appropriated their loyalty to his selfish ends. More to the point, the supremacists believed "the big lie"—that the election had been stolen. Enthralled by their white savior, they adhered to his stealth plan to storm the Capitol on January 6, at the very hour that the ceremonial counting of ballots was scheduled to declare Biden as the winner of the 2020 election. As the crazed mob unleashed death and destruction on the nation's capital, Trump retreated to the White House to watch the havoc and violence unfold on television. Reality TV, indeed.

IMMIGRATION AND THE WHITE BACKLASH (OR WHITELASH)

As a senator from Texas, Lyndon Johnson vetoed legislation against lynching. As president, at the pinnacle of the civil rights revolution, he signed the Voting Rights Act. At a commencement address to students at Howard University on June 4, 1965, he concluded by exclaiming, in his Southern drawl, "And we shall overcome."

For Southerners, this was the final straw. For decades there had been an "unholy alliance" in the Democratic Party between Northern Democrats and Southern "Dixiecrats." Johnson knew all too well that the passage of the Voting Rights Act was the death knell of this "unholy alliance." Even before passage of the Voting Rights Act, George Wallace surprised everyone by making inroads among working-class voters in Democratic primaries in the industrial North. The tarot cards were in place for a fateful realignment of the two parties.

When Johnson overwhelmingly defeated Barry Goldwater in the 1964 election, pundits declared that Goldwater's defeat portended "the death of conservatism." However, by 1968 the tables had turned. Though Goldwater had been defeated in a landslide, Republican operatives regarded this as a turning point that would ultimately resurrect the Republican Party after years of liberal hegemony. Nixon prevailed in the 1968 election, thanks to his "Southern strategy" that lured disaffected whites into the Republican Party.

Nixon wasted no time in nominating two outright racists to the Supreme Court (Clement Haynsworth and G. Harrold Carswell). Both were rebuffed since liberals still controlled the Senate. However, this was an unmistakable sign that the Supreme Court was on the cusp of falling under Republican control.

With the election of Ronald Reagan in 1980, Republicans occupied the White House for twenty-eight of the next forty years. The only outliers were two Southern Democrats—Jimmy Carter from Georgia and Bill Clinton from Arkansas. Given the Republican upsurge, Clinton was compelled to move the Democratic Party decisively to the right, which he did by dismantling the welfare system that had existed since the Depression, backing away from affirmative action, and signing the crime bill that set the stage for mass incarceration. Equally significant was the Republican takeover of the Supreme Court after decades of liberal domination dating back to the Depression.

In his 1969 book *The Emerging Republican Majority*, Kevin Phillips, a strategist in the Nixon campaign, declared that Nixon's election augured the end of New Deal hegemony and the ascendency of the Republican Party. By 1992, Thomas Byrne Edsall and Mary D. Edsall—in their book *Chain Reaction: The Impact of Race, Rights, and Taxes on American Politics*—declared that Republicans had become "the party of segregation.[36] The unexpected election of Barack Obama in 2008 signaled a turning point for the Democrats. Note, however, that Obama secured his victory with only 43 percent of the white vote. In other words, if only whites had voted, Obama would have lost in a landslide. Obama's victory was made possible by the unprecedented influx of Black voters, especially Black women. At first there was doubt whether Latinx would provide significant support for Obama, but they turned out in large numbers along with Asians. Young voters were the only white constituency that voted overwhelmingly for Obama.

Trump's narrow win in 2016 was unpredicted. Nevertheless, Trump wasted no time in delivering on his promise to remember those "forgotten white Americans." As Denvir notes: "Until Trump's election, it had been almost a century since nativism had stood among the country's explicit and central governing ideologies." Trumpism was born in the crucible of an unabashed and fierce white backlash.

As Denvir observed, this backlash was fueled by a long history of African Americans migrating from the South into schools, neighborhoods, and workplaces in the cities of the North, Midwest, and West. The backlash was also compounded by a new wave of immigration in the years following passage of the 1968 Immigration Act, which also stoked anti-immigrant resentment, especially among white supremacists.[37]

Only in retrospect can we clearly see that the unholy alliance between Democrats and Dixiecrats had kept racism and nativism in check within the bounds of the Democratic Party. With the genie out of the bottle, Republicans evolved overnight into the party of segregation, as Thomas and Mary Edsall had predicted in 1992. Trump instantly conveyed his willingness to violate the norms that previously restrained race-baiting in political discourse. His base reacted with delirium, which Trump brought to new heights of unabashed racism and nativism.

WHITENESS AND THE TICKING TIME BOMB

We have come to regard whiteness as a monolithic whole, defined by skin color and other biological signifiers. Every schoolchild knows that the American colonies were first settled by the English, and prior to the American Revolution, the colonists regarded themselves as subjects of the English monarchy. However, on closer examination, the people we consider "white" have their roots in a host of European nations, defined by nationality, language, and phenotype. Furthermore, many of these "whites" were once regarded as aliens and subject to nativist recrimination and policies.

For example, in 1751 Benjamin Franklin railed at the influx of Germans in the American colonies. He grumbled: "Why should the Palatine boars be suffered to swarm into our settlements and, by herding together, establish their language and manners, to the exclusion of ours. Why should Pennsylvania, founded by the English, become a colony of aliens, who will shortly be so numerous as to Germanize us, instead of us Anglifying them?"[38]

Here was a clear sign that whiteness was predicated on nationality as much as on race or color. Furthermore, like "the Palatine boars," other Europeans who emigrated to the United States were hardly welcomed as white brethren, though over time they were accepted as "honorary whites." Indeed, sociologists have propagated an entire canon of "whiteness studies," with book titles like *How Jews Became White Folk*, *How the Irish Became White*, *Working toward Whiteness*, *Are Italians White?* and *Whiteness of a Different Color*.[39] It was not until the aftermath of the Second World War that these discordant nationalities melted into a sea of whiteness.

Yet there is another historical irony to this saga: whites are a declining proportion of the American population. One factor is the influx of over 40 million immigrants following passage of the 1965 Immigration Act, and the number is projected to reach 78 million by 2065. The 1968 immigration reform annulled the national origin quotas from the 1924 Immigration Act that discriminated against immigrants from Eastern and Southern Europe (read: Jews and Italians). The post-1968 act opened up immigration to nations the world over, though the three most preponderant groups are Latinx, Asians, and people from the Caribbean islands. Given the rapid integration of these new immigrants into the nation's body politic, the United States is losing its image as "a nation of immigrants" and is rapidly evolving into "a hybrid nation."

The other factor is the low birthrate among whites in the United States. This has not escaped notice by the editors of the Breitbart News, a right-wing news outlet. Today the birthrates of whites are well below the replacement levels in every state and the District of Columbia.[40] Clearly, these demographic trends are unfavorable to the electoral interests of Republicans, whose median age is higher than that of the Democrats. Another risk comes from Gen Z children, the oldest of whom were born after 1996 and turned 23 in 2019, at which time 24 million of them were eligible to vote beginning in the November election. Their political clout will grow in coming years as more of them reach voting age.[41]

This is problematic for a Republican Party that ostracizes immigrants and whose core constituency is white male voters. Consider these additional facts:

- By 2020, 81 percent of Republican voters were white and 57 percent were male.[42]
- There is a yawning gender gap within the Republican Party: only 42 percent of women voted for Trump, compared to 57 percent of males.

According to Pew Research Center, white eligible voters are sharply declining, both in absolute numbers and in terms of regional distribution:

- The number of white eligible voters has declined from 76 percent in 2000 to 72 percent in 2010, to 67 percent in 2018.
- The number of white eligible voters declined in all fifty states between 2000 and 2018.
- Ten states had double-digit drops in white voters.
- Between 2000 and 2018, ten states experienced a 10 percent decline in white voters.
- In battleground states in 2018, whites declined 13 percent in Florida, 12 percent in Arizona, 7 percent in Pennsylvania, 6 percent in North Carolina, 5 percent in Wisconsin, and 3 percent in Michigan.[43]
- The U.S. electorate is aging. Currently, 52 percent are fifty or older, up from 41 percent in 1996. More than half of Republican and GOP-leaning voters are fifty or older, up from 39 percent in 1996.

Given these trends, it seems doubtful that the Republican Party will be able to win elections except in states with a large plurality of white voters. In the 2020 election, this trend was already evident in such states as Pennsylvania, Nevada, Arizona, and Georgia. Even Texas is now considered a swing state. Political parties typically pay lip service to putting up a big tent and expanding their base, but Republicans seem to be moving in the opposite direction, threatened by changing demographics as well as the discourse and politics of inclusion.

Under these circumstances, the last resort is voter suppression. According to the Brennan Center of Justice, since February 18, 2021, forty-three states have already introduced 250 bills to restrict voting.[44] The proposals sought to (1) limit mail voting access, (2) impose stricter voter ID requirements, (3) slash voter registration opportunities, and (4) enable more aggressive voter purges. One such device is to sharply limit voting on Sundays, when Black voters follow church services with "souls to the polls" bus rides to cast ballots. Whether these proposals will survive scrutiny by the Supreme Court is unknown at this point in time. These efforts are a replay of voting suppression tactics that existed before the passage of the Voting Rights Act in 1968. Furthermore, in a 5 to 4 vote, the 2013 *Shelby* decision dismantled many of the provisions that had protected the vote for African Americans. As this book goes to press, state legislatures are falling over each other to pass voter suppression bills that are a throwback to the worst days of Jim Crow.[45]

I do not claim to have a crystal ball, but one thing is certain: if the founding fathers had not created the Electoral College to preserve slavery and to facilitate white supremacy, we would not be in this quandary about the nation's political future. As the saying goes, the past is prologue, and the Electoral College could once again undermine representative democracy as it did in the 2016 election of Donald Trump. We are left with the vain hope that our democracy is sufficiently anchored to withstand another shock, like the storming of the Capitol on January 6. Only history will tell whether this calamitous event signifies the dying gasp of white supremacy. Or whether it is a forewarning of perils ahead.

NOTES

Introduction

An earlier version of this chapter appeared as "Race Relations: The Problem with the Wrong Name" in *New Politics*, Winter 2001, © Stephen Steinberg.

1. Lerone Bennett Jr., "The White Problem in America," *Ebony* 20, no. 10 (August 1965): 29.

2. Charles Blow, "Call a Thing a Thing," *New York Times*, July 9, 2020.

3. Betty Friedan, *The Feminine Mystique* (New York: Dell, 1963).

4. Helen Hacker, "Women as a Minority Group," *Social Forces* 30, no. 1 (October 1951): 60–69.

5. According to Fred R. Shapiro, the term *sexism* was most likely coined on November 18, 1965, by Pauline M. Leet during a student-faculty forum at Franklin and Marshall College. Shapiro also contends that the first time the term *sexism* appeared in print was in Caroline Bird's speech "On Being Born Female," published November 15, 1968, in *Vital Speeches of the Day* (p. 6). In this speech, she asserted that "there is recognition abroad that we are in many ways a sexist country. Sexism is judging people by their sex when sex doesn't matter. "Sexism," Wikipedia, last edited May 17, 2021, https://en.wikipedia.org/wiki/Sexism.

6. Daniel Horowitz, *Betty Friedan and the Making of The Feminine Mystique* (Amherst: University of Massachusetts Press, 2000).

7. Horowitz, *Betty Friedan*, 201.

8. Horowitz, 201.

9. Karen E. Fields and Barbara J. Fields, *Racecraft: The Soul of Inequality in American Life* (New York: Verso, 2014), 39–40.

10. Fields and Fields, *Racecraft*, 149. Italics in original.

11. Henry Hughes, *Treatise on Sociology, Theoretical and Practical* (Philadelphia: Lippincott and Grambo, 1854; repr., New York: Negro Universities Press, 1968); and George Fitzhugh, *Cannibals All! or Slaves Without Masters*, ed. C. Vann Woodward (Cambridge, MA: Belknap Press of Harvard University Press, 1960). See also Stanford M. Lyman, *Militarism, Imperialism, and Racial Accommodation* (Fayetteville: University of Arkansas Press, 1992).

12. To state the obvious, the name per se is of little significance. It is the *context* that matters. In 1895, Frederick Douglass wrote with palpable ire in the *New York Times*: "They could call it some other name—it is fertile in names; it has been called 'the peculiar institution,' the 'impediment,' etc., and it will again turn up under some new and hateful guise to curse and destroy this nation." It is rather the semiotics that are instantiated in the name, together with the hidden meanings and devious uses of that name, that are critical. The ultimate test is whether a name elucidates or whether, as in the case of *race relations*, it is a sinister obfuscation. "The Anti-Slavery Society: Exciting Debate and Final Action on Mr. Garrison's Resolution of Dissolution," *New York Times*, May 11, 1865, https://www .nytimescom/1865/05/11/archives/the-antislavery-society-exciting-debate-and-final-action -on-mr.html.

13. Bob Blauner, *Racial Oppression in America* (New York: Harper & Row, 1972). Full disclosure: as a doctoral student at UC, Berkeley, I was a student of Bob's, and he headed my dissertation committee. Some years later, I asked him via email where he got the word *oppression*. He answered with a shrug: "Well, I don't know. *Oppression* was commonly used on the Left." In an autobiographical essay, Bob divulged that as a youthful radical in Chicago in the 1950s, he was a member of the Communist Party, which did not shirk from calling oppression by its rightful name.

14. "I think one of the great fallacies we have had in the field of race relations for many, many decades has been to worry about attitudes rather than about conditions." Thomas F. Pettigrew, "Transcript of the American Academy Conference on the Negro American. May 14–15, 1965," in "The Negro American," vol. 2, *Daedalus* 95, no. 1 (Winter 1966): 312.

15. Barton Meyers, "Minority Group: An Ideological Formation," *Social Problems* 32, no. 1 (October 1984): 1–15.

16. Oliver Cromwell Cox, *Caste, Class, and Race* (New York: Modern Reader, 1948), 476.

17. Leah Gordon, *From Power to Prejudice: The Rise of Racial Individualism in Mid-century America* (New York: Oxford University Press. 2016).

18. Stephen Steinberg, *Turning Back: The Retreat from Racial Justice in American Thought and Policy*, 2nd ed. (1995; Boston: Beacon Press, 2001).

19. Blauner, *Racial Oppression in America*, ch. 3.

20. Stokely Carmichael (Kwame Ture) and Charles V. Hamilton, *Black Power: The Politics of Liberation in America* (New York: Vintage Books, 1967).

21. See Joe R. Feagin's groundbreaking study *Systemic Racism: A Theory of Oppression* (New York: Routledge, 2006).

22. Dinesh D'Souza, *The End of Racism* (New York: Free Press, 1995), 554.

23. Noel A. Cazenave and Darlene Alvarez Maddern, "Defending the White Race: White Male Opposition to a 'White Racism' Course," *Race and Society* 2, no. 1 (1999): 25–50.

24. Charles W. Mills, *The Racial Contract* (Ithaca: Cornell University Press, 1997); Eduardo Bonilla-Silva, *White Supremacy and Racism in the Post–Civil Rights Era* (Boulder, CO: Lynne Rienner, 2001); Joe R. Feagin, *Systematic Racism: A Theory of Oppression*; and Noel Cazenave, *Conceptualizing Racism* (Lanham, MD: Rowman & Littlefield, 2015).

25. See the useful entry "Critical Race Theory," Wikipedia, last edited May 16, 2021, https://en.wikipedia.org/wiki/Critical_race_theory.

26. Edward Said, *Representations of the Intellectual* (New York: Vintage, 1996).

27. Adolph Reed Jr., "Yackety-Yak about Race," *Progressive*, December 1997.

28. Karen R. Miller, *Managing Inequality: Northern Racial Liberalism in Interwar Detroit* (New York: New York University Press, 2015), 266.

29. Miller, *Managing Inequality*, 267.

30. Miller, 271.

31. Miller, 267–68. Italics in original.

32. Miller, 272.

Part I: Counterrevolution in Historical and Theoretical Perspective

1. Hannah Arendt, *On Revolution* (New York: Penguin Books, 1963), 133.

2. Arendt, *On Revolution*, 133.

3. Arendt, 133.

4. Stephen Eric Bronner, "Notes on the Counter-Revolution," *Logos* 10, no. 1 (2011), http://www.logosjournal.com/notes-counter-revolution.php. Also, Stephen Eric Bronner, "Back to Basics: Trump's Counter-Revolution, Resistance, and Solidarity," *Logos* 17, no. 1 (Winter 2017), http://logosjournal.com/2017/back-to-basics-trumps-counter-revolution-resistance-and-solidarity/.

5. W. E. B. Du Bois, *Black Reconstruction in America, 1860–1880* (1935; New York: Oxford University Press, 2014), 30, 67.

6. Du Bois, *Black Reconstruction in America*, 57.

7. Eric Foner, *Reconstruction: America's Unfinished Revolution, 1863–1877* (New York: Harper & Row, 1988), 281.

8. Quoted in Foner, *Reconstruction*, 271–72.

9. Lerone Bennett Jr., "The Second Time Around," *Ebony*, October 1981. For an informative analysis of Bennett and the role he played at *Ebony*, see John Thomas, "*Ebony* Magazine and Lerone Bennett Jr.: Popular Black History in Postwar America," Bookshelf, *Quill*, April 15, 2020, https://www.quillmag.com/2020/04/15/bookshelf-ebony-magazine-and-lerone-bennett-jr-popular-black-history-in-postwar-america/.

10. Du Bois, *Black Reconstruction in America*, 30.

11. Homer Plessy was an activist for racial justice, a forerunner of Rosa Parks's protest half a century later.

Chapter 1: Nails in the Coffin of the Civil Rights Revolution

An earlier version of this chapter appeared as "Race and Democracy: The American Oxymoron," in *Where Do We Go From Here? American Democracy and the Renewal of the Radical Imagination*, edited by Mark Major, 159–86 (Lanham, MD: Lexington Books, 2010). Reproduced by permission of Rowman & Littlefield.

1. W. E. B. Du Bois, *Black Reconstruction in America, 1860–1880* (1935; New York: Free Press, 1998), 708.

2. "Southern Manifesto on Integration (March 12, 1954)," *Congressional Record* 104, part 4 (Washington, DC: Government Printing Office, 1956), posted by Thirteen/WNET,

December 2006, https://www.thirteen.org/wnet/supremecourt/rights/sources_document2
.html.

3. For a thoughtful analysis of whether the civil rights movement was a revolution,
see Daniel Little, "Was the Civil Rights Movement a Revolution?" *Understanding Society* (blog), January 20, 2015, https://understandingsociety.blogspot.com/2015/01/was-civil
-rights-movement-revolution.html. Also, Thomas J. Sugrue, *Sweet Land of Liberty: The
Forgotten Struggle for Civil Rights in the North* (New York: Random House, 2008).

4. Center for Individual Freedom, "We Couldn't Have Had Reagan in 1980 without First Having Carter in 1976," Freedom Line, posted November 6, 2008, https://www
.cfif.org/htdocs/freedomline/current/in_our_opinion/We-Couldnt-Have-Had-Reagan-in
-1980-Without-First-Having-Carter-In-1976.html.

5. "Clement Haynsworth and C. Harrold Carswell," Supreme Court Nomination Battles, *Time*, n.d., http://content.time.com/time/specials/packages/article/0,28804,1895379
_1895421_1895542,00.html. Richard Nixon had two high-profile Supreme Court nomination strikeouts. In 1969, he nominated Judge Clement Haynsworth—a Southerner reviled
by labor and civil rights groups for rulings related to union representation and school
desegregation. Hoping to derail the Haynsworth nomination, labor activists disclosed that
the judge had a possible financial stake in a case he decided while on the Fourth Circuit.
The Senate voted 55–45 against his nomination. A year later, Nixon nominated another
Southerner, G. Harrold Carswell, reviled by civil rights groups for his earlier support for
segregation. He went down in flames as well. One senator argued that "even if he is mediocre, there are a lot of mediocre judges and people and lawyers, and they are entitled to a
little representation, aren't they?"

6. Carol Anderson, *White Rage* (New York: Bloomsbury USA, 2016), 5.

7. David Swinton, quoted in Anderson, *White Rage*, 123.

8. Jason Hackworth, *Manufacturing Decline* (New York: Columbia University Press,
2019), x.

9. Glenn Kessler, "When Did McConnell Say He Wanted to Make Obama a 'One-
Term President'?" *Washington Post*, September 25, 2012, https://www.washingtonpost
.com/blogs/fact-checker/post/when-did-mcconnell-say-he-wanted-to-make-obama-a
-one-term-president/2012/09/24/79fd5cd8-0696-11e2-afff-d6c7f20a83bf_blog.html?utm
_term=.1c12116889fc.

10. Andy Barr, "The GOP's No-Compromise Pledge," *Politico*, October 28, 2010,
https://www.politico.com/story/2010/10/the-gops-no-compromise-pledge-044311.

11. Jason M. Breslow, "The Opposition Strategy," *Frontline*, January 17, 2017.

12. See Gerald Horne's brilliant study *The Counter-Revolution of 1776: Slave Resistance and the Origins of the United States of America* (New York: New York University
Press, 2014).

13. Kevin P. Phillips, *The Emerging Republican Majority* (1969; Princeton, NJ: Princeton University Press, 2015), 25.

14. Thomas B. Edsall with Mary D. Edsall, *Chain Reaction: The Impact of Race,
Rights, and Taxes on American Politics* (New York: Norton, 1992).

15. Udi Ofer, "How the 1994 Crime Bill Fed the Mass Incarceration Crisis," ACLU
(blog), June 4, 2019, https://www.aclu.org/blog/smart-justice/mass-incarceration/how-1994
-crime-bill-fed-mass-incarceration-crisis.

16. Alison Mitchell, "Two Clinton Aides Resign to Protest New Welfare Law," *New York Times*, September 12, 1996, https://www.nytimes.com/1996/09/12/us/two-clinton-aides-resign-to-protest-new-welfare-law.html.

17. Stephen Eric Bronner, "Notes on the Counter-Revolution," *Logos* 10, no. 1 (2011), 4, http://www.logosjournal.com/notes-counter-revolution.php.

18. Thomas Byrne Edsall and Mary D. Edsall, "When the Official Subject Is Presidential Politics, Taxes, Welfare, Crime, Rights, or Values . . . the Real Subject Is Race," *Atlantic*, May 1991, 62. Obama's triumph in 2008 was an exception to this pattern. Obama won with only 43 percent of white votes nationally, despite the meltdown of capitalism and the debility of McCain's campaign. However, his triumph owed less to stemming white defection than to the unprecedented turnout of Black voters, together with the fact that the two-thirds of Latinos who supported Hillary Clinton in the primaries voted for Obama in the general election. White youth provided another notable base of support, keeping the partisans of counterrevolution in check.

19. See Christopher Bonastia, *Knocking on the Door: The Federal Government's Attempt to Desegregate the Suburbs* (Princeton, NJ: Princeton University Press, 2006).

20. Hugh Davis Graham, *The Civil Rights Era: Origin and Development of National Policy, 1960–1972* (New York: Oxford University Press, 1990), 334–35. For other viewpoints, see Jennifer L. Hochschild, "The Strange Career of Affirmative Action," *Ohio State Law Journal* 59, no. 3 (1998): 997–1038, https://scholar.harvard.edu/jlhochschild/publications/strange-career-affirmative-action.

21. David Hamilton Golland, "Arthur Allen Fletcher, 'The Father of Affirmative Action,'" Blackpast, October 30, 2011, http://www.blackpast.org/perspectives/arthur-allen-fletcher-father-affirmative-action.

22. Herman Belz, *Equality Transformed: A Quarter Century of Affirmative Action*, Studies in Social Philosophy and Policy, no. 15 (Bowling Green, OH: Social Philosophy and Policy Center; New Brunswick, NJ: Transaction, 1991). "Harvard, Affirmative Action, and Diversity," interview with Richard A. Epstein, *Libertarian*, Hoover Institution, podcast, August 17, 2018, https://www.hoover.org/research/libertarian-harvard-affirmative-action-and-diversity.

23. David Roediger, *The Wages of Whiteness*, new ed. (New York: Verso, 2007).

24. Nancy MacLean, *Freedom Is Not Enough: The Opening of the American Workplace* (Cambridge, MA: Harvard University Press, 2008), 218–36.

25. Richard Herrnstein, "On Challenging an Orthodoxy," *Commentary*, April 1973.

26. MacLean, *Freedom Is Not Enough*, 230–31.

27. MacLean, 235. James Kilpatrick went so far as to say that the egalitarians were "worse racists—much worse racists—than the old Southern bigots" and that "the bureaucrats of HEW have done more to destroy good race relations in the past ten years than the Ku Klux Klan did in a century." Quoted in MacLean, 236.

28. Charles Murray, *Losing Ground: American Social Policy, 1950–1980*, 10th anniversary ed. (New York: Basic Books, 1995).

29. Adolph Reed Jr., "Looking Backward," *Nation*, November 28, 1994, 661–62.

30. Daniel Patrick Moynihan, *Family and Nation* (New York: Houghton Mifflin Harcourt, 1986); and Conference Proceedings, "The Negro American," vol. 2, *Daedalus* 95, no. 1 (Winter 1966): 288–80.

31. David P. Bryden, "The False Promise of Compromise," *Public Interest*, Winter 1998, 55; Richard Kahlenberg, *The Remedy* (New York: Basic Books, 1995), 118–19. Among the others whom Kahlenberg cites as supporting a class-based affirmative action are Jack Kemp, George Pataki, Christine Todd Whitman, and Bill Clinton. Stephen Steinberg, "Confronting the Misuse of Class-Based Affirmative Action," *New Politics*, Winter 1999, http://ww3.wpunj.edu/newpol/issue26/steinb26.htm.

32. MacLean, *Freedom Is Not Enough*, 101.

33. Bob Herbert, "The Ugly Side of the GOP," *New York Times*, September 25, 2007, http://www.nytimes.com/2007/09/25/opinion/25herbert.html; and http://en.wikipedia.org/wiki/Lee_Atwater. See also Ian Haney López, *Dog Whistle Politics* (New York: Oxford University Press, 2014).

34. Edsall and Edsall, "When the Official Subject," 62.

35. Gillian Brockell, "She Was Stereotyped as 'the Welfare Queen'; The Truth Was More Disturbing, a New Book Says," *Washington Post*, May 21, 2019, https://www.washingtonpost.com/history/2019/05/21/she-was-stereotyped-welfare-queen-truth-was-more-disturbing-new-book-says/.

36. Linda Gordon, "How Welfare Became a Dirty Word," *Chronicle of Higher Education*, July 20, 1994, B-1. Jane Quadagno, *The Color of Welfare: How Racism Undermined the War on Poverty* (New York: Oxford, 1995); Michael K. Brown, *Race, Money, and the Welfare State* (Ithaca, NY: Cornell, 1999); Kenneth J. Neubeck and Noel A. Cazenave, *Welfare Racism: Playing the Race Card Against America's Poor* (New York: Routledge, 2001); Ellen Reese, *Backlash against Welfare Mothers, Past and Present* (Berkeley: University of California, 2005); Betty Reid Mandell, "The Crime of Poverty," *New Politics*, Winter 2011, http://newpol.org/node/395.

37. See Miguel A. Centeno and Joseph N. Cohen, "The Rise and Fall of Neoliberalism," *Annual Review of Sociology* 37 (August 2011). Also, Catherine Kingfisher and Jeff Maskovsky, "The Limits of Neoliberalism," *Critique of Anthropology* 28 (2008): 115–24.

38. Glenn Beck, "Radio Clips," July 23, 2009, http://www.glennbeck.com/content/articles/article/198/28317/.

39. Steven Pitts, "Black Workers and the Public Sector," UC Berkeley Labor Center, April 4, 2011, http://laborcenter.berkeley.edu/blackworkers/blacks_public_sector11.pdf.

40. Glen Ford, "The Blackenization of Public Sector Employment," Black Agenda Radio, March 16, 2011, https://www.blackagendareport.com/content/blackenization-public-sector-employment.

41. George Wilson and V. J. Roscigno, "End of an Era? Managerial Losses of African American and Latinos in the Public Sector," *Social Science Research*, November 2015; George Wilson and V. J. Roscigno, "Neo-liberal Reform: The Public Sector and Black-White Inequality," *Sociology Compass*, November 2016; and Patricia Cohen, "Public-Sector Jobs Vanish, Hitting Blacks Hard," *New York Times*, May 24, 2015.

For still earlier studies of the diminishing foothold of Blacks in the public sector, see Algernon Austin, "Uneven Pain–Unemployment by Metropolitan Area and Race," Economic Policy Institute, June 8, 2010, http://www.epi.org/publications/entry/ib278/; Glen Ford, "Black Jobs Disappearing at Depression-Era Rates," Black Agenda Radio, August 5,

2009, http://www.blackagendareport.com/content/black-jobs-disappearing-depression-era
-rates; and Kirk Johnson, "Black Workers Bear Big Burden as Jobs in Government Dwin-
dle," *New York Times*, February 2, 1997, http://www.nytimes.com/1997/02/02/nyregion/
black-workers-bear-big-burden-as-jobs-in-government-dwindle.html.

42. Eduardo Porter. "Illegal Immigrants Are Bolstering Social Security with Billions,"
New York Times, April 5, 2005.

43. Mae Ngai, *Impossible Subjects: Illegal Aliens and the Making of Modern America*,
updated ed. (2004; Princeton, NJ: Princeton University Press, 2014).

44. Steven M. Gillon, *"That's Not What We Meant To Do"* (New York: W. W. Norton,
2000), ch. 4, 163–99. Hugh Davis Graham, *Collision Course: The Strange Convergence
of Affirmative Action and Immigration Policy in America* (New York: Oxford University
Press, 2003), ch. 3.

45. Haya El Nasser, "Black Populations Fall in Major Cities," *USA Today*, March 22,
2011, http://www.usatoday.com/news/nation/census/2011-03-22-1Ablacks22_ST_N.htm.

46. William Frey, a demographer at Brookings, has argued that the suburb was no brass
ring for Blacks. William H. Frey, "Black Populations Dropping in Big Cities," Brookings,
March 22, 2011, https://www.brookings.edu/on-the-record/black-populations-dropping-in
-big-cities/.

47. Thomas Sugrue, "A Dream Still Deferred," *New York Times*, March 26, 2011, http://
www.nytimes.com/2011/03/27/opinion/27Sugrue.html?_r=1&scp=1&sq=sugrue%20
-%20suburbs%20-%200p%20ed%20-&st=cse.

48. Edward Goetz, *Clearing the Way: Deconcentrating the Poor in Urban America*
(Washington, DC: Urban Institute Press; Lanham, MD: Rowman & Littlefield, 2003), 256.

49. Stephen Steinberg, "The Myth of Concentrated Poverty," in *The Integration
Debate*, ed. Chester Hartman and Gregory D. Squires (New York: Routledge, 2010),
213–28.

50. James Baldwin, excerpt from interview by Kenneth Clark, 1963, posted on You-
Tube, https://youtu.be/T8Abhj17kYU. Jacob Wagner, "'Negro Removal' Revisited: Urban
Planning and the New Jim Crow in Kansas City," Progressive City, March 12, 2017, https://
www.progressivecity.net/single-post/2017/03/12/negro-removal-revisited-urban-planning
-and-the-new-jim-crow-in-kansas-city; Kwame Shakir, "Gentrification Is 'Negro Removal':
A Parasitically Vicious Attack against POC Communities," Afropunk, March 6, 2018,
http://afropunk.com/2018/03/gentrification-negro-removal-parasitically-vicious-attack
-poc-communities/.

51. Goetz, *Clearing the Way*, 256.

52. Danny Weil, "Neoliberalism, Charter Schools and the Chicago Model," *Counter-
punch*, August 24, 2009, http://counterpunch.org/weil08242009.html. Jitu Brown, Eric
(Rico) Gutstein, and Pauline Lipman, "Arne Duncan and the Chicago Success Story: Myth
or Reality?" *Rethinking Schools* 23, no. 3 (Spring 2009), https://rethinkingschools.org/
articles/arne-duncan-and-the-chicago-success-story-myth-or-reality/; Paul Tough, "The
Harlem Project," *New York Times Magazine*, March 20, 2004.

53. Loic Wacquant, *Punishing the Poor: The Neoliberal Government of Social Insecurity* (Durham, NC: Duke University Press, 2009).

54. "In some states, black men have been admitted to prison on drug charges at rates twenty to fifty times greater than those of white men. And in major cities wracked by the drug war, as many as 80 percent of young African American men now have criminal records and are thus subject to legalized discrimination for the rest of their lives." Michelle Alexander, *The New Jim Crow: Mass Incarceration in the Age of Colorblindness* (New York: New Press, 2010), 7. Harry Levine, "The Epidemic of Pot Arrests in New York City," *Alternet*, August 10, 2009; Charles Blow, "Smoke and Horrors," Opinion, *New York Times*, October 22, 2010, http://www.nytimes.com/2010/10/23/opinion/23blow.html.

55. Alexander, *The New Jim Crow*, 59, 174–75. Also see Khalil Gibran Muhammad, *The Condemnation of Blackness: Race, Crime, and the Making of Modern Urban America* (Cambridge, MA: Harvard University Press, 2010).

56. Quoted in Ari Berman, "Voter Suppression: The Confederacy Rises Again," *Nation*, September 4, 2012, https://www.thenation.com/article/voter-suppression-confederacy-rises -again/.

57. Ari Berman, "How the GOP Rigs Elections: Gerrymandering, Voter ID Laws, Dark Money," *Rolling Stone*, January 24, 2018, https://www.rollingstone.com/politics/ news/gop-rigs-elections-gerrymandering-voter-id-laws-dark-money-w515664; Nina Totenberg, "Supreme Court Upholds Controversial Ohio Voter-Purge Law," *All Things Considered*, NPR, June 11, 2018, https://www.npr.org/2018/06/11/618870982/supreme-court -upholds-controversial-ohio-voter-purge-law%C2%A0.

58. Ari Berman, "The Supreme Court Gives the Green Light to Voter Purges: Trump's Justice Department Isn't Wasting Any Time," *Mother Jones*, June 15, 2018, https://www .motherjones.com/politics/2018/06/the-supreme-court-gave-the-green-light-to-voter-purges -trumps-justice-department-isnt-wasting-any-time/.

59. Quoted in Berman, "Voter Suppression," 2.

60. Lerone Bennett Jr., "Is History Repeating Itself?" *Ebony*, October 1981.

Chapter 2: How Daniel Patrick Moynihan
Derailed the Civil Rights Revolution

An earlier version of this chapter appeared as "The Moynihan Report at Fifty: The Long Reach of Intellectual Racism" in *Boston Review*, June 24, 2015, © Stephen Steinberg.

1. Quoted in Pamela Kirkland, "For Howard Grads, LBJ's 'To Fulfill These Rights' Remarks Are Still Relevant Half a Century Later," *Washington Post*, June 4, 2015, https:// www.washingtonpost.com/news/post-nation/wp/2015/06/04/for-howard-grads-lbjs-to -fulfill-these-rights-remarks-are-still-relevant-half-a-century-later/.

2. Lee Rainwater and William L. Yancey, *The Moynihan Report and the Politics of Controversy, including the Text of Daniel Patrick Moynihan's* The Negro Family: The Case for National Action (Cambridge, MA: MIT Press, 1967), 9.

3. Martin Luther King Jr., quoted in "Showdown for Non-Violence," *Look*, April 16, 1968, 24.

4. Daniel Patrick Moynihan, "The President and the Negro: The Moment Lost," *Commentary*, February 1967, https://www.commentarymagazine.com/article/the-president-the -negro-the-moment-lost/:31.

5. Whitney Young Jr., "Domestic Marshall Plan," 129, and Kyle Haselden, "Parity, not Preference," 128, in "Should There Be 'Compensation' For Negroes?" *New York Times Magazine*, October 6, 1963.

6. Mae M. Ngai, *Impossible Subjects: Illegal Aliens and the Making of Modern America*, updated ed. (2004; Princeton, NJ: Princeton University Press, 2014), 234–64.

7. Nathan Glazer, *Affirmative Discrimination: Ethnic Inequality and Public Policy* (New York: Basic Books, 1975), 221.

8. "Liberalism and the Negro: A Round-Table Discussion," *Commentary* 37 (March 1964): 25.

9. "Liberalism and the Negro," 31.

10. Richard N. Goodwin, *Remembering America: A Voice from the Sixties* (Boston: Little Brown, 1988), 342–43.

11. Godfrey Hodgson, *The Gentleman from New York* (New York: Houghton Mifflin, 2000), 96. There is also some ambiguity concerning how Goodwin and Moynihan staged this collaboration. Here is Moynihan's account: "The report went to the White House on May 4. One month later, on June 4, it provided the thesis for the commencement address given at Howard University by the President. The idea to do this was that of Bill D. Moyers. The speech was written by Richard Goodwin and me in a twenty-four-hour period starting about noon on June 2. There were two drafts; first mine, then a joint product of which Goodwin was the principal author." Daniel Patrick Moynihan, *Family and Nation*, Godkin Lectures, Harvard University, 1985 (New York: Harcourt Brace Jovanovich, 1986), 29–30.

12. James Patterson, *Freedom Is Not Enough* (New York: Basic Books, 2010), xii. Patterson also quotes Allen Matusow describing Moynihan in 1984 as having "a penchant for ambition," 23.

13. Lyndon B. Johnson, "To Fulfill These Rights," commencement address at Howard University, June 5, 1965, http://www.lbjlib.utexas.edu/johnson/archives.hom/speeches.hom/650604.asp.

14. Johnson, "To Fulfill These Rights," 126–27.

15. Nathan Glazer, "Negroes and Jews: The New Challenge to Pluralism," *Commentary*, December 1964, 32.

16. Nathan Glazer and Daniel P. Moynihan, *Beyond the Melting Pot: The Negroes, Puerto Ricans, Jews, Italians, and Irish of New York City*, 2nd ed. (Cambridge, MA: MIT Press, 1970), xcviii.

17. Glazer and Moynihan, *Beyond the Melting Pot*, 49–50.

18. As Daryl Michael Scott has put it: "Among this rising group of neoconservatives led by Eric Hoffer and Nathan Glazer, damage imagery effectively placed the onus for Black social problems on Black people rather than on society." Daryl Michael Scott, *Contempt and Pity: Social Policy and the Image of the Damaged Black Psyche, 1880–1996* (Chapel Hill: University of North Carolina Press, 1997), 92.

19. In his critique of the Moynihan Report, Herbert Gans also observed that "Moynihan's initial knowledge of research about the Black community appears to come from the work of Nathan Glazer (1963), who had begun his own discussion of the Negro family in *Beyond the Melting Pot* with observations on the female-headed family, illegitimacy, child

abandonment, and related problems." Herbert J. Gans, "The Moynihan Report and Its Aftermaths: A Critical Analysis," *Du Bois Review* 8, no. 2 (2011): 318.

20. Paul E. Peterson, "Nathan Glazer on Revisiting the Moynihan Report," *Education Next* 15, no. 2 (Spring 2015), https://www.educationnext.org/nathan-glazer-revisiting -moynihan-report/.

21. Nathan Glazer, introduction to *Slavery*, by Stanley Elkins (New York: Universal Library, Grosset & Dunlap, 1963). Glazer's introduction was previously published as a review of Elkins's book. Nathan Glazer, "*Slavery: A Problem in American Institutional and Intellectual Life* by Stanley M. Elkins," *Commentary*, May 1960. Also see Ann J. Lane, *The Debate over Slavery: Stanley Elkins and His Critics* (Champaign: University of Illinois Press, 1971).

22. Glazer, introduction to *Slavery*, xii.

23. Glazer reviewed Elkins's book in *Commentary*, May 1960.

24. Nathan Glazer, "Is 'Integration' Possible in the New York Schools," *Commentary*, September 1960, https://www.commentarymagazine.com/article/is-integration-possible-in -the-new-york-schools/.

25. Nathan Glazer, foreword to *The Negro Family in the United States*, rev. and abr. ed. (Chicago: University of Chicago Press, 1966). Glazer adds with an air of innocence: "As I write, the *New York Times* reports that the President and his advisers now see the Negro family as a key element in their efforts to wipe out the gap between the social, educational, and economic position of Negro and white."

26. Anthony M. Platt, *E. Franklin Frazier Reconsidered* (New Brunswick, NJ: Rutgers University Press, 1991), 137.

27. Platt, *E. Franklin Frazier Reconsidered*, 141.

28. In Rainwater and Yancey, *Moynihan Report and the Politics of Controversy*, 410.

29. "'Semantic infiltration' is a term coined by the foreign policy expert Fred Iklé and popularized by the late Senator Daniel Patrick Moynihan." Michael Lind, "How Right-Wingers Use Semantic Tricks to Kill Government," *Salon*, May 18, 2013, https://www .salon.com/2013/05/18/how_right_wingers_use_semantic_tricks_to_kill_government/. After public consternation about the source of *semantic infiltration*, Fred Iklé revealed his identity in "Semantic Infiltration," *American Spectator*, July-August, 2010, http://spectator .org/articles/39311/semantic-infiltration.

30. Rainwater and Yancey, *Moynihan Report and the Politics of Controversy*, Preface.

31. Goodwin, *Remembering America*, 344.

32. Review of the Week, *New York Times*, June 6, 1965, 10.

33. Quoted in Rainwater and Yancey, *Moynihan Report and the Politics of Controversy*, 135.

34. It was widely rumored that Moynihan leaked the report to the press. Steve Estes, *I Am a Man* (Chapel Hill: University of North Carolina Press, 2005), 117.

35. Rainwater and Yancey, *Moynihan Report and the Politics of Controversy*, 139.

36. Rainwater and Yancey, 141.

37. Rainwater and Yancey, 141.

38. Robert Dallek, *Flawed Giant: Lyndon Johnson and His Times, 1961–1973* (New York: Oxford University Press, 1998), 225–26.

39. Goodwin, *Remembering America*, 348.

40. Stephen Steinberg, "Race and Counterrevolution," *New Politics*, no. 53 (Winter 2013).

41. Daniel Patrick Moynihan, "The New Racialism," *Atlantic Monthly*, August 1968, https://www.theatlantic.com/past/politics/race/moynihan.htm.

42. Rainwater and Yancey, *Moynihan Report and the Politics of Controversy*, 3.

43. Daniel Patrick Moynihan, "The President and The Negro: The Moment Lost," *Commentary*, February 1967, https://www.commentarymagazine.com/article/the-president -the-negro-the-moment-lost/.

44. "The Negro American," vol. 2, *Daedalus*, Winter 1966, 288–89. Italics in original.

45. "Neglect, but Not 'Benign,'" *New York Times*, March 3, 1970, 40.

46. Iklé, "Semantic Infiltration."

47. Goodwin, *Remembering America*, 542.

48. Earl Shorris, "The Jews of the New Right," *Nation*, May 8, 1982, 557.

49. Nathan Glazer, "In Defense of Preference," *New Republic*, April 6, 1988. See also James Traub, "'I Was Wrong': Nathan Glazer Comes to Terms with Multiculturalism," review of *We Are All Multiculturalists Now*, *Slate*, May 15, 1997, http://www.slate.com/ articles/arts/books/1997/05/i_was_wrong.html. In the wake of Glazer's defection, *Commentary* ran a symposium of twenty prominent figures, including Glazer, most of whom were adamantly opposed to affirmative action.

50. One key player was James E. Jones, who provides rich detail on the genesis of the Philadelphia Plan in his autobiography, *Hattie's Boy* (Madison: University of Wisconsin Law School, 2006).

51. Hugh Davis Graham, *The Civil Rights Era: The Origins and Development of National Policy, 1960–1972* (New York: Oxford University Press, 1990), 325. Rick Perlstein also subscribes to the theory that the Plan "drove a wedge through the Democratic coalition at its most vulnerable joint: between Blacks and hard hats." Rick Perlstein, *Nixonland* (New York: Scribner, 2008), 515.

52. Dean J. Kotlowski, *Nixon's Civil Rights* (Cambridge, MA: Harvard University Press, 2001), 107.

53. Kotlowski, *Nixon's Civil Rights*, 107; Graham, *The Civil Rights Era*, 344–45.

54. Benjamin Balint, *Running* Commentary: *The Contentious Magazine That Transformed the Jewish Left into the Neoconservative Right* (New York: Public Affairs, 2010), 90.

55. Balint, *Running* Commentary, 138.

56. MacLean, *Freedom Is Not Enough*, 230–37. Also see Patterson, *Freedom Is Not Enough*, 101–2. Patterson writes: "The simplest and in general most accurate label for Moynihan's ideas during these years following the release of his report on Black family life is that they had become moderately neoconservative. Hence, Moynihan's appeal to readers of journals such as *Commentary* and *The Public Interest* (which he had helped to found and on which he served as a member of the Publication Committee). Hence, too, his close association with leading neoconservatives such as Glazer, Wilson, and Irving Kristol."

57. MacLean, *Freedom Is Not Enough*, 198.

Chapter 3: The Life and Death of Affirmative Action

Earlier versions of this chapter appeared as "Nathan Glazer and the Assassination of Affirmative Action" in *New Politics* 9, no. 3, whole no. 35 (Summer 2003), © Stephen Steinberg; and as "Confronting the Misuse of Class-Based Affirmative Action" in *New Politics* 7, no. 2, whole no. 26 (Winter 1999), © Stephen Steinberg.

1. Lerone Bennett Jr., "Tea and Sympathy: Liberals and Other White Hopes," in *The Negro Mood*, by Lerone Bennett Jr. (Chicago: Johnson Publishing, 1964), 75–104.

2. James Traub, "Nathan Glazer Changes His Mind, Again," *New York Times Magazine*, June 28, 1998.

3. Nathan Glazer, "Negroes and Jews: The New Challenge to Pluralism," *Commentary*, December 1964, 43. Italics in original.

4. Glazer, "Negroes and Jews," 42.

5. Herbert Hill: "Black Labor and Affirmative Action: A Historical Perspective," in *The Question of Discrimination*, ed. Steven Shulman and William Darity (Middletown, CT: Wesleyan University Press, 1989), 230.

6. Personal dialogue with Joseph Bensman, CUNY Graduate Center, circa 1980.

7. Ira Katznelson, *When Affirmative Action Was White: An Untold History of Racial Inequality in Twentieth-Century America* (New York: W. W. Norton, 2006).

8. Nathan Glazer and Daniel Patrick Moynihan, *Beyond the Melting Pot: The Negroes, Puerto Ricans, Jews, Italians, and Irish of New York City* (Cambridge, MA: MIT Press, 1963), 53.

9. Nathan Glazer and Daniel Patrick Moynihan, *Beyond the Melting Pot*, 2nd ed. (Cambridge, MA: MIT Press, 1970), xix–xx.

10. Gunnar Myrdal, *An American Dilemma* (New York: Harper & Row, 1944).

11. Howard Schuman, "Sociological Racism," *Transaction* 7, no. 2 (December 1969): 44–48.

12. Glazer and Moynihan, *Beyond the Melting Pot*, 2nd ed., xxxiii.

13. Glazer and Moynihan, xxxiii.

14. Glazer and Moynihan, xxxiii.

15. Glazer and Moynihan, 49–50.

16. Jim Sleeper, "In Fragments," Book Review, *New York Times*, April 27, 1997, https://www.nytimes.com/1997/04/27/books/in-fragments.html.

17. Nathan Glazer, *Affirmative Discrimination: Ethnic Inequality and Public Policy* (New York: Basic Books, 1975), 200.

18. Ira Katznelson, "What America Taught the Nazis: In the 1930s, the Germans Were Fascinated by the Global Leader in Codified Racism—the United States," *Atlantic Monthly*, November 2017.

19. Nathan Glazer, "From Socialism to Sociology," in *Authors of Their Own Lives*, ed. Bennett M. Berger (Berkeley: University of California Press, 1990). Also Nathan Glazer, "My Life in Sociology," *Annual Review of Sociology* 38 (August 2012): 1–16, http://dx.doi.org/10.1146/annurev-soc-071811-145506.

20. Glazer, "From Socialism to Sociology," 190–209.

21. Glazer, "From Socialism to Sociology."

22. *Arguing the World*, directed and written by Joseph Dorman, featuring Daniel Bell, Nathan Glazer, Irving Howe, and Irving Kristol (New York: First Run Features, 1998).

23. Nathan Glazer, *The Social Basis of American Communism* (1961; repr., New York: Praeger, 1974).

24. Glazer, "From Socialism to Sociology," 25.

25. Traub, "Nathan Glazer Changes His Mind, Again." According to Peter Skerry, this was Glazer's first regular teaching post. In 1966 Moynihan secured a position as a tenured professor of education and urban policy at Harvard, and three years later, Glazer also moved to Harvard. Peter Skerry, "Nathan Glazer—Merit before Meritocracy," *American Interest*, April 3, 2019, https:///www.the-american-interest.com/2019/04/03/nathan-glazer.

26. Nathan Glazer, new introduction, *Affirmative Discrimination*, updated ed. (Cambridge, MA: Harvard University Press, 1987).

27. Nathan Glazer, *We Are All Multiculturalists Now* (Cambridge, MA: Harvard University Press, 1997).

28. Glazer, *We Are All Multiculturalists Now*, 119.

29. Traub, "Nathan Glazer Changes His Mind, Again."

30. Glazer, *We Are All Multiculturalists Now*, 147.

31. Barry Goldberg, "Let Them Eat Multiculturalism," review of Nathan Glazer, *We Are All Multiculturalists Now*, *New Politics* 6, no. 3 (Summer 1997), https://archive.newpol.org/issue23/goldbe23.htm.

32. Goldberg, "Let Them Eat Multiculturalism."

33. Murray Kempton was a popular *New York Times* columnist; his obituary described him as "unmatched in his moral insight into the hypocrisies of politics and their consequences for the poor and powerless." Richard Severo, "Murray Kempton, 79, a Newspaperman of Honor and Elegant Vinegar Is Dead," *New York Times*, May 6, 1997, https://www.nytimes.com/1997/05/06/nyregion/murray-kempton-79-a-newspaperman-of-honor-and-elegant-vinegar-is-dead.html. For Moynihan's anecdote about Kempton , see "The Negro American," vol. 2, *Daedalus* 95, no. 1 (Winter 1966): 410.

Chapter 4: The Comeback of the Culture of Poverty
An earlier version of this chapter appeared as "Poor Reason: Culture Still Doesn't Explain Poverty" in *Boston Review*, January 13, 2011, © Stephen Steinberg.

1. Patricia Cohen, "'Culture of Poverty' Makes a Comeback," *New York Times*, October 17, 2010, 1.

2. Mario Luis Small, David J. Harding, and Michèle Lamont, eds., "Reconsidering Culture and Poverty," special issue, *Annals of the American Academy of Political and Social Science* 629 (May 11, 2010).

3. Small, Harding, and Lamont, "Introduction to Special Issue," in "Reconsidering Culture and Poverty."

4. Daniel Patrick Moynihan, *The Negro Family: The Case for National Action* (Washington, DC: Office of Policy Planning and Research, United States Department of Labor, March 1965), https://www.dol.gov/general/aboutdol/history/webid-moynihan, or https://web.stanford.edu/~mrosenfe/Moynihan%27s%20The%20Negro%20Family.pdf.

5. Daniel Patrick Moynihan, interview, *Meet the Press*, December 1965, posted on YouTube, December 22, 2015, by C-SPAN3, *Reel America*, https://youtu.be/mnE_NseoS6U.

6. William Julius Wilson, "Why Both Social Structure and Culture Matter in a Holistic Analysis of Inner-City Poverty," in Small, Harding, and Lamont, "Reconsidering Culture and Poverty."

7. Moynihan, *The Negro Family*, 30.

8. Moynihan, 47.

9. Herbert Gans, "The Negro Family: Reflecting on the Moynihan Report," *Commonweal*, October 15, 1965, 47–51.

10. Moynihan, *The Negro Family*, 47.

11. Carol B. Stack, *All Our Kin: Strategies for Survival in a Black Community* (New York: Basic Books, 1983).

12. Elliott Liebow, *Tally's Corner: A Study of Negro Streetcorner Men* (New York: Little Brown, 1967).

13. Liebow, *Tally's Corner*, 144.

14. Michael Harrington, *The Other America* (New York: Penguin, 1962).

15. Gunnar Myrdal, *Challenge to Affluence* (New York: Pantheon, 1962).

16. Ken Auletta, "The Underclass—1," "The Underclass—2," and "The Underclass—3," *New Yorker*, November 8, 1981, November 15, 1981, and November 22, 1981.

17. Myron Magnet, "America's Underclass: What to Do?" *Fortune*, May 11, 1987, 130. Like other iterations of the culture of poverty, "the underclass" reified culture and obscured political economy. In her classic study *Exotics at Home*, Micaela di Leonardo reveals the face of power that lurks behind the mask of culture (Chicago: University of Chicago Press, 1998).

18. Adolph Reed, "The Underclass Myth," *Progressive*, August 1, 1991.

19. Wilson, "Why Both Social Structure and Culture Matter," 200, 204.

20. Douglas G. Glasgow, *The Black Underclass: Poverty, Unemployment, and Entrapment of Ghetto Youth* (New York: Vintage, 1981).

21. Liebow, *Tally's Corner*, 222.

22. Will Dobbie and Roland G. Fryer, "Are High-Quality Schools Enough to Increase Achievement among the Poor? Evidence from the Harlem Children's Zone," *American Economic Journal Allied Economics* 3, no. 2 (July 2011): 158–87.

23. Office of Elementary and Secondary Education, Department of Education, "2011 Promise Neighborhood Grant Winners Announced," News, December 19, 2011, https://oese.ed.gov/2011/12/2011-promise-neighborhoods-grant-winners-announced/.

Part II: Deconstructing Victim-Blaming Discourses

1. Miranda Fricker, "What Is the Point of Blame? A Paradigm-Based Explanation," *Noûs* 50 (2016): 165–83.

2. William Ryan, *Blaming the Victim*, rev. ed. (1971; New York: Vintage, 1976).

3. Robert Fogelson, *Violence as Protest: A Study of Riots and Ghettos* (New York: Doubleday, 1971).

4. Elizabeth Hinton, *America On Fire: The Untold History of Police Violence and Black Rebellion since the 1960s* (New York: Liveright, 2021): 4.

5. Otto Kerner et al., *Report of the National Advisory Commission on Civil Disorders* (Washington, DC: US Government Printing Office, 1968), 1, https://catalog.hathitrust.org/Record/000339500.

6. Murray Friedman, "The White Liberal's Retreat," *Atlantic Monthly* 211 (January 1963): 43.

7. Murray Friedman, *What Went Wrong?: The Creation and Collapse of the Black-Jewish Alliance* (New York: Free Press, 1994).

8. Edward Banfield, "Rioting Mainly for Fun and Profit," in *The Unheavenly City: The Nature and Future of Our Urban Crises* (Boston: Little, Brown, 1970).

9. Friedman, "The White Liberal's Retreat," 109.

10. Martin Luther King Jr., *Why We Can't Wait* (New York: Harper & Row, 1964), 130.

11. Martin Luther King Jr., *Where Do We Go from Here? Chaos or Community* (Boston: Beacon Press, 1968), 12. Italics added.

12. King, *Where Do We Go from Here?* 68.

13. Jelani Cobb, "How Parties Die," *New Yorker*, March 15, 2021, 26.

14. William Ryan, *Blaming the Victim* (New York: Vintage, 1971), 6–7.

15. Jim Sleeper, *Liberal Racism: How Fixating on Race Subverts the American Dream* (New York: Viking, 1997).

16. Brian K. Landsberg, *Enforcing Civil Rights: Race Discrimination and the Department of Justice* (Lawrence: University Press of Kansas, 1997).

17 For an excellent recent study, see Amaka Okechukwu, *To Fulfill These Rights: Political Struggle over Affirmative Action and Open Admissions* (New York: Columbia University Press, 2019). Despite her passionate defense of affirmative action and despite the noble efforts to shape affirmative action to the narrow restraints allowed by court decisions, Okechukwu is pessimistic about the future of affirmative action.

18. Dinesh D'Souza, *The End of Racism* (New York: Free Press, 1995), 289.

19. Ta-Nehisi Coates, "How to Steal Things, Exploit People, and Avoid Responsibility," *Atlantic Monthly*, October 5, 2014, https://www.theatlantic.com/business/archive/2014/10/the-road-to-reparations/373578/. Also, David Frum, "The Impossibility of Reparations," *Atlantic Monthly*, June 3, 2014; and Adolph Reed, "The Case against Reparations," *Progressive*, December 2000.

20. William Julius Wilson, *The Declining Significance of Race* (Chicago: University of Chicago Press, 1978). Kenneth Clark asserted that the idea that racism was declining was "a pitiful delusion." Kenneth Clark, "Contemporary Sophisticated Racism," in *The Declining Significance of Race: Myth or Reality*, ed. J. R. Washington (Philadelphia: University of Pennsylvania Press, 1980).

21. In *The Truly Disadvantaged*, Wilson sought to present his policy proposals for addressing the high rates of unemployment and underemployment among Blacks and ghetto youth in particular. However, his main policy proposal was for a WPA-like program to provide jobs for ghetto youth, and it lacked details or a plan for implementation. Nor does Wilson frontally address the pervasive racism in job markets or the lack of enforcement of

laws against job discrimination in the 1964 Civil Rights Act. William Julius Wilson, *The Truly Disadvantaged* (Chicago: University of Chicago Press, 1987.).

22. "In an unapologetic embrace of liberal Democratic Party values, President Clinton declared Wednesday that affirmative action has been 'good for America' and urged the nation to 'mend it, not end it.'" Paul Richter, "Clinton Declares Affirmative Action Is 'Good for America,'" *Los Angeles Times*, July 20, 1995, https://www.latimes.com/archives/la-xpm -1995-07-20-mn-26049-story.html.

23. D'Souza, *The End of Racism*, 554.

24. David Hollinger, *Postethnic America: Beyond Multiculturalism* (New York: Basic Books, 1995). Among the prominent exponents of "race over," see Paul Gilroy, *Against Race: Imagining Political Culture Beyond he Color Line* (Cambridge, MA: Harvard University Press, 2000); David Hollinger, *Postethnic America: Beyond Multiculturalism* (New York: Basic Books, 1995); Antonia Darder and Rodolfo D. Torres, *After Race: Racism after Multiculturalism* (New York: New York University Press, 2000); Orlando Patterson, "Race Over," *New Republic* 222 (January 10, 2000); Orlando Patterson, "Race by the Numbers," *New York Times*, May 8, 2001; Adolph Reed, "Class-ifying the Hurricane," *Nation*, October 3, 2005; and Adolph Reed, "The Real Divide," *Progressive*, November 2005.

On the other hand, criticism emanated from two sources: David Roediger, "The Retreat from Race and Class," *Monthly Review* 58, no. 3 (July-August, 2006); and Michael K. Brown, Martin Carnoy, Elliott Currie, Troy Duster, David B. Oppenheimer, Marjorie M. Schultz, and David Wellman, *Whitewashing Race: The Myth of a Color-Blind Society* (Berkeley: University of California Press, 2005).

25. Ryan, *Blaming the Victim*, 25.

26. Ryan, *Blaming the Victim*, 28–29. Italics in original.

27. Alyson M. Cole, *The Cult of True Victimhood: From the War on Welfare to the War on Terror* (Stanford, CA: Stanford University Press, 2007), 112.

28. Cole, *The Cult of True Victimhood*, 112.

Chapter 5: Social Science and the Occlusion of Political Economy

An earlier version of this chapter appeared as "The Role of Social Science in the Legitimation of Racial Hierarchy" in *Race & Society* 1, no. 1 (1998): 5–14. Reprinted with permission from Elsevier.

1. W. E. B. DuBois, *Black Reconstruction in America, 1860–1880* (1935; New York: Free Press, 1998), 727.

2. Charles W. Mills, *The Racial Contract* (Ithaca, NY: Cornell University Press, 1997), 19.

3. George Fredrickson, *White Supremacy: A Comparative Study of American and South African History* (New York: Oxford University Press, 1982), 7.

4. Dinesh D'Souza, *The End of Racism* (New York: Free Press, 1995).

5. D'Souza, *The End of Racism*, 483.

6. D'Souza, 482, 486.

7. D'Souza, 456.

8. Thomas Pettigrew, "The Negro American," *Daedalus* 95, no. 1 (Fall 1965): 312.

9. Leah N. Gordon, *From Power to Prejudice: The Rise of Racial Individualism in Midcentury America* (Chicago: Oxford University Press, 2015).

10. For a critique of urban ethnography, see Robin D. G. Kelley, "Looking for the 'Real' NIGGA: Social Scientists Construct the Ghetto," in *YO' mama's disfunktional!* (Boston: Beacon Press, 1997), ch. 1.

11. One of the few contemporaneous critics to challenge the cultural deprivation model was Kenneth Clark. In *Dark Ghetto*, he wrote: "To what extent are the contemporary social deprivation theories merely substituting notions of environmental immutability and fatalism for earlier notions of biologically determined educational unmodifiability?" Kenneth Clark, *Dark Ghetto* (New York: Harper & Row, 1965), 131.

12. Lewis's original explication of the "culture of poverty" concept was in *La Vida* (New York: Knopf, 1964), xlii–lii. Also see Oscar Lewis, "The Culture of Poverty," *Scientific American* 215 (October 1966): 19–25. For critiques of the culture of poverty canon, see Hylan Lewis, *Class, Culture, and Poverty* (Washington, DC: Cross-Tell, 1967); Eleanor Burke Leacock, ed., *The Culture of Poverty: A Critique* (New York: Simon & Schuster, 1971); Herbert J. Gans, "Culture and Class in the Study of Poverty," in *People, Plans, and Policies* (New York: Columbia University Press, 1993), ch. 20; William Ryan, *Blaming the Victim*, rev. ed. (New York: Vintage Books, 1976); Stephen Steinberg, "The Culture of Poverty Reconsidered," in *The Ethnic Myth* (Boston: Beacon Press, 1989), ch. 4.

13. Myron Magnet, "America's Underclass: What to Do?" *Fortune* 115 (May 11, 1987): 130. For critiques of the underclass discourse, see William Kornblum, "Lumping the Poor: What Is the Underclass?" *Dissent*, September 1984, 295–302; Michael Katz, *The Undeserving Poor* (New York: Pantheon Books, 1989), ch. 5; Herbert Gans, "The Dangers of the Underclass: Its Harmfulness as a Planning Concept," in *People, Plans, and Policies* (New York: Columbia University Press, 1993), ch. 21; and Stephen Steinberg, *Turning Back: The Retreat from Racial Justice in American Thought and Policy*, 2nd ed. (1995; Boston: Beacon Press, 2000), ch. 6.

14. "Resistance theory" has its origin in the writing of Pierre Bourdieu, *Outline of a Theory of Practice* (Cambridge: Cambridge University Press, 1977); Paul Willis, *Learning to Labor* (London: Routledge, 1977); and Henry Giroux, *Theory and Resistance in Education* (South Hadley, MA: Bergin & Garvey, 1983). See Jay MacLeod, *Ain't No Makin' It*, 2nd ed. (Boulder, CO: Westview, 1995). In *When Work Disappears*, William Julius Wilson embraces the assumptions of the resistance theorists. He argues that, in response to persistent joblessness, ghetto residents develop a cultural repertoire and patterns of "ghetto-related behavior" that "hinder rational planning" and otherwise prevent them from taking advantage of even the scarce opportunities that exist for work. William Julius Wilson, *When Work Disappears* (New York: Vintage, 1997). For a critique of *When Work Disappears*, see Stephen Steinberg, "The Role of Racism in the Inequality Studies of William Julius Wilson," *Journal of Blacks in Higher Education*, no.15 (Spring 1997): 109–17.

15. Orlando Patterson, "A Poverty of the Mind," Op-Ed, *New York Times*, March 26, 2006.

16. The term *civility* emerged as a recurrent trope in political discourse. For an astute analysis, see Benjamin De Mott, "Seduced by Civility," *Nation* 263 (December 9, 1996), 19.

17. Elliot Liebow, *Tally's Corner: A Study of Negro Streetcorner Men* (New York: Little Brown, 1967), 222.

18. Liebow, *Tally's Corner*, 223.

19. The "sin of reification" is Abraham Kaplan's coinage: "Reification is more than a metaphysical sin, it is a logical one. It is the mistake of treating a notational device as though it were a substantive term, what I have called a construct as though it were observational, a theoretical term as though it were a construct or indirect observable." Abraham Kaplan, *The Structure of Science* (San Francisco: Chandler, 1964), 61.

20. Gerald D. Berreman, "Race, Caste, and Other Invidious Distinctions in Social Stratification," *Race*, 13 (1972): 4.

21. Abram Kardiner and Lionel Ovesey, *The Mark of Oppression* (New York: W. W. Norton, 1951).

22. C. Wright Mills, *The Power Elite* (1956; New York, Oxford University Press, 2000).

23. Mustafa Emirbayer and Matthew Desmond, "Race and Reflexivity," *Ethnic and Racial Studies* 34, no. 4 (2012): 574–99. Italics in original.

24. Aldon Morris, *The Scholar Denied: W.E.B. Du Bois and the Birth of Modern Sociology* (Berkeley: University of California Press, 2015).

Chapter 6: Education as a False Panacea

1. James D. Anderson, *The Education of Blacks in the South, 1860–1935* (Chapel Hill: University of North Carolina Press, 1988), 83.

2. Denzell Jobson, "Is the Harlem Children's Zone Accomplishing Its Goal?" Yale Education Studies, May 4, 2017, http://debsedstudies.org/harlem-childrens-zone/.

3. Winifred Raushenbush, *Robert E. Park: Biography of a Sociologist*, with foreword and epilogue by Everett C. Hughes (Durham, NC: Duke University Press, 1979), 67.

4. Daniel Breslau, "The American Spencerians: Theorizing a New Science," in *Sociology in America: A History*, ed. Craig Calhoun, ASA Centennial Publication (Chicago: University of Chicago Press, 2007), 46.

5. Pamela Barnhouse Walters, "Betwixt and Between Discipline and Profession: A History of Sociology of Profession," in Calhoun, *Sociology in America*, 641–42.

6. Booker T. Washington, *Up from Slavery* (1901; New York: W. W. Norton, 1966), 13. It is not clear whether Max Thrasher, Washington's ghostwriter, was the author of these words.

7. Louis R. Harlan, *Booker T. Washington: The Wizard of Tuskegee, 1901–1945* (New York: Oxford, 1983), 144.

8. These words ("complete the education begun under slavery") were spoken by Hollis B. Frissell, principal of Hampton Institute, at a conference for education in the South, Capon Springs, West Virginia, circa 1900. Anderson, *The Education of Blacks in the South*, 83.

9. Anderson, 89.

10. Anderson, 90.

11. Winifred Raushenbush, "The Convergence of William I. Thomas and Robert Park," in Raushenbush, *Robert E. Park*, 29–30.

12. Quoted in Stephen Steinberg, *Race Relations: A Critique* (Stanford, CA: Stanford University Press, 2006), 29.

13. John Stanfield, *Philanthropy and Jim Crow in American Social Science* (New York: Praeger, 1985), 38. In a recent paper, Aldon Morris also contends that Park was the purveyor of Booker T. Washington's worldview, and that W. E. B. Du Bois is the unheralded founder of the sociology of race. Aldon Morris, "W. E. B. Du Bois and Robert E. Park: Origins of the Sociology of Race," paper delivered at the 2010 Annual Meeting of the American Sociological Society; and Aldon Morris, "Sociology of Race and W. E. B. Du Bois," in Calhoun, *Sociology in America*, 503–34.

14. Stanford Lyman, *The Black American in Sociological Thought: New Perspectives on Black America* (New York: Capricorn, 1972), 36.

15. Robert Ezra Park and Ernest Burgess, *Introduction to the Science of Sociology* (Chicago: University of Chicago Press, 1921). This is often credited as the first textbook in sociology, though there was a precursor twenty-seven years earlier: Albion Woodbury Small and George E. Vincent, *An Introduction to the Study of Society* (New York: American Book, 1894).

16. Robert E. Park, *Race and Culture* (New York: Free Press, 1950), 151.

17. Gunnar Myrdal, *An American Dilemma* (New York: Harper, 1944).

18. Andrew Abbott, *Department and Discipline* (Chicago: University of Chicago Press, 1999), 9.

19. Abbott, *Department and Discipline*, 11.

20. Albion Small, "Scholarship and Social Agitation," *American Journal of Sociology* 1, no. 5 (March 1896): 569.

21. Small, "Scholarship and Social Agitation," 38. Also see Mary O. Furner, *Advocacy and Objectivity: A Crisis in the Professionalization of American Social Science, 1865–1905* (Lexington: University of Kentucky Press, 1975), 177.

22. Herman Schwendinger and Julia R. Schwendinger, *The Sociologists of the Chair* (New York: Basic Books, 1974), 100.

23. Schwendinger and Schwendinger, *Sociologists of the Chair*, 106. Italics in original.

24. Karl Marx, *The Poverty of Philosophy* (Mayfield Center, CT: Martino Publishing, 2014), 121.

25. Aldon Morris, *The Scholar Denied: W. E. B. Du Bois and the Birth of Modern Sociology* (Berkeley: University of California Press, 2015), 4.

26. Morris, *The Scholar Denied*, 4.

27. Morris, 17.

28. Morris, 50.

29. Morris, 48.

30. Morris, 54.

31. Schwendinger and Schwendinger, *Sociologists of the Chair*, 504.

32. Quoted in Schwendinger and Schwendinger, 504.

33. According to Du Bois, "After a time no Negro institution could collect funds without the recommendation or acquiescence of Mr. Washington. Few political appointments were made anywhere in the United States without his consent. Even the careers of rising

young colored men were very often determined by his advice and certainly his opposition was fatal." Quoted in Schwendinger and Schwendinger, 505.

34. Quoted in Morris, *The Scholar Denied*, 112, from W. E. B. Du Bois, "The Evolution of the Race Problem," *Proceedings of the National Negro Conference*, May 31–June 1, 1909, New York (New York [?]: The Conference, 1909 [?]), 146–47.

35. Morris, *The Scholar Denied*, 99.

36. Shedding light on the "cultural turn" that "began to take hold in the sociology of race" after World War I, Howard Winant writes: "The culturalist trend appealed to many mainstream sociologists disaffected with social Darwinist and Spencerian evolutionism, and dismayed by the intractability the biologistic paradigm assigned to race. So racial themes and race itself now began to be recognized as 'social problems.' Initial challenges to biologism were timid, merely replacing its overtly 'natural' framework with one based on concepts of cultural backwardness and disadvantage. These were handicaps, matters that could be transformed, but only gradually over many generations." Howard Winant, "The Dark Side of the Force: One Hundred Years of the Sociology of Race," in Calhoun, *Sociology in America*, 548.

37. Thomas D. Fallace, "Was John Dewey Ethnocentric? Reevaluating the Philosopher's Early Views on Culture and Race," *Educational Researcher* 19, no. 6 (2012): 471–77.

38. At the turn of the nineteenth century, Charles W. Dabney, president of the University of Tennessee, averred: "We must use common sense in the education of the negro. . . . We must recognize in all its relations that momentous fact that the negro is a child race, at least two thousand years behind the Anglo-Saxon in its development. . . . Nothing is more ridiculous than the programme of the good religious people from the North who insist upon teaching Latin, Greek, and philosophy to the negro boys who come to their schools." Quoted in Anderson, *The Education of Blacks in the South*, 85.

39. Robert Park, "Education in its Relation to the Conflict and Fusion of Cultures," in *Race and Culture*, 267, 268.

40. Park, *Race and Culture*, 282.

41. Stanford Lyman, "Race Relations as Social Process: Sociology's Resistance to a Civil Rights Orientation," in *Race in America*, ed. Herbert Hill and James E. Jones (Madison: University of Wisconsin Press, 1993), 394.

42. Lyman, "Race Relations as Social Process," 397.

43. Paul Tough, *Whatever It Takes: Geoffrey Canada's Quest to Change Harlem and America* (New York: Mariner Books, 2008). "President Obama Cites HCZ as an Innovator," Harlem Children's Zone, n.d., https://hcz.org/news/president-obama-cites-hcz-as-an-innovator/; "Promise Academy Student Bowls over President Obama," Harlem Children's Zone, n.d., https://hcz.org/news/promise-academy-student-bowls-over-president-obama/; Michelle Croft and Grover J. "Russ" Whitehurst, "The Harlem Children's Zone, Promise Neighborhoods, and the Broader, Bolder Approach to Education," Brookings, July 20, 2010, https://www.brookings.edu/research/the-harlem-childrens-zone-promise-neighborhoods-and-the-broader-bolder-approach-to-education/; Jobson, "Is the Harlem Children's Zone Accomplishing Its Goal?"

44. Lorraine Hansberry, *Les Blancs*, ed. Robert Nemiroff (New York: Vintage Books, 1972).

45. Harvey Kantor, "Education Can't Solve Poverty—So Why Do We Keep Insisting That It Can?" interview by Jennifer Berkshire, *AlterNet*, September 24, 2017, https://www.alternet.org/2017/09/education-cant-solve-poverty/. Harvey Kantor is the author, with Robert Lowe, of "Educationalizing the Welfare State and Privatizing Education," Marquette College of Education Faculty Research and Publications, 2016, https://epublications.marquette.edu/edu_fac/433/. The authors emphasize the deleterious consequences of No Child Left Behind.

46. Lee D. Baker, *Anthropology and the Racial Politics of Culture* (Durham, NC: Duke University Press, 2010), 63.

47. For example, Danny Weil, "Neoliberalism: The Leveraging of Charter Schools with Public and Private Funds," *Dissident Voice*, November 24, 2009.

48. In the acknowledgments to *When Work Disappears*, Wilson lists no less than twenty foundations and funding sources that contributed to three of his research projects. William Julius Wilson, *When Work Disappears* (New York: Vintage, 1997), xi.

49. Weil, "Neoliberalism."

50. Obama championed the Harlem Children's Zone and used it as his model for his education policy nationally. "The *Washington Post* Spotlights Obama's Plan to Reproduce HCZ Model, Harlem Children's Zone, n.d., https://hcz.org/news/the-washington-post-spotlights-obamas-plan-to-reproduce-hcz-model/.

51. Tough, *Whatever It Takes*, 53.

52. Tough, 54.

53. Will Dobbie and Roland G. Fryer Jr., "Are High-Quality Schools Enough to Close the Achievement Gap?" National Bureau of Economic Research, Working Paper 15473, November 2009, https://www.nber.org/papers/w15473.

54. "Hope or Hype in Harlem," special issue, *City Limits* 34, no. 1 (March 2010), www.citylimits.org.

55. Broad Foundation, http://www.broadfoundation.org/about_foundations.html.

56. William Julius Wilson, "Why Both Social Structure and Culture Matter in a Holistic Analysis of Inner-City Poverty," in "Reconsidering Culture and Poverty," special issue, *Annals* 629, no. 1 (May 2010): 215.

57. Dobbie and Fryer, "Are High-Quality Schools Enough?" 1. Soon after the publication of the Dobbie-Fryer study, David Brooks rushed into print with a column entitled "The Harlem Miracle." Brooks revealed that he received an email message from Fryer, along with a copy of his report, saying that "the attached study has changed my life as a scientist because I am no longer interested in marginal changes." Brooks then added rapture of his own: "Basically, the no-excuses schools pay attention to behavior and attitudes. They teach students how to look at the person who is talking, how to shake hands. . . . They also smash the normal bureaucratic structures that bind leaders in regular schools. . . . The approach works. Ever since welfare reform, we have had success with government programs that combine paternalistic leadership, sufficient funding and a ferocious commitment to

traditional, middle-class values." David Brooks, "The Harlem Miracle," *New York Times.*
May 8, 2009, http://www.nytimes.com/2009/05/08/opinion/08brooks.html.

58. Merryl Tisch, "Shaping Success," in "Hope or Hype in Harlem," 16. Also to be considered is selective bias, since parents elect to enter the lottery for the Promise Academies, and there are fewer special-need students.

59. David F. Labaree, "The Winning Ways of a Losing Strategy: Educationalizing Social Problems in the United States," *Educational Theory* 58, no. 4 (2008): 447.

60. Brooks, "The Harlem Miracle."

61. For a penetrating analysis of the relationship between social class and educational achievement, see Richard Rothstein, *Class and Schools* (New York: Economic Policy Institute and Teachers College Press, 2004), ch.1.

62. Tough, *Whatever It Takes*, 166.

63. John U. Ogbu, *The Next Generation: An Ethnography of Education in an Urban Neighborhood* (New York: Academic Press, 1974), xvii.

64. John U. Ogbu, *Black American Students in an Affluent Suburb* (New York: Routledge, 2003).

65. John Ogbu, *Minority Education and Caste: The America System in Cross-Cultural Perspective* (New York: Academic Press, 1978), 370.

66. Ogbu, *Minority Education and Caste.*

67. Children's Defense Fund, "Child Poverty," *The State of America's Children 2021,* 2021, https://www.childrensdefense.org/state-of-americas-children/soac-2021-child-poverty/.

Chapter 7: Theories of Ethnic Success

An earlier version of this chapter appeared as "The Myth of Ethnic Success: Old Wine in New Bottles," in *The Oxford Handbook of American Immigration and Ethnicity,* ed. Ronald Baylor (New York: Oxford University Press, 2016), 338–54. Reproduced by permission of Oxford University Press.

1. Quoted in Leonard Covello, *The Social Background of the Italo-American School Child* (Totowa, NJ: Rowman & Littlefield, 1967), 256. Covello's book was originally a 1944 doctoral dissertation at New York University and was based on research in both Italy and New York City.

2. Personal conversation with Queens College student, circa 1985.

3. Thomas Sowell, *Ethnic America* (New York: Basic Books, 1981), 98.

4. Stephen Steinberg, *The Ethnic Myth* (Boston: Beacon Press, 1989). Israel Rubinow, "The Economic Condition of Jews in Russia," *Bulletin of the Bureau of Labor,* no. 72 (Washington, DC: Government Printing Office, 1907), 487–583.

5. U.S. Immigration Commission, *Immigrants in Industries,* vol. 8 (Washington, DC, 1911). "In his study of Russian Jewish immigrants in Providence, Rhode Island, Joel Perlmann found that a very considerable number of East European Jewish immigrants made their way into the American economy through commercial pursuits rather than as members of the working class as that term is usually understood." Joel Perlmann, "Beyond New York: The Occupations of Russian Jewish Immigrants in Providence, R. I., and in Other Small Jewish Communities, 1900–1915," *Journal of American Jewish History* 1, 72, no. 3 (March 1983): 309–32.

6. Selma C. Berrol, "Education and Economic Mobility: The Jewish Experience in New York City, 1880–1920," *American Jewish Historical Quarterly*, March, 1976, 271. Italics in original.

7. Calvin Goldscheider and Alan S. Zuckerman, *The Transformation of the Jews* (Chicago: University of Chicago Press, 1984), 107.

8. Louise Farkas, "Occupational Genealogies of Jews in Eastern Europe and America, 1880–1924," (master's thesis, Queens College, 1982). Stephen Steinberg, "The Rise of the Jewish Professional," *Ethnic and Racial Studies* 9, no. 4 (October 1986): 502–13.

9. Toni Morrison, "On the Backs of Blacks," *Time*, December 2, 1993.

10. Nathan Glazer, *American Judaism* (Chicago: University of Chicago Press, 1957), 12.

11. Nathan Glazer, "The American Jew and the Attainment of Middle Class Rank: Some Trends and Explanations," in *The Jews*, ed. Marshall Sklare (New York: Free Press, 1958) 143.

12. Thomas Sowell, *Ethnic America* (New York: Basic Books, 1981).

13. Richard Gambino, *Blood of My Blood: The Dilemma of the Italian-Americans* (Garden City, NY: Anchor Press, 1975). Andrew Greeley, "The Ethnic Miracle," *Public Interest*, Fall 1976, 20–36; Richard Novak, *The Rise of the Unmeltable Ethnics* (New York: Macmillan, 1972); and Betty Lee Sung, *The Story of the Chinese in America* (New York: Collier, 1975). Note that all these works were published during the "ethnic revival" of the early 1970s.

14. William A. McIntyre, "Chinatown Offers Us a Lesson," *New York Times*, October 6, 1957.

15. McIntyre, "Chinatown Offers Us a Lesson."

16. William Petersen, "Success Story: Japanese-American Style," *New York Times Magazine*, January 9, 1966: 20–43.

17. Petersen, "Success Story," 21.

18. Petersen, "Success Story."

19. "Liberalism and the Negro: A Round-Table Discussion," *Commentary* 37 (March 1964): 25–42.

20. William Petersen, review of *Discriminating against Discrimination: Preferential Admissions and the* DeFunis *Case*, by Robert M. O'Neil, *Commentary*, June 1976, 88. *DeFunis v. Odegaard*, 416 U.S.312 (1974).

21. William Petersen, review of *Affirmative Discrimination: Ethnic Inequality and Public Policy*, by Nathan Glazer, *Commentary*, May 1976, 78–80.

22. William Petersen, review of *Ethnic America*, by Thomas Sowell, *Commentary*, October 1981, 76–78.

23. "Success Story of One Minority Group in U.S.," *U.S. News and World Report*, December 26, 1966.

24. "Success Story: Outwhiting the Whites," *Newsweek*, June 21, 1971, 24–25.

25. Thomas K. Nakayama, "'Model Minority' and the Media: Discourse on Asian America," *Journal of Communication Inquiry* 12, no. 1 (1988): 65–73.

26. David A. Bell, "The Triumph of Asian-Americans: America's Greatest Success Story," *New Republic*, July 15 and 22, 1985, 24–31.

27. Kiyoshi Ikeda, "A Different Dilemma," review of *Japanese Americans: Oppression and Success*, by William Petersen, *Social Forces* 51 (June 1973): 498–99.

28. Arthur Sakamoto and Keng-Loong Yap, "The Myth of the Model Minority Myth," paper presented at the annual meeting of the American Sociological Association, Montreal Convention Center, August 11, 2006.

29. Sakamoto and Yap, "The Myth of the Model Minority Myth," 2.

30. Theodore Hsien Wang and Frank H. Wu, "Beyond the Model Minority Myth," in *The Affirmative Action Debate*, ed. George E. Curry (Cambridge: Perseus Books, 1996), 191–207.

31. Nakayama, "'Model Minority' and the Media."

32. Louis Winnick, "America's 'Model Minority,'" *Commentary*, August 1990, 24.

33. Signithia Fordham and John Ogbu, "Black Students' School Success: Coping with the Burden of 'Acting White,'" *Urban Review* 18, no. 3 (September 1986): 176–206. In a subsequent study of a high school that was more than 99 percent Black, Fordham made the acting-white thesis the centerpiece of her analysis. She contended that these students had cultivated a "Black identity" in opposition to the stigmatizing and dehumanizing stereotypes associated with white racism, and school success amounted to a liquefaction of their Black selves. Signithia Fordham, *Blacked Out: Dilemmas of Race, Identity, and Success at Capital High* (Chicago: University of Chicago Press, 1996), 283.

34. Two professors of education described the "acting-white" postulate as providing one of the dominant theories used to explain the Black-white achievement gap. Erin McNamara Horvat and Kristine S. Lewis, "Reassessing the 'Burden of Acting White': The Importance of Peer Groups in Managing Academic Success," *Sociology of Education* 76, no. 4 (October 2003): 265.

35. Barack Obama, 2004 Democratic National Convention Keynote Address, July 27, 2004, http://obamaspeeches.com/002-Keynote-Address-at-the-2004-Democratic-National-Convention-Obama-Speech.htm.

36. Karolyn Tyson, William Darity Jr., and Domini R. Castellino, "It's Not 'a Black Thing': Understanding the Burden of Acting White and Other Dilemmas of High Achievement," *American Sociological Review* 70, no. 4 (August 2005): 582–605.

37. No doubt, Capital High, the school that Signithia Fordham studied in Washington, DC, had a different youth culture than the eight schools studied in North Carolina. This suggests that "acting white" might be more characteristic of inner-city schools in the urban North.

38. Paul Willis, *Learning to Labor: How Working Class Kids Get Working Class Jobs*, 2nd ed. (New York: Columbia University Press, 1981).

39. John Ogbu, *Minority Education and Caste* (New York: Academic Press, 1978), 357.

Chapter 8: "Making It"

An earlier version of this chapter appeared as "Tiger Couple Gets It Wrong on Immigrant Success" in *Boston Review*, March 11, 2014, © Stephen Steinberg.

1. Daria Roithmayr, "The Flaw at the Heart of *The Triple Package*," *Slate*, February 12, 2014.

2. Thomas Sowell, *Ethnic America: A History* (New York: Basic Books, 1981), 265. Italics in original.

3. Stephen Steinberg, *The Ethnic Myth* (Boston: Beacon Press, 1989), 103.

4. Beth Fertig and Jennifer Hsu, "Around Sunset Park, Tutoring Is Key to Top Schools," *Schoolbook* (blog), WNYC, March 12, 2013, https://www.wnyc.org/story/301916-around-sunset-park-tutoring-is-key-to-top-high-schools/.

5. Kyle Spencer, "Centers See New Faces Seeking Test Prep," *New York Times*, April 2, 2013, https://www.nytimes.com/2013/04/03/nyregion/cram-schools-no-longer-just-an-asian-pursuit.html.

6. Amy Chua and Jed Rubenfeld, "What Drives Success?" Opinion, *New York Times*, January 26, 2014, https://www.nytimes.com/2014/01/26/opinion/sunday/what-drives-success.html.

7. Jennifer Szalai, "Confessions of a Tiger Couple," *New York Times Magazine*, January 29, 2014, https://www.nytimes.com/2014/02/02/magazine/confessions-of-a-tiger-couple.html.

8. Sandra Tsing Loh, "Secrets of Success," review of *The Hybrid Tiger: Secrets of the Extraordinary Success of Asian-American Kids*, by Quanyu Huang, *New York Times*, January 31, 2014, https://www.nytimes.com/2014/02/02/books/review/the-hybrid-tiger-and-the-triple-package.html.

9. Toni Morrison, "On the Back of Blacks," *Time*, December 2, 1993, http://content.time.com/time/magazine/article/0,9171,979736,00.html.

Chapter 9: The Goose-Gander Myth

1. Quoted in German Lopez, "The False Equivalency of Trump Blaming 'Many Sides' in Charlottesville," *Vox*, August 12, 2017, https://www.vox.com/identities/2017/8/12/16138982/trump-charlottesville-false-equivalency.

2. Margaret Sullivan, "This Week Should Put the Nail in the Coffin of 'Both Sides' Journalism," *Washington Post*, August 16, 2017, https://www.washingtonpost.com/lifestyle/style/this-week-should-put-the-nail-in-the-coffin-for-both-sides-journalism/2017/08/16/77c6668a-8292-11e7-b359-15a3617c767b_story.html?utm_term=.775b78bfa959.

3. *Merriam-Webster*, s.v. "what's sauce for the goose is sauce for the gander," https://www.merriam-webster.com/dictionary/what%27s%20sauce%20for%20the%20goose%20is%20sauce%20for%20the%20gander; *Merriam-Webster*, s.v. "what's good for the goose is good for the gander," https://www.merriam-webster.com/dictionary/what%27s%20good%20for%20the%20goose%20is%20good%20for%20the%20gander.

4. "Herstory," Black Lives Matter, n.d., https://blacklivesmatter.com/herstory/. The Black Lives Matter movement evolved from a coalition of over sixty organizations, under the umbrella of "A Vision for Black Lives: Policy Demands for Black Power, Freedom and Justice." For an incisive analysis of the sources and goals of the movement, see the riveting article "What Does Black Lives Matter Want?" by Robin D. G. Kelley in *Boston Review*, August 17, 2016. http://bostonreview.net/books-ideas/robin-d-g-kelley-movement-black

-lives-vision. Kelley writes: "'A Vision for Black Lives' is a plan for ending structural racism, saving the planet, and transforming the entire nation—not just black lives."

5. Jonathan Capehart, "No, 'Black Lives Matter' Is Not Inherently Racist," Opinion, *Washington Post*, July 13, 2016, https://www.washingtonpost.com/blogs/post-partisan/wp/2016/07/13/no-black-lives-matter-is-not-inherently-racist/?utm_term=.1ad3f3ff5538.

6. This is not to deny that whites are also slain without provocation by police. For example, see Adam Rothman and Barbara J. Fields, "The Death of Hannah Fizer," *Dissent*, July 24, 2020, https://www.dissentmagazine.org/online_articles/the-death-of-hannah-fizer.

7. "All Lives Matter," Wikipedia, last edited July 12, 2021, https://en.wikipedia.org/wiki/All_Lives_Matter.

8. "President Obama Defends Black Lives Matter Movement," *CBS News*, October 23, 2015, https://www.cbsnews.com/news/president-barack-obama-defends-black-lives-matter-movement/.

9. "All Lives Matter," Wikipedia.

10. "Black Lives Matter or All Lives Matter?" *Rasmussen Reports*, August 20, 2015, http://www.rasmussenreports.com/public_content/politics/general_politics/august_2015/black_lives_matter_or_all_lives_matter.

11. Lopez, "The False Equivalency of Trump."

12. Chris Suarez, "Charlottesville City Council Renames Lee, Jackson Parks," *Daily Progress*, June 5, 2017, http://www.dailyprogress.com/news/local/charlottesville-city-council-renames-lee-jackson-parks/article_2c849c98-4a5f-11e7-9781-7f23c7cf1163.html. On July 10, 2021, the Robert E. Lee statue was removed. Deon J. Hampton and Henry Austin, "Charlottesville, Virginia, Removes 3rd Monument Hours after Lee, Jackson Statues Come Down," *NBC News*, July 10, 2021, https://www.nbcnews.com/news/us-news/robert-e-lee-statue-removed-charlottesville-n1273612.

13. Joel Gunter, "A Reckoning in Charlottesville," *BBC News*, August 13, 2007, http://www.bbc.com/news/world-us-canada-40914748.

14. Gunter, "A Reckoning in Charlottesville."

15. Joe Helm, "Recounting a Day of Rage, Hate, Violence and Death," *Washington Post*, August 14, 2017, https://www.washingtonpost.com/graphics/2017/local/charlottesville-timeline/?utm_term=.6f68537d53e7.

16. Helm, "Recounting a Day of Rage."

17. Libby Nelson and Kelly Swanson, "Full Transcript: Donald Trump's Press Conference Defending the Charlottesville Rally," *Vox*, August 15, 2017, https://www.vox.com/2017/8/15/16154028/trump-press-conference-transcript-charlottesville.

18. "David Duke," Wikipedia, last edited May 31, 2021, https://en.wikipedia.org/wiki/David_Duke.

19. Libby Nelson, "Why We Voted for Donald Trump": David Duke Explains the White Supremacist Charlottesville Protests," *Vox*, August 12, 2017, https://www.vox.com/2017/8/12/16138358/charlottesville-protests-david-duke-kkk. Alan Pyke, Ryan Koronowski, and Joshua Eaton, "Virginia White Supremacist Rally Turns Violent, Shut Down by Police," ThinkProgress, August 12, 2017, https://thinkprogress.org/white-supremacist-rally-charlottesville-9dc4fa92f40c/.

20. Sullivan, "This Week Should Put the Nail in the Coffin."

21. Eric Alterman, "How False Equivalence Is Distorting the Election Coverage," *Nation*, June 2, 2016, https://www.thenation.com/article/how-false-equivalence-is-distorting-the-2016-election-coverage/.

22. This is not an argument for epistemological relativism, but only an acknowledgement that opposing sides will summon logic and facts to buttress their respective viewpoints. The debate over "the false equivalency of Trump" demonstrates this principle. For example, German Lopez argued in *Vox*: "In short, there aren't multiple moral equivalent sides here. There's one side—white supremacists—that has long oppressed other groups of people. Their protests aim to ensure that oppression continues, even if it means using violence. The people counterprotesting, on the other hand, are trying to end that oppression." Lopez, "The False Equivalency of Trump."

23. "Ironically, the focus of the Court has been far more on limiting affirmative action and protecting whites than remedying discrimination and advancing equality for racial minorities. The Court has failed to realize that there is a world of difference between the government using race to subordinate minorities and using race to benefit minorities and advance equality." Edward Chemerinsky, *The Conservative Assault on the Constitution* (New York: Simon & Schuster, 2010) 268–69.

24. Civil Rights Cases, Supreme Court of the United States, 109 U.S. 3; 3 S.Ct. 18; 1883 U.S. Lexis 928; 27 L. Ed. 835. Italics added.

Chapter 10: The Political Uses of "Concentrated Poverty"

An earlier version of this chapter appeared as "The Myth of Concentrated Poverty" in *The Integration Debate: Competing Futures for American Cities*, ed. Chester Hartman and Gregory Squires (New York: Routledge, 2010), © 2010, Routledge. Reproduced by permission of Taylor & Francis Group.

1. Quoted in Susan D. Greenbaum, *Blaming the Poor: The Long Shadow of the Moynihan Report on Cruel Images about Poverty* (New Brunswick, NJ: Rutgers University Press, 2015), 68.

2. Elvin Wyly and Daniel Hammel, "Islands of Decay in Seas of Renewal: Urban Policy and the Resurgence of Gentrification," *Housing Policy Debate* 10, no. 4 (1999): 711–71.

3. James Rosenbaum and Stefanie DeLuca, *Is Housing Mobility the Key to Welfare Reform? Lessons from the Gautreaux Program* (Washington, DC: Brookings Institution, 2000), 1–8.

4. Jordan Lebeau, "Boston Changed Malcolm X, and Malcolm X Changed Me," Boston.com, May 19, 2015, https://www.boston.com/news/commentary/2015/05/19/boston-changed-malcolm-x-and-malcolm-x-changed-me; "Malcolm X's Roxbury Home Should be Preserved," editorial, *Boston Globe*, June 15, 2012, https://www.bostonglobe.com/opinion/editorials/2012/06/14/malcolm-home-should-preserved/27uG57rA5cvAioGbmoPKHK/story.html.

5. Matthew Hughey, *The White Savior Film: Content, Critics, and Consumption* (Philadelphia: Temple University Press, 2014).

6. Edward G. Goetz, *Clearing the Way: Deconcentrating the Poor in Urban America* (Washington, DC: Urban Institute Press; Lanham, MD: Rowman & Littlefield, 2003), 256.

7. Larry Bennett and Adolph Reed Jr., "The New Face of Urban Renewal: The Near North Redevelopment Initiative and the Cabrini-Green Neighborhood," in *Without Justice for All*, ed. Adolph Reed Jr. (Boulder, CO: Westview Press, 1999), 175–211. Also, the following chapters in Larry Bennett, Janet L. Smith, and Patricia A. Wright, eds., *Where Are Poor People to Live? Transforming Public Housing Communities* (Armonk, NY: M. E. Sharpe, 2006): Patricia A. Wright, with Richard M. Wheelock and Carol Steele, "The Case of Cabrini-Green," 168–184; Larry Bennett, Nancy Hudspeth, and Patricia Wright, "A Critical Analysis of the ABLA Redevelopment Plan," 185–215; Patricia A. Wright, "Community Resistance to CHA Transformation: The History, Evolution, Struggles, and Accomplishments of the Coalition to Protect Public Housing," 25–67; William P. Wilen and Rajess D. Nayak, "Relocated Public Housing Residents Have Little Hope of Returning: Work Requirements for Mixed-Income Public Housing Developments," 216–38; and Janet L. Smith, "Mixed-Income Communities: Designing Out Poverty or Pushing Out the Poor," 259–81.

8. Wright, with Wheelock and Steele, "The Case of Cabrini-Green," 169.

9. Greenbaum, *Blaming the Poor*.

10. Wilen and Nayak, "Relocated Public Housing Residents."

11. Chicago Real Estate Blog, http://www.chicagorealestateblog.com/parkside-of-old-town-brings-development-to-cabrini/.

12. Wilen and Nayak, "Relocated Public Housing Residents," 220.

13. Douglas S. Massey and Nancy A. Denton, *American Apartheid: Segregation and the Making of the Underclass* (Cambridge, MA: Harvard University Press: 1993); Douglas Massey and Shawn M. Kanaiaupuni "Public Housing and the Concentration of Poverty," *Social Science Quarterly* 74, no. 1 (1993): 109–22; Paul Jargowsky, *Poverty and Place: Ghettos, Barrios, and the American City* (New York: Russell Sage, 1997).

For a thoughtful analysis of the logic of "concentration effects," see Marta Tienda, "Poor People and Poor Places: Deciphering Neighborhood Effects on Poverty Outcomes," *RePEc*, January 1991. She faults existing studies for failing to specify the mechanisms through which these putative effects are enacted and concludes on a skeptical note: "Given the nature of available data, it is virtually impossible to determine with any degree of confidence the existence of neighborhood effects on poverty behaviors" (258).

14. Manuel Castells, *The Urban Question: A Marxist Approach* (Cambridge, MA: MIT Press, 1979).

15. Yet the cheerleaders of deconcentration turn a blind eye to the extensive body of research that goes against their pet idea. For a critical review of "The Dispersal Consensus," see David Imbroscio, "United and Actuated by Some Common Impulse of Passion: Challenging the Dispersal Consensus Quoted in American Policy Research," *Journal of Urban Affairs* 30, no. 2 (March 31, 2008): 114. See also the responses in that issue by Xavier de Souza Briggs, 131; John Goering and Judith Feins, 139–48; and rejoinder by Imbroscio, 149–54. Note that Imbroscio assails "The Dispersal Consensus" for trampling over what Chester Hartman has called "the right to stay put." Chester Hartman, "The Right to Stay Put," Opinions, *Washington Post*, September 21, 2018, https://www.washingtonpost.com/opinions/the-right-to-stay-put/2018/09/21/395cc5d8-b90f-11e8-94eb-3bd52dfe917b_story.html.

16. Hanna Rosin, "Missed-Income Communities: Designing Out Poverty or Pushing Out the Poor?" in Bennett, Smith, and Wright, *Where Are Poor People to Live?*

17. Xavier de Souza Briggs, "Introduction" and "More Pluribus, Less Unum? The Changing Geography of Race and Opportunity," in *The Geography of Opportunity: Race and Housing Choice in Metropolitan America* (Washington, DC: Brookings Institution Press, 2005), 36.

18. Susan Greenbaum, Cheryl R. Rodriquez, Ashley Spalding, and Beverly G. Ward, "Scattering Urban Poverty: Displacement and Deconcentration in Tampa," *Anthropology News*, December 2008.

19. Early ethnographic studies that portray the poor and/or public housing in a more positive light are Elliott Liebow, *Tally's Corner: A Study of Negro Streetcorner Men* (New York: Little Brown, 1967); Carol B. Stack, *All Our Kin: Strategies for Survival in a Black Community* (New York: Basic Books, 1983); and Ida Susser, *Norman Street: Poverty and Politics in an Urban Neighborhood* (New York: Oxford, 1982).

20. Jeff Crump, "Deconcentration by Demolition: Public Housing, Poverty, and Urban Policy," *Environment and Planning* 20, no. 5 (October 1, 2002): 581.

21. Peter Marcuse, "The Enclave, the Citadel, and the Ghetto: What Has Changed in the Post-Fordist U.S. City," *Urban Affairs Review* 33, no. 2 (1997): 228–64.

22. J. Philip Thompson, "Universalism and Deconstruction: Why Race Still Matters in Poverty and Economic Development," *Politics and Society* 26, no. 2 (1998): 181–219. Solomon Moore, "As Program Moves Poor to Suburbs, Tensions Follow," *New York Times*, August 8, 2008, https://www.nytimes.com/2008/08/09/us/09housing.html.

23. Rick Perlstein, "How to Sell Off a City," *In These Times*, January 21, 2015. https://inthesetimes.com/article/how-to-sell-off-a-city.

24. For example, "Reauthorization of the Hope VI Program," Hearing Before the Subcommittee on Housing and Community Opportunity of the Committee on Financial Services, U.S. House of Representatives, 110th Congress, First Session, June 21, 2007, http://frwebgate.access.gpo.gov/cgi-bin/getdoc.cgi?dbname=110_house_hearings&docid=f:37561.wais.

25. Neil Smith, *The New Urban Frontier: Gentrification and the Revanchist City* (New York: Routledge, 1996), 45–47.

26. Jonathan Springston, "Activists Mobilize to Save Atlanta Public Housing, Seek Legal Options," *Atlanta Progressive News*, April 11, 2007, https://atlantaprogressivenews.com/2007/04/11/activists-mobilize-to-save-atlanta-public-housing-seek-legal-options/; and Alex Perlstein, "Atlanta to Demolish Nearly All Its Public Housing," Planetizen, February 15, 2007, http:///www.planetizen.com/node/22899.

27. For a view of the protest before the New Orleans City Council, see "New Orleans City Council Shuts Down Public Housing Debate," YouTube, December 21, 2007, http://www.youtube.com/watch?v=cMBWAXfGsc4.

28. Bruce Katz and William Julius Wilson, interview with Ray Suarez, *Newshour with Jim Lehrer*, transcript from American Archive of Public Broadcasting, September 16, 2005, https://americanarchive.org/catalog/cpb-aacip_507-fb4wh2f181.

29. The petition can be found at Adolph Reed and Stephen Steinberg, "Liberal Bad Faith in the Wake of Hurricane Katrina," *Black Commentator* 182 (May 4, 2006), http://www.blackcommentator.com/182/182_cover_liberals_katrina.html. For critical commentary, see Reed and Steinberg, "Liberal Bad Faith"; and David Imbroscio, "United and Actuated

by Some Common Impulse of Passion: Challenging the Dispersal Consensus Quoted in American Policy Research," *Journal of Urban Affairs* 30, no. 2 (March 31, 2008). Also see Susan Greenbaum, Sudhir Alladi Venkatesh, and Xavier de Souza Briggs, "Symposium on Hurricane Katrina," *City & Community* 5, no. 2 (June 2006): 107–28 Also, on the failure of planning in the reconstruction of New Orleans, see Nicolai Ouroussoff, "Reflections: New Orleans and China," *New York Times*, September 14, 2008, https://www.nytimes .com/2008/09/14/weekinreview/14ouroussoff.html.

30. Susan Greenbaum, "Comments on Katrina," *City & Community* 5, no. 2 (June 2006): 109–13.

31. Goetz, *Clearing the Way*, 252.

32. Edward Goetz, *The One-Way Street of Integration: Fair Housing and the Pursuit of Racial Justice in American Cities* (Ithaca, NY: Cornell University Press, 2018).

Chapter 11: Decolonizing Race Knowledge

1. Daniel Breslau, "'The American Spencerians': Theorizing a New Science," in *Sociology in America: A History*, ed. Craig Calhoun, ASA Centennial Publication (Chicago: University of Chicago Press, 2007), 46.

2. Pierre Saint-Arnaud, *African American Pioneers of Sociology: A Critical History* (Toronto: University of Toronto Press, 2009).

3. Parsons quoted in Breslau, "'The American Spencerians,'" 46.

4. Breslau, 46.

5. Herman Schwendinger and Julia R. Schwendinger, *The Sociologists of the Chair: A Radical Analysis of the Formative Years of North American Sociology (1883–1922)* (New York Basic Books, 1974), 107.

6. Oliver Cromwell Cox, *Caste, Class, and Race* (New York: Modern Reader, 1948), 476.

7. Schwendinger and Schwendinger, *Sociologists of the Chair*.

8. The full text reads as follows: "The preceding discussion has emphasized the degree to which foreign and domestic imperialism had transformed the United States into a brutally exploitative racist society. It might be concluded on this basis that although the pioneering sociologists were racists, they were also 'men of their time' and therefore indistinguishable in this respect from most of the white population. This conclusion, however, minimizes their special contribution to the ongoing development of racist ideologies in the United States. It also ignores the fact that Marx had developed a materialism strategy for analyzing historical relations *before* the rise of sociology. Marx's writings certainly cannot be regarded as the last word on the topic of nineteenth-century exploitation, colonialism, and imperialism. But they certainly were superior to Spencer's point of view. If applied creatively and systematically to American conditions, a Marxian analysis would have linked racial and national oppression to the historical development of imperialism under changing capitalist condition. It certainly would not have interpreted these forms of oppression, as did the founding sociologists, in the context of a universal struggle for existence among biologically superior and inferior races. A Marxian analysis would *not* have justified imperialist oppression in the United States." Schwendinger and Schwendinger, 107. Italics in original.

9. Karl Marx, *The Poverty of Philosophy* (Mayfield Center, CT: Martino Publishing, 2014), 121.

10. Mary O. Furner, *Advocacy and Objectivity: A Crisis in the Professionalization of American Social Science, 1865–1905* (Lexington: University Press of Kentucky, 1975), 165.

11. Schwendinger and Schwendinger, "Academic Freedom Is a Sometime Thing," ch. 63, *Sociologists of the Chair*, 490–548.

12. Ernest W. Burgess, cited by Fred Matthews, *Quest for an American Sociology: Robert E. Park and the Chicago School* (Toronto: University of Toronto Press, 1977), 116. Burgess is the source of this anecdote about Robert Park.

13. Howard Winant, "The Dark Side of the Force: One Hundred Years of the Sociology of Race," in Calhoun, *Sociology in America*, 535–36. Mia Bay, an African American intellectual historian, depicts 1890s sociology similarly: "In its analysis of race relations especially, 1890s sociology was based on theoretical speculations rather than on empirical research. Bent on creating 'grand theories' of society that could be employed to analyze and solve the social problems of Gilded Age America, the founding fathers of American sociology invariably explained racial inequities with reference to natural laws. These natural laws offered little support to Du Bois's search for the scientific principles that would foster Black progress." Quoted in Reiland Rabaka, *Against Epistemic Apartheid* (New York: Lexington Books, 2010), 100. Rabaka adds that this was precisely the sociology that Du Bois was working against.

14. Schwendinger and Schwendinger, *Sociologists of the Chair*, 107n5. Italics in original.

15. R. W. Connell, "Why Is Classical Theory Classical?" *American Journal of Sociology* 102 (May 1997): 1516–17. Also, see Julian Go's penetrating analysis, "Sociology's Imperial Unconscious: The Emergence of American Sociology in the Context of Empire," in *Sociology and Empire*, ed. George Steinmetz (Durham, NC: Duke University Press, 2013), 83–105.

16. Stanford M. Lyman, *Color, Culture, Civilization* (Chicago: University of Illinois, 1994), 55.

17. Robert Ezra Park, "An Autobiographical Note," *Race and Culture* (New York: Free Press, 1950), 5.

18. Charles W. Mills, *The Racial Contract* (Ithaca: Cornell University Press, 1997), 18.

19. Roger A. Salerno, "Was There a Black Chicago School?" in *The Chicago School Diaspora: Epistemology and Substance*, ed. Jacqueline Low and Gary Bowden (Montreal: McGill-Queen's University Press, 2013), 58.

20. Salerno, "Was There a Black Chicago School?" 58.

21. Salerno, 58.

22. Salerno, 58–59.

23. Salerno, 57.

24. Saint-Arnaud, *African American Pioneers of Sociology*, 283.

25. Salerno mentions two other Black students in the 1930s: H.M. Bond and Bertram Wilber Doyle. Salerno, "Was There a Black Chicago School?" 56.

26. Du Bois remained at Atlanta from 1897 until 1910, when he took a position as publisher of *Crisis*, the journal of the NAACP. In this makeover from scholar to activist,

Du Bois devoted himself to advancing the goals of the nascent civil rights movement. Saint-Arnaud, *African American Pioneers of Sociology*, 118; Pierre Saint-Arnaud, *L'invention de la sociologie noire aux Etats-Unis d'Amérique: Essai en sociologie de la connaissance scientifique* (Quebec: Presses de l'Université Laval, 2003).

27. Martin Bulmer, "Charles S. Johnson, Robert E. Park and the Research Methods of the Chicago Commission on Race Relations, 1919–22," *Ethnic and Racial Studies* 4 (1981): 300.

28. Anthony Platt, *E. Franklin Frazier Reconsidered*. New Brunswick: Rutgers University Press, 1991: 204.

29. Thanks to Shawn Leigh Alexander, professor of African American studies and director of the Langston Hughes Center at the University of Kansas, for uncovering the story of Frazier's flight from danger. Shawn Alexander, "The Pathology of Delusions," *Diverse Issues in Higher Education*, August 31, 2017, https://diverseeducation.com/article/101015/.

30. J. G. St. Clair Drake and Horace A. Cayton, *Black Metropolis: A Study of Negro Life in a Northern City* (Chicago: University of Chicago Press, 1945) chs. 1–12.

31. Drake and Cayton, *Black Metropolis*, ch. 14.

32. Drake and Cayton, 381.

33. Oliver Cromwell Cox, *Class, Caste, and Race* (New York: Modern Reader, 1948), 476.

34. Cox, *Class, Caste, and Race*, 474.

35. Schwendinger and Schwendinger, *Sociologists of the Chair*, 476–77.

36. Schwendinger and Schwendinger, 512.

37. Quoted in *The Black Sociologists: The First Half Century*, ed. John Bracey, August Meier, and Elliot Rudwick (Belmont, CA: Wadsworth , 1971), 6.

38. Peter M. Ascoli, *Julius Rosenwald: The Man Who Built Sears, Roebuck and Advanced the Cause of Black Education in the South* (Bloomington: Indiana University Press, 2006).

39. Editorial, *Pittsburgh Courier*, February 12, 1938.

40. W. E. B. Du Bois, *Dusk of Dawn: An Essay toward an Autobiography of Race Concept* (New York: Oxford University Press, 2007), 49.

41. Aldon D. Morris, *The Scholar Denied* (Oakland: University of California Press, 2015), ix. Many commentators date Du Bois's "first awakening to the color line" to his earlier experience as a schoolboy of getting his card rejected by a young white girl. See "On Our Spiritual Strivings" in *The Souls of Black Folk*, ch. 1. Thanks to Charles W. Mills for this insight.

42. Morris, *The Scholar Denied*, xv.

43. Morris, 4.

44. Morris, 4.

45. Morris, 8.

46. Morris, 54.

47. Morris, 68.

48. Morris, 30.

49. Morris, 30.

50. Morris, 32.

51. Morris, 141.

52. "Marx had developed a materialist strategy for analyzing historical relations *before* the rise of American sociology" (italics in original). Schwendinger and Schwendinger, *Sociologists of the Chair*, 107; Mills, *The Racial Contract*; Stephen Steinberg, *Race Relations: A Critique* (Stanford, CA: Stanford University Press, 2006).

53. Morris, *The Scholar Denied*, 162.

54. W. E. B. Du Bois, "My Evolving Program for Negro Freedom," in *What the Negro Wants*, ed. Rayford W. Logan (Chapel Hill, NC: University of North Carolina Press, 1944), 52, http://www.webdubois.org/dbMyEvolvingPrgm.html. Italics added.

55. Du Bois, "My Evolving Program," 134, 165.

56. Morris, *The Scholar Denied*, 195.

57. Saint-Arnaud, *African American Pioneers of Sociology*.

58. For a provocative critique of "assimilation scholarship" and its perverse role in providing legitimacy to the prevailing racial order, see Vilna Bashi Treitler, "Social Agency and White Supremacy in Immigration Studies," *Sociology of Race and Ethnicity* 1, no. 1 (January 2015), https://researchgate.net/publication/282859377.

Chapter 12: The Myth of Black Progress

1. Quote by Malcolm X, goodreads.com. The full quote is as follows: "You don't stick a knife in a man's back nine inches and then pull it out six inches and say you are making progress. Even if you pull it all the way out, that is not progress. Progress is healing the wound, and America hasn't even begun to pull out the knife."

2. Derrick Bell, "Racial Realism," *Connecticut Law Review*, 24, no. 3 (Winter 1992): 558.

3. Roopali Mukherjee, "'Ghetto Fabulous' in the Imperial United States: Black Consumption and the 'Death of Civil Rights,'" in *The Imperial Homeland in the 21st Century*, ed. Jeff Maskovsky and Ida Susser (New York: Routledge, 2009). Mukherjee is an associate professor of media studies at Queens College and a faculty member in film studies, Asian American studies, and Africana studies. Also see Robin D. G. Kelley, *Race Rebels: Culture, Politics, and the Black Working Class* (New York: Free Press, 1994). Kelley comments, "I chose the title *Race Rebels* because this book looks at forms of resistance—organized and unorganized—that have remained outside of (and even critical of) what we've come to understand as the key figures and institutions in African American politics," 4–5.

4. Mukherjee, "'Ghetto Fabulous' in the Imperial United States," 152.

5. Mukherjee, 152.

6. Ibram X. Kendi, "Racial Progress Is Real, But So Is Racist Progress," Sunday Review, *New York Times*, January 22, 2017, 2, https://wwww.nytimes.com/2017/01/21.

7. John Nichols, "Barack Obama Charts an Arc of History That Bends Toward Justice," *Nation*, January 21, 2013. Obama derived this phrase from Martin Luther King. For the full history, see Mychal Denzel Smith, "The Truth about "The Arc of the Moral Universe," *Huffington Post*, January 18, 2018, https://www.huffpost.com/entry/opinion-smith-obama-king_n_5a5903e0e4b04f3c55a252a4.

8. Kendi, "Racial Progress Is Real," 2.

9. Kendi, 2.

10. Hannah Arendt, *On Revolution* (New York: Penguin Books, 1963), 133.

11. Lyndon B. Johnson, "To Fulfill These Rights," commencement address at Howard University, June 5, 1965, http://www.lbjlib.utexas.edu/johnson/archives.hom/speeches .hom/650604.asp.

12. Steven J. Allen, "'We Have Lost the South for a Generation'": What Lyndon Johnson Said, or Would Have Said If Only He Had Said It," Capital Research Center, October 7. 2014, https://capitalresearch.org/article/we-have-lost-the-south-for-a-generation-what -lyndon-johnson-said-or-would-have-said-if-only-he-had-said-it/.

13. Ilyana Kuziemko and Ebonya Washington, "Why Did the Democrats Lose the South? Bringing New Data to an Old Debate," *American Economic Review* 108, no. 10 (October 2018): 2830–67.

14. Martin Luther King, *Where Do We Go From Here? Chaos or Community* (Boston: Beacon Press, 1968), 2.

15. King, *Where Do We Go From Here?* 4–5.

16. King, 4.

17. King, 12.

18. Alphonso Pinkney, *The Myth of Black Progress* (New York: Cambridge University Press, 1984), ix.

19. Pinkney, *The Myth of Black Progress*, x.

20. Pinkney, ix.

21. Steve Pinker, *Enlightenment Now: The Case for Reason, Science, Humanism, and Progress* (New York: Penguin Books, 2019).

22. Janelle Jones, John Schmitt, and Valerie Wilson, *50 Years after the Kerner Commission*, report, Economic Policy Institute, February 26, 2018, https://www.epi.org/publication/ 50-years-after-the-kerner-commission/.

23. Jill Lepore, "The History of the 'Riot' Report: How Government Commissions Became Alibis for Inaction," *American Chronicles*, June 15, 2020.

24. Michael Lipsky and David J. Olson, *Commission Politics: The Processing of Racial Crisis in America* (New Brunswick, NJ: Transaction, 1977). Quoted in Lepore, "The History of the 'Riot' Report," 4.

25. Lepore, 4.

26. Nathalie Baptiste, "Staggering Loss of Black Wealth Due to Subprime Scandal Continues Unabated," *American Prospect*, October 13, 2014.

27. Elise Gould and Valery Wilson, *Black Workers Face Two of the Most Lethal Preexisting Conditions for Coronavirus—Racism and Economic Inequality*, report, Economic Policy Institute, June 1, 2020, https://www.epi.org/publication/black-workers-covid/.

28. Gould and Wilson, *Black Workers*.

Chapter 13: Systemic Racism

1. Martin Luther King, "A Testament of Hope," *Playboy*, January 1969, 175ff, repr. in *A Testament of Hope: The Essential Writings and Speeches of Martin Luther King Jr.*, ed. James Melvin Washington (New York: HarperCollins, 1991), 315.

2. Michael Eric Dyson, *Long Time Coming: Reckoning with Race in America* (New York: St. Martin's Press, 2020), 214.

3. Gordon Allport, *The Nature of Prejudice* (Cambridge, MA: Addison-Wesley, 1954): 2.

4. Leah Gordon, *From Power to Prejudice: The Rise of Racial Individualism in Midcentury America* (Chicago: Oxford University Press, 2015), 2.

5. Oliver Cromwell Cox, *Class, Caste, and Race* (New York: Modern Reader, 1948), 531.

6. Mel Watkins, "Black Revolution in Books," *New York Times Book Review*, August 10, 1969, 71.

7. Bob Blauner, *Racial Oppression in America* (New York: Harper & Row, 1972), 5n.

8. Blauner, *Racial Oppression in America*, 9. Blauner added that "social science experts assumed that this movement toward equality depended primarily on the reduction of prejudice in the white majority, rather than upon the collective actions of the oppressed groups themselves or upon basic transformations in the society."

9. Blauner, 9.

10. Blauner, 9.

11. Blauner, 10–11.

12. "Black Lives Matter," Wikipedia, last edited June 10, 2021, https://en.wikipedia.org/wiki/Black_Lives_Matter.

13. Ashby Southall and Michael Gold, "Why 'Stop and Frisk' Inflamed Black and Hispanic Neighborhoods," *New York Times*, November 17, 2019, https://www.nytimes.com/2019/11/17/nyregion/bloomberg-stop-and-frisk-new-york.html; NYCLU, "Annual Stop and Frisk Data," https://www.nyclu.org/en/Stop-and-Frisk-data.

14. Gretchen Sorin, *Driving While Black: African American Travel and the Road to Civil Rights* (New York: W. W. Norton, 2020).

15. Henry Ordower, J. Onésimo Sandoval, and Kenneth Warren, "Out of Ferguson: Misdemeanors, Municipal Courts, Tax Distribution and Constitutional Limitations," *Howard Law Journal* 61, no. 113 (October 18, 2016), Saint Louis University Legal Studies Research Paper no. 2016–14, https://ssrn.com/abstract=2854372.

16. Kelly Moffitt, "SLU Law School Professors, Arch City Defenders Propose Changes to Municipal Courts in Missouri," *St. Louis Business Journal*, September 5, 2014, https://www.bizjournals.com/stlouis/blog/2014/09/slu-law-school-professors-arch-city-defenders.html.

17. Brian Mann, "Democrats in Albany Rethink Using NY's Prison System as an Economic Engine," North Country Public Radio, July 1, 2019, https://www.northcountrypublicradio.org/news/story/39019/20190701/democrats-in-albany-rethink-using-ny-s-prison-system-as-an-economic-engine.

18. Alice Speri, "The FBI Has Quietly Investigated White Supremacist Infiltration of Law Enforcement," *Intercept*, January 31, 2017, https://theintercept.com/2017/01/31/the-fbi-has-quietly-investigated-white-supremacist-infiltration-of-law-enforcement/.

19. Speri, "The FBI Has Quietly Investigated," 3.

20. Speri, 5.

21. Speri, 15.

22. *The Racism Review* provides a forum for journalists, professors, students, and the general public to discuss matters of race (racismreview.com).

23. Joe R. Feagin, *Systemic Racism: A Theory of Oppression* (New York: Routledge, 2006), 7. For another groundbreaking study of systemic racism, see Eduardo Bonilla-Silva, *White Supremacy and Racism in the Post-Civil Rights Era* (Boulder, CO: Lynne Rienner, 2001).

24. Feagin, *Systemic Racism*, 7.

25. Feagin, 297. Italics in original.

26. Samuel Freeman, "Rawls on Distributive Justice and the Difference Principle," in *The Oxford Handbook of Distributive Justice*, ed. Serena Olsaretti (Oxford Handbooks Online, online publication June 2018), https://www.oxfordhandbooks.com/view/10.1093/oxfordhb/9780199645121.001.0001/oxfordhb-9780199645121-e-2.

27. Feagin, *Systemic Racism*, 310.

28. Feagin, quoting W. E. B. Du Bois, *The Gift of Black Folk: Negroes in the Making of America* (Boston: Stratford, 1924), 138. Italics added.

Chapter 14: Bring Back Affirmative Action

An earlier version of this chapter appeared as "The Birth and Death of Affirmative Action: Is Resurrection Possible?" in *Intergroup Conflict and Cooperation*, ed. Robert S. Chang and Greg Robinson (Jackson: University Press of Mississippi, 2016).

1. Dahlia Lithwick, "The Courts: The Conservative Takeover Will Be Complete," *Washington Monthly*, January-February 2012.

2. Nick Kotz, "'When Affirmative Action Was White': Uncivil Rights," book review, *New York Times*, August 28, 2005, https://www.nytimes.com/2005/08/28/books/review/when-affirmative-action-was-white-uncivil-rights.html.

3. "The Slow and Tortured Death of Affirmative Action," *Black Commentator* 49 (July 3, 2003).

4. Nancy MacLean, *Freedom Is Not Enough: The Opening of the American Workplace* (Cambridge, MA: Harvard University Press, 2008), chs. 6, 7.

5. Neil R. McMillen, *Dark Journey: Black Mississippians in the Age of Jim Crow* (Urbana: University of Illinois Press, 1990), 7.

6. Charles W. Mills, *The Racial Contract* (Ithaca: Cornell University Press, 1997), 130-31.

7. Martin Luther King Jr., *Where Do We Go from Here? Chaos or Community* (Boston: Beacon Press, 1968), 5.

8. King, *Where Do We Go from Here?* 5. Also cited in *Look*, April 16, 1968, 24.

9. Whitney Young and Kyle Haselden, "Should There Be 'Compensation' for Negroes? A Debate," *New York Times Magazine*, October 6, 1963, 43ff.

10. Whitney M. Young Jr., *To Be Equal* (New York: McGraw-Hill, 1963), 54.

11. Haselden, "Parity, Not Preference" in "Should There Be 'Compensation for Negroes?'"

12. Charles Silberman, *Crisis in Black and White* (New York: Random House, 1964).

13. Martin Luther King Jr., *Why We Can't Wait* (New York: Harper & Row, 1964), 147.

14. John David Skrentny, *The Ironies of Affirmative Action* (Chicago: University of Chicago Press, 1996), chs. 11-13.

15. According to John David Skrentny, in defeating the Congressional rider, "the Nixon forces came through, despite almost no help from the civil rights community, save for a few written statements coaxed from Roy Wilkins and Whitney Young," 20. But he also notes that at the local level, CORE and the NAACP worked with a coalition of churches in support of the Plan. Skrentny, *The Ironies of Affirmative Action*, 208, 285.

16. Hugh Davis Graham, *The Civil Rights Era: The Origins and Development of National Policy, 1960–1972* (New York: Oxford University Press, 1990), 325.

17. Hugh Davis Graham, "Race, History, and Policy: African Americans and Civil Rights since 1964," *Journal of Policy History* 6, no. 1 (1994): 23.

18. Graham, *The Civil Rights Era*, 334–35.

19. "Promoting affirmative action was another demonstration that the President flirted with liberal reforms during his first two years in office." Terry Anderson lists a number of such reforms, including set-asides in contracts to socially disadvantaged firms and a family assistance plan that guaranteed a family wage that "horrified conservatives helped defeat in Congress." Terry H. Anderson, *The Pursuit of Fairness: A History of Affirmative Action* (New York: Oxford, 2004), 119.

20. Arthur Fletcher, *The Silent Sell-Out* (New York: Third Press, 1974), 65.

21. MacLean, *Freedom Is Not Enough*, 100–101.

22. Graham, "Race, History and Policy," 19–20.

23. Skrentny, *The Ironies of Affirmative Action*, 141.

24. Jacob Heilbrunn, *They Knew They Were Right: The Rise of the Neocons* (New York: Doubleday, 2008), 88.

25. Benjamin Balint, *Running Commentary: The Contentious Magazine That Transformed the Jewish Left into the Neoconservative Right* (New York: BBS Public Affairs, 2010), 138. In an endnote, Balint lists thirteen articles during the 1990s that railed against affirmative action.

26. For example, Herman Belz, *Equality Transformed: A Quarter-Century of Affirmative Action. Transaction Publishers*, Studies in Social Philosophy and Policy, no. 15 (Bowling Green, OH: Social Philosophy and Policy Center; New Brunswick, NJ: Transaction, 1991); and Richard Epstein, *Forbidden Grounds: The Case Against Employment Discrimination Laws* (Cambridge, MA: Harvard University Press, 1995).

27. Alan Wolfe, "Affirmative Action: The Fact Gap," *New York Times Book Review*, October 25, 1998, 15.

28. Ellen Willis, "Race and the Ordeal of Racial Optimism," in *Don't Think, Smile!* (Boston: Beacon Press, 1999), 91–113.

29. I am indebted to Sharon Collins, University of Illinois at Chicago Circle, for this insight.

30. Stephen Steinberg, *The Ethnic Myth* (Boston: Beacon Press, 1989), 238–46. Jerome Karabel, *The Chosen: The Hidden History of Admission and Exclusion at Harvard, Yale, and Princeton* (New York: Mariner Books, 2006).

31. David Hollinger, "Group Preferences, Cultural Diversity and Social Democracy: Notes toward a Theory of Affirmative Action," in *Race and Representation: Affirmative Action*, ed. Robert Post and Michael Rogin (New York: Zone Books, 1998), 99.

32. Peter Schrag, "So You Want to Be Color-Blind: Alternative Principles for Affirmative Action," *American Prospect*, Summer 1995, 45.

33. Richard Herrnstein, "On Challenging an Orthodoxy," *Commentary* 55, no. 4 (April 1973).

34. Richard Herrnstein and Charles Murray, *The Bell Curve: Intelligence and Class Structure in American Life* (New York: Free Press, 1996).

35. MacLean, *Freedom Is Not Enough*, 230.

36. Quoted in MacLean, *Freedom Is Not Enough*, 235.

37. Heilbrunn, *They Knew They Were Right*, 165.

38. Jean Stefancic and Richard Delgado, *No Mercy: How Social Conservatives and Think Tanks Changed America's Social Agenda* (Philadelphia: Temple University Press, 1996).

39. Joe Klein, "The End of Affirmative Action," *Newsweek*, February 12, 1995, http://newsweek.com/1995/02/12/the-end-of-affirmative-action.html, 36–37.

40. Klein, "The End of Affirmative Action."

41. James P. Sterba, *Affirmative Action for the Future* (Ithaca, NY: Cornell University Press, 2009), 21–22.

42. Sharon M. Collins, "Diversity in the Post Affirmative Action Labor Market: A Proxy for Racial Progress?" *Critical Sociology* 37 (2011): 524

43. Peter Schmidt, "From 'Minority' to 'Diversity,'" *Chronicle of Higher Education*, February 3, 2006, https://www.chronicle.com/article/from-minority-to-diversity/. Also see Ben Gose, "The Rise of the Chief Diversity Officer," *Chronicle of Higher Education*. September 29, 2006, https://www.chronicle.com/article/the-rise-of-the-chief-diversity-officer/.

44. Steven M. Teles, *The Rise of the Conservative Legal Movement* (Princeton, NJ: Princeton University Press, 2008), 135–80.

45. Keeanga-Yamahtta Taylor, *From #Blacklivesmatter to Black Liberation* (Chicago: Haymarket Books, 2016).

Chapter 15: Trump, Trumpism, and the Resurgence of White Supremacy

1. Barbara Perry, "'White Genocide': White Supremacists, and the Politics of Reproduction," in *Home-Grown Hate*, ed. Amy L. Ferber (New York: Routledge, 2003), 1.

2. Robin D. G. Kelley, "After Trump," *Boston Review*, November 15, 2016.

3. "Transcript of Barack Obama's Victory Speech," NPR, November 5, 2008, https://www.npr.org/templates/story/story.php?storyId=96624326.

4. Michael Kimmel, *Angry White Men: American Masculinity at the End of an Era* (New York: Nation Books, 2013), 236–37.

5. Associated Press, "Supremacists Hope for Boost from Obama Win," *NBC News*, August 8, 2008, https://www.nbcnews.com/id/wbna26087413.

6. Associated Press, "Supremacists Hope," 2.

7. Mark Potok, "Rage on the Right," special issue, *Intelligence Report*, March 2, 2010, https://www.splcenter.org/fighting-hate/intelligence-report/2010/rage-right. Charles M. Blow, "Whose Country Is It?" Opinion, *New York Times*, March 26, 2010, https://www.nytimes.com/2010/03/27/opinion/27blow.html.

8. Daniel Bell, ed., *The Radical Right* (New York: Anchor Books, 1955), 47.

9. Seymour Martin Lipset, "The Sources of the Radical Right," in Bell, *The Radical Right*, 307.

10. Kimmel, *Angry White Men*, 308.

11. Lipset, "The Sources of the Radical Right," 309.

12. Richard Hofstadter, "The Pseudo-Conservative Revolt," in Bell, *The Radical Right*, 76.

13. Daniel Denvir, *All-American Nativism: How the Bipartisan War on Immigrants Explains Politics as We Know It* (New York: Verso, 2020), 5.

14. "Great Lakes Economic Initiative," Brookings Institution, September 3, 2010, https://web.archive.org/web/20100903175731/http://www.brookings.edu/projects/great-lakes/GLEI-about.aspx.

15. "Great Lakes Economic Initiative."

16. John Aidan Byrne, "Manufacturing Jobs Vanishing from City," *New York Post*, February 18, 2015.

17. Kimmel, *Angry White Men*, 243. Many of the protesters who stormed the Capitol were Southerners with roots in the Ku Klux Klan and other hate groups. There were also a significant number of women among hate groups. See Abby L. Ferber, *Home-Grown Hate* (New York: Routledge, 2004); Kathleen M. Blee, *Understanding Racist Activism* (New York: Routledge, 2017); and Jesse Daniels, *White Lies: Race, Class, Gender, and Sexuality in White Supremacist Discourse* (New York: Routledge, 1997).

18. Kimmel, 55–56.

19. Kimmel, 245.

20. Kimmel, 256.

21. Kimmel, 3.

22. Jeff Maskovsky, "Trumpism and the Collapse of the Liberal Racial Consensus in the United States," in *Beyond Populism: Angry Politics and the Twilight of Neoliberalism*, ed. Jeff Maskovsky and Sophie Bjork-James (Morgantown: West Virginia University Press, 2020), 171.

23. Kimmel, *Angry White Men*, 263. On February 10, 2021, the *Boston Globe* ran a story by Todd C. Frankel titled "A Majority of the People Arrested for Capitol Riot Had a History of Financial Trouble," https://www.bostonglobe.com/2021/02/10/nation/majority-people-arrested-capitol-riot-had-history-financial-trouble/. According to Pippa Norris, a political science professor at Harvard University who has studied radical political movements, "the participation of people with middle- and upper-middle-class positions fits with research suggesting that the rise of right-wing extremist groups in the 1950s was fueled by people in the middle of society who felt they were losing status and power." Smerconish, "WaPo: Majority of Capitol Riot Defendants Have History of Financial Troubles," CNN, February 13, 2021, https://www.cnn.com/videos/tv/2021/02/13/wapo-majority-of-capitol-riot-defendants-have-history-of-financial-troubles.cnn.

24. David Neiwert, *Alt-America: The Rise of the Radical Right in the Age of Donald Trump* (New York: Verso, 2017), 6.

25. "Trump Stands by Statements on Mexican Illegal Immigrants, Surprised by Backlash," Fox News, July 4, 2015, https://www.foxnews.com/politics/trump-stands-by-statements-on-mexican-illegal-immigrants-surprised-by-backlash.

26. Denvir, *All-American Nativism*, 3.

27. Denvir, 3.

28. Denvir, 4.

29. Alvin Felzenberg, "How William F. Buckley, Jr., Changed His Mind on Civil Rights," *Politico*, May 13, 2017.

30. Felzenberg, "How William F. Buckley, Jr."

31. Nancy Fraser, *The Old Is Dying and the New Cannot Be Born: From Progressive Neoliberalism to Trump and Beyond* (New York: Verso, 2019). This provocative title was coined by Antonio Francesco Gramsci, an Italian Marxist philosopher (1891–1937).

32. Fraser, *The Old Is Dying*, 24.

33. Maskovsky, "Trumpism and the Collapse."

34. Fraser, *The Old Is Dying*.

35. Fraser, *The Old Is Dying*.

36. Thomas B. Edsall with Mary D. Edsall. *Chain Reaction: The Impact of Race, Rights, and Taxes on American Politics* (New York: Norton, 1992).

37. Denvir, *All-American Nativism*, 4, 7. Also see Thomas B. Edsall, "Why Trump Still Has Millions of Americans in His Grip," *New York Times*, May 5, 2021.

38. Matthew Iglesias, "Swarthy Germans," *Atlantic*, February 4, 2008, https://www.theatlantic.com/politics/archive/2008/02/swarthy-germans/48324/.

39. Noel Ignatiev, *How the Irish Became White* (New York: Routledge, 1995); Karin Brodkin, *How Jews Became White Folk* (Rutgers, NJ: Rutgers University Press, 1998); Matthew Frye Jacobson, *Whiteness of a Different Color: European Immigrants and the Alchemy of Race* (Cambridge, MA: Harvard University Press, 1999); Jennifer Gugliano and Salvatore Salerno, *Are Italians White? How Race Is Made in America* (New York: Routledge, 2003); David R. Roediger, *Working toward Whiteness: How American's Immigrants Became White* (New York: Basic Books, 2005); and David R. Roediger, *Colored White: Transcending the Racial Past* (Berkeley: University of California Press, 2002).

40. John Binder, "Data: White American Births below Replacement Level in Every State," Breitbart News, January 13, 2019, https://www.breitbart.com/politics/2019/01/13/states-birth-rate-2017/#.

41. Kim Parker and Ruth Igielnik, "On the Cusp of Adulthood and Facing an Uncertain Future: What We Know About Gen Z So Far," Pew Research Center, May 14, 2020, https://www.pewresearch.org/social-trends/2020/05/14/on-the-cusp-of-adulthood-and-facing-an-uncertain-future-what-we-know-about-gen-z-so-far-2/.

42. Jelani Cobb, "How Parties Die," *New Yorker*, March 15, 2021, 27.

43. See Ruth Igielnik and Abby Budiman, "The Changing Racial and Ethnic Composition of the U.S. Electorate," Pew Research Center, September 23, 2020, https://www.pewresearch.org/2020/09/23/the-changing-racial-and-ethnic-composition-of-the-u-s-electorate/, comparing 2018 and 2000.

44. Cobb, "How Parties Die," 29. According to the *New York Times* on February 28, 2021, a year ago only twenty-five such bills in fifteen states were filed. Also see Ari Berman, "How the GOP Rigs Elections: Gerrymandering, Voter ID Laws, Dark Money," *Rolling Stone*, January 24, 2018, https://www.rollingstone.com/politics/politics-news/how

-the-gop-rigs-elections-121907/; and Nina Totenberg, "Supreme Court Upholds Contro-versial Ohio Voter-Purge Law," *All Things Considered*, NPR, June 11, 2018, https://www.npr.org/2018/06/11/618870982/supreme-court-upholds-controversial-ohio-voter-purge-law%C2%A0.

45. Sasha Abramsky, "GOP-Led Voter Suppression Is Being Implemented Step by Step—Just Like Jim Crow," Truthout, July 11, 2021, https://truthout.org/articles/gop-led-voter-suppression-is-being-implemented-step-by-step-just-like-jim-crow/.

INDEX

acting white, myth of, 137–40
Adorno, Theodore, 227
Advocacy and Objectivity (Furner), 173
affirmative action, 22–26, 59, 72; compensatory
  programs (1963–1965), 210–11; dismantling
  by Supreme Court, 222; Fletcher as father
  of, 55; Glazer as critic of, 59–61; golden years
  (1972–1988), 215–17; Moynihan as critic of,
  50–52; opposition to, 25; possibility of resurrecting, 221–23; unraveling of (1988–2012),
  217–21. *See also* anti-affirmative-action
  discourse, fallacies of
Affirmative Discrimination: Ethnic In-
  equality and Public Polity (Glazer), 40,
  64, 67, 133
African American Pioneers of Sociology
  (Saint-Arnaud), 177
Aid for Dependent Children (AFDC), 28
Alcove I, 66
Alexander, Michelle, 35
All-American Nativism (Denvir), 228, 233
All Our Kin (Stack), 75
Allport, Gordon, 198
Alt-America: The Rise of the Radical Right
  in the Age of Trump (Neiwert), 232
Alterman, Eric, 154
An American Dilemma (Myrdal), 108
American Judaism (Glazer), 66, 131
America on Fire (Hinton), 84, 257
Anderson, Carol, 19
Anderson, James D., 105, 106
Anderson, Nels, 179

Angry White Men (Kimmel), 225
anti-affirmative-action backlash, 219
anti-affirmative-action discourse, fallacies of,
  208–10
Arendt, Hannah, 11–12, 190
Asian immigrants, success story of, 130–37
Atlanta school of sociology, 185–86
Atwater, Lee, 27, 29
Auletta, Ken, 76
The Authoritarian Personality (Adorno),
  227

Bakke, Allan, 155, 217
Baldwin, James, 34, 41–42, 91, 162, 199, 203
Balint, Benjamin, 56–57, 216
Banfield Edward, 86
Barrett, Amy Coney, 221
Battle Hymn of the Tiger Mother (Chua),
  146
Beck, Glenn, 29
Bell, Daniel, 226, 233
Bell, David, 134–35
Bell, Derrick, v, 8, 18, 187, 189, 195, 275n2
The Bell Curve (Herrnstein and Murray), 24,
  25, 218, 219
Bennett, Lerone, Jr., 1, 13–14, 18, 19, 36–37, 58
Berkshire, Jennifer, 115
Berman, Ari, 36
Berreman, Gerald, 102
Berrol, Selma, 128
Betty Friedan and the Making of the The
  Feminine Mystique (Horowitz), 2